*no. 17 in a series of research reports
sponsored by the NCTE Committee
on Research

Children's *Categorization of Speech Sounds in English

By CHARLES READ
University of Wisconsin

ERIC Clearinghouse on Language and Linguistics
ERIC Clearinghouse on Reading and Communication Skills
   National Institute of Education

National Council of Teachers of English
1111 Kenyon Road, Urbana, Illinois 61801

NCTE Stock Number: 06307

Published October 1975
ERIC Clearinghouse on Language and Linguistics
ERIC Clearinghouse on Reading and Communication Skills,
National Institute of Education
and
National Council of Teachers of English
1111 Kenyon Road, Urbana, Illinois 61801

Library of Congress Cataloging in Publication Data

Read, Charles, 1940-
    Children's categorization of speech sounds in
English.

    (NCTE research reports; no. 17)
    Bibliography: p.
    1. English language—Phonetics. 2. Children—
Language. 3. English language—Orthography and
spelling. I. Title. II. Series: National
Council of Teachers of English. Research report;
no. 17.
PE1011.N295 no. 17 [PE1135]   421'.52
ISBN 0-8141-0630-7   75-26122

The material in this publication was prepared pursuant to a contract with the National Institute of Education, U.S. Department of Health, Education and Welfare. Contractors undertaking such projects under government sponsorship are encouraged to express freely their judgment in professional and technical matters. Prior to publication, the manuscript was submitted to the National Council of Teachers of English for critical review and determination of professional competence. This publication has met such standards. Points of view or opinions, however, do not necessarily represent the official view or opinions of either the National Council of Teachers of English or the National Institute of Education.

National Council of Teachers of English
Research Report No. 17

Charles Read's study is significant primarily for what it tells us about children's tacit grouping of speech sounds. Secondarily, it is significant for what it reveals about the potential for cooperatively funded research. Since large grants from a single agency are increasingly hard to come by, it is reassuring to see an example of what can be done through pooled resources.

Read's research contributes substantially to what is known about children's phonological competence—a topic which, unlike syntactic competence, has received little research emphasis. Read found evidence in several instances that children's grouping of speech sounds differs from the groupings embodied in standard English spelling. His findings concerning the differences between these two implicit groupings contribute to our understanding of the tasks children face in learning to read and write the English language.

The following comment excerpted from Peter Rosenbaum's critique of the manuscript is appropriate as an introduction to Read's monograph:

"Were I to speculate on the force of Read's monograph, I would note that Read's presentation calls direct attention to the existence in school children at primary levels of a surprisingly rich phonological sense that is organized in ways that are not at all obvious or intuitive. At the very least, the mere existence of this organization calls into question the veracity of instructional schemes that attempt to impose a one-to-one sound-symbol correspondence on the reading and spelling curricula (e.g., Pitman and Gattegno). Perhaps even more interesting is the notion that existing phonological competence can be harnessed in some productive way in the instructional process. I have no doubt that Read's understated arguments will raise considerable controversy; perhaps they will even stimulate research toward a new synthesis."

Roy C. O'Donnell
For the Committee on Research

PREFACE

This monograph presents the results of extensive research on children's categorization of speech sounds in English, including analyses of prominent patterns in children's spelling and experimental studies of children's judgments of relationships among speech sounds. From this research we draw both psycholinguistic and pedagogical conclusions.

Chapter one presents the basic argument in its theoretical context and relates this research to other studies of children's phonology. Chapter two presents the analysis of patterns in children's early invented spelling, an analysis which suggested the direction for each of the subsequent experimental studies. The data for this analysis are quantitative; the main features appear in tables in the text, and a complete tabulation of sound-spelling correspondences in the corpus of children's spelling appears in Appendices A through I. Chapter three presents the first set of experimental studies, dealing with children's judgments of initial [tr] clusters. Chapter four reports a set of experiments dealing with children's (and adults') judgments of nasals that immediately precede stop consonants, another case in which children's spelling has special characteristics. Chapter five discusses relationships among the front vowels of English, again through a set of related experiments. This is perhaps the most general of the experimental topics, and the chapter concludes with a map of this vowel territory, as putatively structured by children. Finally, chapter six reports a set of investigations of the relationship between [s] and [z], a peculiarly close relationship, both phonetically and orthographically. These studies specifically attempt to distinguish the influence of standard spelling from phonetic and phonological sources of children's judgments.

Each of the investigations compared two principles which might account for an aspect of children's categorization of speech sounds and consequently their expectations concerning the spelling of English. The issues are different in each case, and each is of general importance in the study of how children group speech sounds into classes. Together the naturalistic and experimental studies include children's judgments of a fair variety of phonetic relationships in English; yet they far from exhaust the topic. The experiments were designed to provide a check on inferences drawn from the invented spelling, and in some cases we find several kinds of evidence converging on a specific conclusion, yet the studies are often less than conclusive or unambiguous. My hope is simply that these investigations will help to open up an area of study, to demonstrate its potential significance, and to illustrate some ways in which it may be approached.

Although children's tacit grouping of speech sounds is the central theoretical issue, each of the studies has practical significance in explaining some very common apparent errors in children's spelling. In these cases, the children's grouping of speech sounds is quite different from that which is embodied in standard English spelling, which also commonly represents distinct sounds with the same spelling. The differences between these two implicit groupings help to define part of what children must acquire in learning to read and write English. Essentially, we have attempted to find out what relationships children might tacitly expect to find embodied in English spelling, so that we can compare these with the relationships that are actually reflected in the standard spelling system. On a more immediately useful level, if we can reveal a phonetic basis for certain very common "errors," we can distinguish between appropriate and inappropriate ways of responding to these errors. Although we have not studied ways of changing children's spelling patterns, it is clear that a teacher ought to respond differently to spelling patterns that are based on phonetic relationships than to those that arise, for example, from visual confusions or from faulty generalizations about sound-spelling correspondences.

Accordingly, each chapter highlights some conclusions and suggestions of interest to teachers and those who teach teachers. Common sense dictates caution, for he who has never taught even one child to read and write should certainly be reticent in offering advice to those who have made it their career. Even though we have applied appropriate statistical tests, one hesitates to generalize about first-graders on the basis of experiments with samples of about 20 children. On the other hand, as our colleagues in the schools point out, teachers make practical choices every day, and it is only reasonable that they should be able to draw on any relevant material in making these choices, especially in the tangled area of reading and writing.

Two matters of notation deserve to be mentioned. The reader will note that phonetic symbols are enclosed in slashes (/ /) in chapter two, but in square brackets ([ ]) in all other sections. Except where the context indicates otherwise, all such transcriptions are intended to refer to phone types, not (ordinarily) to detailed phonetic transcriptions or to phonemes in the classical sense. The reason for the notational differences is that in chapter two it was necessary to refer to some rather broad classes of phones, particularly with respect to certain vowel-types. As the text indicates, the circumstances under which the children's early spelling was collected did not usually permit a phonemic analysis of each child's dialect or detailed transcription of a child's speech. The experimental studies did allow a finer discrimination among phone-types—thus the notational difference. With this qualification, the phonetic symbols used have quite traditional values. In connection with the tables in the appendices, the reader should note that the computer printout symbol "@" represents an apparent omission in a child's spelling; for example, in Appendix B, Table 4, the "spelling" @/N indicates the spelling N for the phonetic sequence [ən]. The nature of such apparent omissions is discussed in the text of chapter two. Throughout the manuscript, children's spellings appear in all uppercase characters, while cited standard spellings appear in lowercase. Footnotes begin on page 146.

ACKNOWLEDGMENTS

One of the genuine pleasures in preparing this work for publication is acknowledging, albeit inadequately, the generous contribution of many people to the research. My first debt is to the children themselves, those who created the original spelling which stimulated the inquiry and the hundreds who have participated in the subsequent studies. They were not aware of the significance which I attached to their judgments, and I literally do not know how to thank them. Likewise, the work could not have proceeded without the cooperation of parents, those who opened their homes and their collections of children's writing to me, and those who gave permission for their children to participate in my studies in schools. I am grateful for their trust.

Many schools, teachers, and administrators have also been helpful. Knowing as I do that teachers encounter an ample number of problems in an ordinary day without the additional disruptions occasioned by research, I am particularly grateful for their contribution.

Private preschools:

Beacon Nursery School, Brookline, Massachusetts
Boston Children's School, Boston, Massachusetts
First Congregational Church Nursery School, Madison, Wisconsin
Woodland Montessori School, Madison, Wisconsin
St. Mary of the Lake Montessori School, Waunakee, Wisconsin

Public and private elementary schools:

Brookline (Massachusetts) Public Schools
   Baker, Devotion, Driscoll, and Lawrence Schools
Lexington (Massachusetts) Public Schools
   Franklin School
Madison (Wisconsin) Public Schools
   Frank Allis and Samuel Gompers Schools
Nahant (Massachusetts) Public Schools
   Johnson School and J. T. Wilson School
Queen of Peace Elementary School, Madison, Wisconsin

Regrettably, listing institutions in this fashion excludes an acknowledgment of the help and cooperation of many fine individuals.

For the equally necessary financial support, I wish to thank the Spencer Foundation and the committee of the School of Education, University of Wisconsin, which administered the Spencer Foundation grant; the National Council of Teachers of English Research Foundation; the National Council of Teachers of English Committee on Research; and the Graduate School Research Committee of the University of Wisconsin. As with any research, there was no way of being certain in advance that the work would be productive, so I am particularly grateful to the people of these agencies who were willing to support the effort with money.

Among the research assistants and aides who helped with the work, I particularly wish to acknowledge the contributions of Tracy Connell, Shirley Lukitsch, Lucy Rava, and Stephanie Shattuck. These people willingly invested effort and ideas, often at considerable inconvenience to themselves. I also wish to thank the staff of the Publications Department of the National Council of Teachers of English, under the direction of Paul O'Dea, and particularly Carol Schanche, for her expert and thoughtful editing of this monograph.

Several scholars have generously given encouragement and advice. Professors Carol Chomsky, Wayne O'Neil, and Israel Scheffler have been associated with this project from the beginning; Carol Chomsky, in particular, is responsible for much of what is good in the research designs. During my term as a Visiting Scientist at M.I.T., I benefited greatly from the advice of Kenneth Stevens, Dennis Klatt, and A. W. F. Huggins, as well as from extensive use of their facilities for speech analysis and synthesis in the Speech Communication Group of the Research Laboratory of Electronics. Professor Morris Halle contributed insights, criticism, and encouragement of a kind so fundamental as to defy summary. My colleagues at Wisconsin, Peter Schreiber, Charles Scott, and Richard Venezky, have also sustained and improved this work with their advice. The influence of all these people is reflected, however dimly, throughout the monograph.

TABLE OF CONTENTS

CHAPTER ONE

A SURVEY OF THE MONOGRAPH

1.1 The topic

The aim of this monograph is to present evidence that young children tacitly categorize the phones of English, sometimes in rather surprising ways. "Categorization" in this case refers to the following type of phenomenon: children and adults can *discriminate* the English phones [t], [s], and [z], as in *tip, sip,* and *zip,* but beyond this phonemic discrimination, they can recognize similarity relations, in that [s] and [z] are regarded as more similar than [s] and [t].[1]

Speech recognition itself is categorial. Without this property, speech communication as we know it would be impossible. If two discriminably different speech sounds could never be regarded as the same, or functionally alike, we would recognize very few words, since almost all normal human utterances are noticeably different in some respect. A male speaker and a female speaker could hardly say the same words, nor could speakers of different dialects, nor could we say the same thing over the telephone that we can say in person; it is even doubtful that we could regard the initial and final sounds of *boob* as the same sound. In fact, quite a range of articulatory and acoustic events may be regarded as a single speech sound, and obviously this categorization is essential to the success of speech.

This observation by itself may suggest that a functional class of sounds, such as /b/, is simply distinct *as a whole* from other functional classes of sounds in a language, such as /a/, /p/, /s/, or /w/. The basic requirements of speech communication seem to be met as long as we can sort speech sounds into discrete categories. Actually, however, speakers can do more than this minimum; they can recognize relations *among* distinct speech sounds based on phonetic similarities and differences, and sometimes can rank these relationships, as in the [s]-[z], [s]-[t] example. This monograph reports a series of studies of the categorization of speech sounds, in this latter sense, by children

---

[1]Footnotes begin on page 146.

from about age four to age eight. It argues that children recognize specific and sometimes subtle phonetic relationships, and that these judgments may influence children's initial encounters with spelling and reading.

Edward Sapir emphasized the linguistic importance of such categorizations in "Sound Patterns in Language," in the first volume of *Language* (1925). He clearly anticipates his article on the psychological reality of the phoneme (1933) with the observation that it is extraordinarily difficult for a native speaker "to make phonetic distinctions that [do] not correspond to 'points in the pattern of his language,'" but the patterns that Sapir refers to primarily concern the speaker's recognition of relationships among *contrasting* speech sounds.

Sapir notes that it is crucial to language that sounds be felt to be "placed" with respect to other sounds. He gives as an example the feeling that "sound A is to sound B as sound X is to sound Y." He notes that such judgments involve more than just contrast: "A 'place' is intuitively found for a sound in such a system because of a general feeling of its phonetic relationship resulting from all the specific phonetic relationships (such as parallelism, contrast, combination, imperviousness to combination, and so on) to all other sounds. These relationships may, or may not, involve morphological processes" (Sapir, 1925). Sapir cites the fact that "in English, *f* is nearer to *v* than *p* is to *b*, but in German this is certainly not true." Although Sapir does not indicate his evidence for this claim, the context indicates that as a basis for this presumed relationship, he was thinking of alternations such as *wife–wives* and *leaf–leaves* in English, as contrasted with the more general terminal obstruent devoicing rule in German.

With Sapir, I assume that these judgments of relationships may be based on several factors, including the phonological and morphophonemic regularities of the language. However, such relationships appear to require a high degree of phonetic similarity among the sounds involved, and they can be described best as choices among possible phonetic-feature bases of classification. In fact, one of the reasons for analyzing phones as bundles of features is that it makes it possible to describe the articulatory (and/or acoustic) bases for such judgments. In the [s]-[z] case, we might say that the similarity in frication between [s] and [z] is more salient than the similarity in voicing between [s] and [t].

The use of phonetic description must not obscure another important observation of Sapir's:

And yet it is most important to emphasize the fact, strange but

indubitable, that a pattern alignment does not need to correspond exactly to the more obvious phonetic one. It is most certainly true that, however likely it is that at last analysis pattern-
ings of sounds are based on natural classifications, the pattern
feeling, once established, may come to have a linguistic reality
over and above, though perhaps never entirely at variance with,
such classifications. . . .

The present discussion is really a special illustration of the
necessity of getting behind the sense data of any type of expression in order to grasp the intuitively felt and communicated
forms which alone give significance to such expression. (Sapir,
in Joos 1957)

Sapir's insistence that "it is not nonsense to say that, e.g., the *s* or *w*
of one linguistic pattern is not necessarily the same thing as the *s* or *w*
of another" may apply to children's judgments versus those of adults,
as well as to one language versus another.

In his anthology, Martin Joos (1957) adds in an end note acknowledging Sapir's genius, "thus we seem captious when we point out
that he also said many things which are essentially uncheckable ('in-
vulnerable') and thus not science." Assuming that Joos's criticism refers
to Sapir's effort to "get behind sense data," including his remarks about
phonetic relationships, we should note that one major goal of this
monograph is to show that relationships like those Sapir discussed
can be studied empirically and turn out to have both psychological
validity and practical significance. If the research has achieved this
goal, it is one illustration of the way in which the boundaries of what
is "checkable" have been expanded in linguistics and psycholinguistics.

One can study not only the phonetic bases for categorial judgments,
but also their reflections in phonology and orthography. For example,
a linguist is not surprised to find that English words ending in [s] and
[z] form their plurals in the same way, whereas words ending in [t]
form plurals in a different way (compare *face–faces* and *phase–phases*
with *fate–fates*). In orthography, [s] and [z] are frequently spelled
with the same letter, as in *this* and *is*, whereas [s] and [t] virtually
never are. The child learning English may make use of any of these
sources of information. At age five, a child may not only recognize the
phonetic relation between [s] and [z], but may also have learned their
similarity in plural formation and orthography (see Berko, 1958, for
evidence of children's production). In some instances, the arguments
to be presented here will concern the existence and nature of children's
phonetic categories without disentangling their phonetic, phonologi-

cal, and orthographic bases; in other cases, it will be possible to distinguish these, at least in part. For example, I will present evidence that children, like adults, judge that [u] *(boot)* is more closely related to [o] *(boat)* than it is to [i] *(beat)*. This judgment must surely be based on the phonetic similarities between [u] and [o] in backness and rounding rather than on the derivational relationship between them (the Great Vowel Shift and its synchronic reflex); furthermore, the children involved did not all know the orthographic similarity between [u] and [o] (e.g., that *boot* and *boat* are both spelled with *o*). In several other cases, a phonetic basis for children's categorizations is present, but phonological and orthographic bases are totally absent; thus the assumption is that the phonetic bases are primary.

In the examples cited, it is possible to distinguish two kinds of judgments: that [u] and [o] are *not* members of two unrelated phonemes of English, but rather members of some more general class, and that this class is more prominent than the one (of high vowels) to which [u] and [i] belong. The former kind of judgment may exist without the latter, and in the data to be presented, there are cases of both types. I will present evidence of several types of phonetic classification by children. What they have in common is that they all reflect a tacit phonetic-feature system that determines which speech sounds are related. With two important exceptions, the examples reported here all deal with supra-phonemic categories, i.e., with categories that include members of different phonemes. A set of discrete phonemes defined by functional contrast (as in *sip–zip* and *boot–boat*) is not the limit of children's phonetic analysis at the age at which they enter school.

1.1.1 Relation to spelling. Viewed in this theoretical light, children's categorization of speech sounds may seem an arcane topic, of interest only to those specializing in children's language acquisition. One focus of this monograph is indeed the significance of children's judgments for the theory of acquisition, but these judgments also relate to the problem of learning English spelling—both producing it and reading it. In fact, the evidence presented in chapter two comes from spellings that children invented for themselves prior to learning the standard system.

The relationship between spelling and speech sound categorization is a rather profound one: all alphabetic spelling represents some level of phonetic or phonological classification. (Klima, 1972, discusses several such levels in an interesting way.) A detailed record of the speech signal, such as a sound spectrogram, proves very difficult to read, and a detailed articulatory representation is not a serious candidate for a practical orthography. Standard English spelling, near the other extreme, is phonetically highly abstract; it adopts a consistent spelling for the phonetically (and phonemically) varying forms of meaningful elements (Venezky, 1970). Only recently have linguists seriously discussed the merits of such a system for the skilled adult reader (Weir and Venezky, 1968; Chomsky and Halle, 1968). Otherwise, the almost universal assumption by linguists and others has been that an optimal orthography would be phonemic, i.e., that it would represent uniquely all and only the functional contrasts in the language. This assumption underlies the Initial Teaching Alphabet (i.t.a.), the most widely adopted pedagogical orthography, and it has been applied to the development of spelling systems in general (e.g., Pike, 1947: 89, 208-209). It is crucial that we recognize, however, that this *is* an assumption; reasonable as it may seem, it is an empirical question whether all and only the phonemic contrasts should be distinguished in orthography for children (or adults).

One holistic approach to answering this question is to develop and test orthographies which embody implicit hypotheses as to what phonetic relationships are "real" or natural to children. This approach has been taken in the development of i.t.a. (Downing, 1967). A more basic approach is to attempt to determine what relationships children might expect to find represented in spelling, through the study of children's phonetic judgments, and to use this information to motivate decisions about orthography, distinctions among different kinds of errors, the organization of learning, and other practical choices. The latter is the means by which this monograph may contribute to the teaching of literacy. Of course, there are many related issues and pedagogical decisions that lie outside the scope of this monograph and, indeed, outside a linguist's professional competence.

As an example of the relation between the study of children's phonetic categories and the design of literacy instruction, consider the case of the initial sounds of *thin* and *then* ([θɪn] and [ðɛn]). These two sounds are phonetically and phonemically different, although both are commonly spelled *th*. On the assumption that, for children at least, it is most natural to distinguish phonemes in spelling, i.t.a. represents these sounds with slightly different symbols (þ and ħ). To question the assumption that this aspect of English spelling is indeed a likely source of difficulty, we must ask (a) whether children of about age six distinguish between these sounds (minimal pairs like *teeth* and *teethe* may not be in their vocabulary), and (b) whether children who distinguish the two sounds nevertheless regard them as so closely related that it is natural to find them spelled in the same way. A similar question applies even to [s] and [z]. The invented spellings reported in chapter two and the experimental studies in subsequent chapters present evidence on this type of question.

1.1.2 Relation to production and perception. The study of children's implicit categorizations of speech sounds is distinct from, but may be related to, somewhat more traditional areas of inquiry. One of these is the study of children's production. Although there has been considerable confusion about what is studied—the production of phones or the acquisition of phonemes, the standard of success in each case, etc. —this area has been enriched by some large studies, notably Templin (1957) and Olmsted (1971) and by an influential set of generalizations in Jakobson (1941). These studies have provided some indication of the relative difficulty of phones, at least an approximate notion of the relation between age and correct production, and some inferences about the general nature of development. In addition there is a large related clinical literature.

The relative difficulty of distinguishing various phones in production does not necessarily coincide with their relatedness in children's categorizations. For example, the common substitution of [w] for [l] in the speech of young children (Olmsted, 1971, p. 71) does not necessarily imply that these phones form a phonetic category. Also, production errors are not generally reciprocal (e.g., [d] substitutes for [t], but [t] substitutes for [k]; Olmsted, 1971, p. 76), whereas children's phonetic categories involve reciprocal relationships (see chapter five). However, many production errors do involve phones that seem similar, at least to adults, such as the substitution of [d] for [ð]. Empirically, even if not necessarily, the two kinds of performance may be related, so when a child indicates in some way that he or she regards two phones as belonging to the same class, it is relevant to ask whether that child pronounces them alike. In the cases to be presented here, the answer is almost always negative; we are dealing with children's grouping of phones that they distinguish in both production and perception. The cases in which children class two phones together and tend to substitute one for the other still leave an open question as to the relationship between these two facts. This is partly the question of whether production errors must have a peripheral (e.g., physiological) basis, or whether they may stem from judgments at a more abstract level of speech processing. This question has been addressed by Fromkin (1971, esp. pp. 35-38) and Shattuck (1974).

In general, the studies reported here have both a methodological advantage and a disadvantage, as compared with studies of production. The disadvantage is that it is far more difficult to elicit phonetic judgments than speech production from children. The advantage is that when we present phones to children and elicit their judgments of relationships among them, we can at least specify the phonetic "input" to the process, whereas the origins of production are obscure. This advantage is parallel to that in the study of comprehension as opposed to production in syntax, illustrated in the work of Carol Chomsky (1969). It was pointed out relatively early in the recent study of language development (Bellugi and Brown, 1964: 42). In principle, this advantage applies to all of the studies reported here, although the phonetic "input" is under practical control mainly in the experimental studies (chapters three through six).

Another distinction between the study of speech sound categorization and the study of speech perception may be less obvious than in the case of production. As examples of the study of perception, consider Liberman, Cooper, Shankweiler, and Studdert-Kennedy (1967), and other research in the framework associated with Haskins Laboratory, and Massaro (1972a, 1971, 1970a, and 1970b). These studies deal with the processing of acoustic information, primarily in the momentary interval between the onset of a speech stimulus and the recognition of it, usually as one of a given set of native-language target syllables. Speech recognition in this sense—recognizing an acoustic signal as belonging to a particular phoneme—is a different kind of performance from the categorizations studied here, most of which involve recognizing a relationship between the members of distinct phonemes. However, we do speak of categorizing [u] and [o] together, as "perceiving" a similarity between them, (with the understanding that phonetically native speakers are not ordinarily conscious of the basis of this judgement). It is clear that both kinds of performance are categorial; in fact, the categorial nature of speech perception has been the topic of much recent research. As in the case of production, however, it is an empirical question whether the bases of speech recognition are the same as the bases of speech sound categorization, that is, whether the cues that are important in speech recognition are also salient in the recognition of higher-order categories.

Given that one set of categories includes the other, we might suppose that speech recognition is a necessary but not sufficient condition for speech sound categorization. However, the order in which we recognize units of different types in speech is not fully understood. For instance, there is some evidence (Savin and Bever, 1970; Massaro, 1972b) that the immediate unit of speech recognition is longer than one segment, and that the recognition of individual phones is temporally secondary. Analogously, the recognition of supra-phonemic categories may either precede or follow phonemic perception, both in speech processing and in development. This issue will not be pursued here.

A special case of the study of perception has been the rather extensive work on inter-phonemic auditory discrimination in both children and adults (e.g., Graham and House, 1971; Miller and Nicely, 1955). The present studies differ from these in that they deal with children's judgments of relationships between phones that they do discriminate. For example, the evidence to be presented in chapters two and five suggest that children tend to group the vowel [ɪ] with the vowel [i] under certain conditions and with the vowel [ɛ] under other conditions. Yet there can hardly be serious doubt that five-year-old children can discriminate these vowels in normal speech recognition. Kamil and Rudegeair (1972) demonstrate that on properly designed auditory discrimination tasks, the error rates of kindergarten and first-grade children are quite low. For the same reason, discrimination studies with adults have almost all used conditions of noise or distortion. Thus we assume, and in marginal cases provide evidence, that in the present studies the classification of one phone with another is not based on discrimination error, but is more abstract judgment of relationships between discriminable (and functionally distinct) stimuli.

The experiments most similar to those reported in chapters three through six are the studies of "perceptual similarity" of consonants (Singh, 1971) and of vowels (Singh and Woods, 1971). In these studies, listeners were asked to choose one of two consonants as most similar to a third "stimulus" consonant in an XAB paradigm (Singh, 1971) or to give numerical dissimilarity judgments for pairs of vowels (Singh and Woods, 1971). Like the present studies, Singh's are concerned with the "different degrees of perceptual distance" associated with various phonetic features. The difference between adult and child subjects, however, is potentially important. In Singh's study the subjects were students in a phonetics class "proficient in phonetic writing" (Singh, 1971, p. 114), and in Singh and Woods (1971) subjects were students in an introductory college speech class. This fact raises the important question of the extent to which the subjects' judgments were reflections of a knowledge of standard and phonetic spelling systems, and of formal phonetic description, rather than reflections of fundamental linguistic competence. The studies reported here help to clarify that issue, since the subjects were children of kindergarten, first- and second-grade age. One of the procedures used was similar to that of Singh (1971), with differences appropriate to the age of the subjects.

In presenting his studies, Singh refers to perception and to the literature on discrimination, but it should be made explicit that the perception of speech in terms of phonemes and the recognition of similarities across phonemes are two different kinds of linguistic performance. Singh compares the relative strength of various phonetic features in distinguishing consonants in his study with the rankings derived from the discrimination studies by Singh and Black (1966) and Miller and Nicely (1955). Table 1 expresses these rankings in a

Table 1

Importance of Phonetic Features
in Studies with Adults

	Discrimination Studies		Similarity Study
	Miller and Nicely (1955)	Singh and Black (1966)	Singh (1971)
Salience	Noise	No Noise	No Noise Condition
Greatest	Nasal	Nasal	Nasal
	Voice	Place	Frication
		Liquid	
	Frication	Voice	Glide
	Duration	Duration	Liquid
		Frication	Place
Least	Place	Aspiration	Voice

strictly ordinal fashion, using the "normal" (no noise, no filtering) condition from Singh (1971).

Singh convincingly accounts for the disparity between Miller-Nicely and the other two studies with respect to the importance of voicing by noting that in the presence of noise (in Miller-Nicely and in the noise conditions in Singh), voicing becomes a more important cue as the noise masks other, higher-frequency information. However, there remain significant disparities among the studies as to the importance of frication and place of articulation. Our evidence from children is largely orthogonal to that presented in Table 1, in that it compares different sets of features and in some instances, different kinds of categorial judgments.

Another attempt to compare the relative "strength" of phonetic features across different tasks is that of Olmsted (1971), who tests the hypothesis that those features that contribute most to discriminability also contribute to success in production. On the basis of Miller and Nicely's ranking of features in discrimination, Olmsted predicts relative success in production with remarkable accuracy: 100% overall and at least 90% for individual children, with respect to mean number of errors of various types. In this large and intricate study, there are certain qualifications to this impressive record, noted by Olmsted, but perhaps the main limitation is the relatively small number of predictions possible with Miller and Nicely's features.

The overall record in comparing the salience of phonetic features across different tasks is left unclear, not only by the relatively small number of studies, but by the fact that different investigators have used different feature systems and different experimental conditions. The extent to which three different tasks—production, discrimination, and judgments of similarity—can be shown to reflect the same basic phonetic structure, certainly remains an open question. The present studies were designed primarily to investigate the existence and nature of children's phonetic categorizations, rather than to relate directly to existing studies of other kinds of performance, but we will examine such relations wherever possible.

1.1.3 Competence and performance. One of the most important issues in recent psycholinguistics has been the distinction between competence and performance; it has also been one of the most confused issues. Two concepts discussed by Fodor and Garrett (1966) may help to clarify the topic of this monograph. They point out that there are at least two parts to the competence-performance distinction. The first is the distinction between studying the mechanisms underlying behavior (thus necessarily idealizing somewhat and predicting beyond any finite corpus) and studying a finite corpus of behavior itself. The second is the distinction between showing that a theory of linguistic competence (a grammar) axiomatizes the knowledge possessed by a native speaker and showing that the grammar itself constitutes a component of a model of performance, that is, that the speaker not only associates sentences and structural descriptions as the grammar predicts, but also that he does so in a manner analogous to the form and organization of the rules of the grammar. Fodor and Garrett point out that this latter distinction has not always been made in studies of syntactic development.

The competence-performance distinction in the first sense is well justified by the nature of linguistic data and by the broader and more insightful analyses that linguists have developed by going beyond inductive generalization from a corpus of utterances. This monograph is intended to be a study of children's developing competence in this first sense. It analyzes children's performance on several kinds of tasks, hypothesizing abstract determinants of that performance, namely implicit categorizations of speech sounds, and relating these categories to a theory of phonetic features. (Whether one considers this underlying competence to be linguistic or psychological is probably an undecidable question in the present state of the field.) In any case, as Fodor and Garrett point out, "both linguistic and psychological models [may be] models of competence" (1966: 138).

The second distinction, applied to phonology, is the distinction between claiming that a given explicit set of rules is the optimal statement of the relation between underlying and phonetic form for a language, and claiming that this phonology directly describes the production and perception of utterances. Unlike its syntactic counterpart, this latter claim has rarely been maintained or investigated, except in some recent studies of laxing and vowel shift in production (Steinberg and Krohn, 1973, and Moskowitz, 1973). The problem does not arise in this form here, in that this monograph deals with phonetic categories rather than generative rules. The relevant analog is the issue discussed in the preceding section: whether the phonetic categories that children employ in spelling and in other judgments play a direct role in the production and recognition of speech.

Related to the competence–performance distinction is the notion of "psychological reality." This is sometimes used in psycholinguistic studies in a way that suggests that linguistic theories require confirmation from performance other than that which formed the linguistic data, which, at its best, may be extremely rich and broad. The suggestion seems to be that a proposed explanation, even if it deals convincingly with a wide range of otherwise puzzling linguistic data, may be put to a direct, and somehow more "real," test by seeing whether it predicts aspects of speech production and recognition. Two assumptions in this view seem to be incorrect: that data which can be most readily observed, controlled and measured are inherently more "real" than the somewhat more abstract data (such as grammaticality judgments) that are characteristic of linguistics; and that all forms of linguistic performance must *directly* reflect linguistic structure. In contrast, the present studies ask, "What phonetic organization underlies certain categorial judgments by children?" Given some answer to this question, we may then compare it with a theory of phonetic structure (see section 1.3.1) and with what is known about other kinds of performance, but always with the recognition that different types of linguistic performance may reflect phonetic structure indirectly and perhaps in differing ways. These studies, which implicitly and explicitly compare children with adults, give some information about the course of development, including what categorizations develop before a child enters school and which ones develop later.

Having attempted to delineate the topic of this monograph, to distinguish it from related topics, and to suggest the nature and interest of the questions involved, I will now indicate the scope of the evidence to be presented, emphasizing its limitations. It is perhaps inevitable, or at least understandable, that the available evidence bears on only some of the many questions that one can ask within the theoretical framework outlined above.

1.2 The nature and scope of the evidence

This section presents a brief overview of the evidence to be presented. It has two main sources: young children's invented spellings, and experimental studies of children's judgments of relationships among phones. Such an overview seems useful because the study of children's phonetic categorization is not a traditional one; accordingly, it may be well to indicate in advance the nature of the evidence and the areas within this potentially broad field that will be dealt with.

1.2.1 Invented spelling. Chapter two presents a spelling system for English created by some preschool children and infers from it aspects of their implicit categorization of speech sounds. Several children independently invented this orthography, beginning at various ages from 2½ to 4, and used it to spell many types of messages until it was replaced by standard English spelling after the child entered school. Most of the spellings which I have been able to date reliably are at ages four and five. Various interesting questions about the origin and development of this invented spelling are discussed in the first section of chapter two: how the spelling began, what influence adults may have had, how it interacted with standard spelling, etc.

Essentially, the children began with a knowledge of the traditional names for the letters of the alphabet. They then learned that a letter may spell a phone or phones in its name: that *A* spells [e], or that *B* spells [b]. They then attempted to extend this insight in order to use the letters to spell various messages at will. Such an extension is not at all straightforward. Most important for our purposes is the simple fact that not all the phonemes of (any dialect of) English are directly represented in letter names. If, for the moment, we make the traditional assumption that the children probably sought to represent English at a phonemic level of detail, we can estimate the magnitude of the problem by noting that there are generally 24 consonant phonemes and at least nine vowel phonemes, the latter forming about 16 simple and complex syllable nuclei. (The precise number depends to a considerable extent on the dialect and the analysis employed.) Of these, 17 consonants and seven vowels are included in the letter-names, in my pronunciation. The seven consonants *not* included in the letter-names are /g, θ, ð, h, š, ž/ and /ŋ/. The seven vowels that *are* included are /e, i, ay, o, yu, ɛ/ and /ʌ/.[2] Obviously, the problem of representing English at will on the basis of the letter-names is severe, particularly with respect to the vowels.

Confronted with these shortcomings, the children might have done one of several things. They might have 1) given up the attempt to spell English on this basis, 2) made up new symbols for those phonemes not included in the letter-names (or used familiar symbols at random), 3) asked adults how to spell just the missing phonemes, as needed, or 4) paired each missing phoneme with one for which a spelling was known using some systematic basis, such as a phonetic similarity between the two. In fact, the children who created the spelling system of chapter two used a combination of methods 3 and 4. They generally obtained from adults the spellings for /g, θ, ð/ and /h/, while they developed for themselves spellings for /š/ and /ŋ/ (/ž/ rarely occurred) and for the vowels, by pairing these phonemes with others for which they knew a spelling, usually from the letter-names. The children evidently constructed these pairings on the basis of phonetic similarity as they perceived it. The outcome of this combination of letter-name analysis and phonetic grouping is a spelling system that is nonstandard in many respects, and it is the nonstandard spellings that are of interest. The standard spellings have little import; although in some instances they may have been invented, we must assume that they were influenced by adults and hence tell us nothing about the children's phonetic judgments. The systematic nonstandard spellings, on the other hand, are quite clearly not borrowed from adults; rather, they indicate the children's own phonetic groupings.

That the children were able to construct such a spelling system at all is of some developmental interest. Among other things, it shows that some children are able, at an early age, to detect relationships that they feel might be represented in spelling, as opposed to merely learning specific sound-spelling correspondences from adults. Other observations about the conditions under which the spellings occurred, how various children began, how the spelling reflected dialect differences, the children's ability to read their own spelling, and how the invented orthography changed as each child developed, have been presented in Read (1970, ch. IV). As interesting as these questions are, our primary concern here is with the phonetic judgments that underlie the orthography.

Essentially, there are four kinds of cases. One is the most typical, particularly for vowels. In the invented orthography, a phone for which no spelling is obvious from the letter-names is spelled in the same way as another phone whose spelling the child knows, either from the letter-names or from standard spelling via adults. In each instance, the phones thus grouped together are in fact phonetically similar in specific respects. To explain this fact, one may hypothesize that the child recognized the phonetic similarity, judged it to be more prominent than other possibilities, and so chose to extend the spelling of the known case to the unknown case. This type of spelling suggests implicit classes of phonemes based on phonetic similarity as judged by children. We can compare various possible phonetic groupings with the ones that the children actually constructed. In some instances, we can conclude that certain phonetic properties are more salient than others as bases for children's phonetic categorizations.

While most of the interesting spellings are of this supra-phonemic type, there are three special cases. The children tended to represent the potentially syllabic consonants [r, l, m, n] and [ŋ] without a preceding vowel, particularly when the sonorant in question was truly syllabic, i.e., when there was in fact no vowel in the syllable. This spelling again suggests an abstract grouping of phonemes (of syllabics as opposed to obstruents), although the grouping is indicated by spelling all phones of this type in the same general manner, rather than with the same letter(s). A second special case is that of the affricated [t] that occurs before [r] in English, as in *truck*. Some children evidently assigned this phone to a category different from /t/, as indicated in their spelling. This possibility is interesting, particularly for what it suggests about a teacher's possible responses to apparent spelling errors. The third special case is that of preconsonantal nasals, such as the [n] of *want*, which the children strongly tended to omit in spelling. This phenomenon has to do with how children categorize nasality in environments with a particular structure.

The invented spellings indicate how children group sounds together for spelling purposes in certain specific situations. These can be regarded as "forced-choice" situations in that the children sought to spell messages at will, using a limited set of known spellings. That is, when the children wished to represent a phone whose spelling is not suggested by the letter-names, they typically chose a known spelling for what seemed to them to be a similar sound. Ordinarily, they knew spellings for several phones, each related to the target phone in different ways, so that the direction in which the children typically made their choice suggests which similarities are most prominent.

In this description, such terms as "perceived"(a phonetic similarity), "judged" (that similarity to be more prominent than other possibilities), and "chose" (one spelling over another) are not intended to imply that every (or any) step of this hypothetical process was a conscious one. It is difficult to determine the degree to which young children are aware of the bases for their actions. In this case, I assume that the underlying phonetic categorizations were largely unconscious, but that the children could bring them to awareness in various degrees, depending partly on the demands of the specific spelling problem. Adult spelling is likewise only partly a matter of conscious decision, although it has very different bases.

Only the nonstandard spellings are informative, and some of them are very far from standard spelling. In fact, the parents involved could not read the spellings in many instances. This fact raises an interesting question of validity: given the spelling BER, how can we be sure that the child was representing the word *bear* and the pronunciation [bɛr]? This is a question of the identification of the word, the influence of the child's dialect, and the level of detail that the children sought to represent. The latter two questions will be dealt with as they arise in specific cases. As for the identification of words, it is important that the children generally produced whole messages, in which words appeared in large contexts. BER, for instance, comes from a story written by a five-year-old. It appeared in a little folded booklet, with a picture on the front, a title page, and the following story: "HOO LICS HANE! HOO LICS HANE WAS OV PONA TIM THER WAS OV BER HOO LOVED HANE THE EAD." Evidently, this story is: "Who likes honey! Who likes honey? Once upon a time there was a bear who loved honey. The end." This supposition is strongly supported by the picture on the cover, which shows a little brown creature standing next to a tree. Conceivably, there is another interpretation, but this one seems well-supported by internal and external evidence (e.g., the well-known tastes of Winnie-the-Pooh).

This example is fairly typical of the extent to which the identification of words is supported by their context and of the mixture of invented and standard spellings to be found in the data. The specific spellings here are relatively sophisticated and obviously influenced by standard spelling; the use of oo for [u], of C for [k], of A for [ʌ], etc. would not be typical of younger children. This example also suggests hypotheses not concerned with phonetic judgments. The use of OV for *u(pon)* and *a (bear)* suggests, not that the child thinks [ə] should be spelled OV on phonetic grounds, but that she has noticed that [ə] and [əv] alternate (as in *one of them*) and that she does not yet know which [ə]'s are really *of*'s. This interpretation is interesting for what it suggests about children's developing syntax, rather than their phonology.

Assuming that the words and even the sounds represented have been correctly identified, one may still question the validity of explaining the spelling in terms of tacit phonetic categories. How can one know that a child used a particular representation because of the similarity between two sounds? Occasionally, there is a nonphonetic explanation available; in the example cited, the A of EAD (end) is actually an unclear letter; it could have been intended as an N. It would hardly be appropriate to seek a phonetic explanation there. Such cases aside, the fact is that an explanation in terms of phonetic similarity is often the only plausible account available. When the children's spellings are nonstandard (so that they could hardly have been dictated by adults), when a given spelling occurs regularly, when several children independently use the same spelling, and when the same general principle seems to have applied in the spelling of several different sounds, it has usually turned out that there is a plausible explanation in terms of phonetic similarity, and rarely is there any other. The experiments reported here have further tested, and generally confirmed, some of the explanations in terms of phonetic categories.

This discussion raises the important question of the extent to which the invented spellings demonstrate a single set of judgments, common to all the children studied. Several factors tend to introduce variation into the spellings. The most important are the influence of standard spelling, which varied from one child to another, and the gradual change in the spellings with age, generally in the direction of standard spelling. Since not all children were spelling at the same age and not all children wrote the same amount, it is not easy to compare the spelling of one with another. Other variable factors are the children's dialects, unclear printing, and spellings that must be considered mistakes with respect to a given child's system at a particular time.

Despite these and other sources of variation, there are striking similarities in the spelling across children. This fact is important because, with the marginal exception of a few siblings, friends, or schoolmates, the children studied were totally unacquainted with the others and their spellings. Previous reports (Read, 1971 and 1975) have been based on impressionistic summaries, but at this writing I have a complete tabulation (performed by computer) of all nonstandard invented spellings available to me as of May, 1973, so that I can give a quantitative indication of the frequency of each spelling.[3] Some of the spellings reported in chapter two are infrequent, though suggestive, but ordinarily the spellings to be discussed are the most frequent nonstandard spellings. Table 2 summarizes the extent of the data contained in this rather massive tabulation.

Table 2

Extent of the Data

Number of children	32
Number of different words spelled (types)	1,201
Number of spellings (tokens)	2,517
(not counting exact repetitions by a given child at a given age)	
Number of spellings of individual phonemes	11,109
Mean phonemes per word	4.4

The data include unequal numbers of examples from different children; some children wrote many stories, letters, and messages of all sorts, which the parents regularly saved; in other cases, the parents were able to pass along only a sentence or two, usually because other examples had been discarded. (Most parents were unaware that the spelling might have any linguistic significance.) Table 3 displays the number of children who contributed various quantities of examples. Note that 11 children contributed 87% of the data, and that these children each contributed from 51 to 468 nonstandard words. In these cases, there is enough evidence to assess whether the child was spelling systematically, particularly for the vowels.

The fact that a number of children independently developed similar

Table 3

Children Contributing Words with Nonstandard Spellings

No. of words contrib'd.	Number of children	Total words	Mean wds/child	% of total contrib'd.
1-10	9	41	4.6	02
11-25	8	134	16.75	05
26-50	5	143	28.6	06
51-100	3	227	75.7	09
101-200	4	616	154.	24
201-300	2	480	240.	19
>400	2	876	438.	35
Total	33	2517	76.3	100

spellings is obviously suggestive. One might even be tempted at first to think of these as optimal or "natural" spellings for children, with immediate pedagogical application. Such an inference is too hasty because the spellings represent the children's choices under certain specific circumstances. Each child knew the standard alphabet and letter-names, and each knew certain aspects of standard spelling. A child's spelling on these bases is obviously not necessarily an absolute optimum, either for that child or for children generally. We can make reasonable inferences only by comparing each child's choices with the alternatives available to him.

1.2.2 Experimental studies. Because of the limitations of the invented spellings, chapter two presents some supplemental evidence. One technique, gathering observations of children who were doing the invented spelling, was limited because some of the children had developed beyond the invented spelling when I studied it (that is, I collected samples that parents had saved); others, who were active, were reluctant to answer questions about it. Their apparent inability to describe what they were doing supports the view that the spelling was only partly a conscious performance. Another kind of supplemental evidence comes from the study of primary-grade spelling, where some characteristics of the invented spelling turn up as extraordinarily frequent "errors."

In any case, the inherent and empirical limitations of the invented spelling suggest a more systematic attempt to study children's categorization of speech sounds. Experimental studies might overcome two fundamental limitations of the inferences from the invented spellings.

The most important is that the spelling problems posed by the standard alphabet and letter-names are limited to certain cases, so that no general description of children's phonetic categories can be constructed on the basis of the invented spelling. Second, in our society only a small minority of children create their own spellings, giving rise to a suspicion (in some quarters, a conviction) that the underlying judgments may be limited to a few children.

My own guess, on the contrary, has been that it is the opportunity for invented spelling that is limited to relatively few children. This opportunity requires the coincidence of a child's interests and inclinations with the minimum of required knowledge and, especially, with a parental tolerance for what appears to be the development of bad spelling "habits." Many parents may quite unknowingly pass along to their children, even at the scribbling stage, the belief that English spelling is governed by a standard of correctness, and that it is hazardous to attempt to predict the spelling of words. This attitude is probably a prevailing one in our society. There are several such circumstantial reasons why relatively few children invent their own spellings, but there is no especially plausible reason why the underlying phonetic categorizations must be restricted to those who do so.

Whatever the merits of the opposing beliefs on this issue, it is obviously pointless and perhaps dangerous to speculate. Whether children implicitly group sounds together, and whether they do so according to certain phonetic similarities, is clearly an empirical question, and one of some developmental and educational significance. The main importance of the invented spellings has been to raise this question and to illustrate some of its empirical consequences. As it turns out, the experimental studies (chapters three through six) indicate that children in kindergarten and first grade often share some of the categorial judgments seen in the invented spellings.

Despite the appeal of attempting to generalize the inferences from the invented spellings through experimental study, it must be acknowledged that this course has its own inherent limitations. A crucial fact about the invented spelling is that it is spontaneous linguistic performance, the phonetic basis of which is quite clear in certain cases. Furthermore, in that the performance involved spelling, it wore its educational significance on its face, so to speak. Such spontaneity and *prima facie* validity are rarely encountered in experimental study, where the need for careful control often conflicts with the need to sample normal linguistic performance. A second problem confronting experimental study is the methodological one: it is not obvious that one can elicit evidence of speech sound classifications from young children, even assuming that such classifications exist. It is distinctly possible that one of the extraordinary characteristics of the children who invented spellings was that their phonetic judgments were more accessible to them (when needed for spelling purposes) than are other children's judgments, just as some adults are especially facile in recognizing phonetic similarities, as in the more subtle forms of rhyme and alliteration. This methodological problem is separate from that of whether children in general recognize categories of speech sounds, so there is the danger of concluding from inadequate methodology that no such categorization exists. Section 2.2.2 discusses one such example.

Recognizing the counterposed difficulties of both experimental and further naturalistic studies, I have undertaken a series of experiments designed to elicit evidence of speech sound categorization from children, primarily from five to seven years of age. These studies tested inferences from the invented spelling, but sought what could never be found in further study of spelling: evidence of how children group sounds in terms of phonetic similarity, without regard to the special problem of spelling English on the basis of letter-names or other specific constraints. There is thus a gain in generality in return for the loss in spontaneity. Nevertheless, English spelling is still a potential confounding influence on the results, and was dealt with in various ways in the several studies.

The explanation for the invented spellings was that when the children spelled two sounds alike, they did so on the basis of a perceived (and real) phonetic similarity between the two. It is this assumption that links the invented spelling with the experimental studies. The experiments did not employ a spelling task, in order to avoid the limitation to specific problems and possibly certain children; rather, the experiments tested children's judgments of phonetic similarity directly. A similarity judgment is inherently relative; there is no point in asking, "Is X similar to A?" since the answer depends entirely on what dimensions of similarity one considers, and what distance along those dimensions one is willing to regard as relatively small. The more meaningful question is, "Is X more similar to A, or to B?" where the comparison can be used to limit the relevant dimensions. This question is especially appropriate for speech sounds, since a theory of phonetic features defines precisely the possible dimensions of similarity. It thus becomes possible to choose A and B such that each differs from X in one dimension, testing quite directly the hypothesis that feature XA is more salient than feature XB as a dimension of phonetic similarity for children.

Accordingly, the experiments typically employed an XAB paradigm, in which the subjects were given sound X and were then asked, "Is X more like A or B?" where X, A, and B were in identical or equivalent contexts, and where X was phonetically like A in all but one feature, and like B in all but one other feature. This paradigm was modified in various details appropriate to the age of the children tested and the specific sounds involved. Thus, the experiments tested several hypotheses:

1. that young children can make judgments in such a task.
2. that these judgments will be consistent for an individual, according to certain phonetic features (rather than to a phonetically irrelevant property such as order of presentation, familiarity, or standard spelling).
3. that children of a given age will choose consistently across individuals.
4. that in certain cases, the children will make different judgments from adults.
5. that overall, certain features will be more salient than others as a basis for similarity judgments.

The features tested against each other were chosen primarily on the basis of the invented spellings. The studies presented in chapters three through six deal with the following categorizations: the affricated [t] in [tr] clusters as an affricate or as a stop; the nasality in words with preconsonantal nasals (e.g., *bent*) with other segments; the vowel [ε] (e.g., *bet*) with vowels related to it in height and in tenseness; phonetic [s] with [z], and [š] and [t]. In exploring the basis for categorizations, some studies deal with nondistinctive features such as duration, or with nonphonetic properties, such as the influence of standard spelling.

1.3 Conclusions and their significance

Overall, the naturalistic and experimental studies reported here do seem to indicate that children tacitly categorize speech sounds according to perceived phonetic similarities, and that these judgments may be elicited by various experimental tests of the type mentioned above. The consistency in these judgments—for individuals and for age groups —depends on the specific phonetic category in question, but there are cases in which children entering school make different judgments from adults. This section will indicate briefly the significance of these conclusions for a theory of phonetic features, for the study of language development, and for educational questions about the learning of reading and writing.

1.3.1 Relation to phonetic feature theory. Children's categorization of speech sounds relates in specific ways to the theory of phonetic features. The essential claim of such a theory is that speech sounds are to be analyzed as bundles of phonetic features, i.e., in terms of the presence or absence of specific phonetic properties. The main constraints that such a theory must meet are that the features chosen must be both narrow enough and broad enough: they must make it possible to describe distinctly the phonetic units in all languages (all possible phonological variation), and yet they must make it possible to describe phonological processes compactly (by picking out phonologically natural classes). Because the subject matter of feature theory is precisely the categorization of speech sounds, children's tacit classifications are a potential source of data, with some important reservations discussed below.

The phonetic feature theory adopted here is that of Chomsky and Halle (1968), with certain recent modifications. This theory is based on a wide variety of phonetic and linguistic data from several languages, and it has been proposed and continuously revised with attention to its adequacy in many respects. Its empirical claims have been developed more explicitly than those of any competing theory. However, in order to make the present description more accessible to some readers, I will not adopt the most recent Chomsky-Halle features in cases where the choice makes no difference to the argument. For example, I will usually refer to the "tense-lax" contrast among vowels, rather than to the feature "advanced tongue root," even though the latter has some justification.

Feature theories in general, including that of Chomsky-Halle, have been developed to account for phonological data. It is a further empirical question whether a particular theory will also provide a compact description of other aspects of performance, such as production, perception, and the categorizations studied here. Essentially feature theory postulates that there is ultimately one set of phonetic material, organized in the same way for all languages. Accordingly, we may expect that this organization underlies various kinds of linguistic performance. There is considerable evidence for this expectation. Consider the nasal-oral contrast for consonants, which is a relatively major class in any feature theory (and traditional articulatory description may be translated into a nonbinary feature theory). Nasals have also turned out to be a major perceptual class in discrimination studies such as Miller and Nicely (see Table 1). One could make parallel arguments concerning a number of major feature distinctions, such as that between obstruents and sonorants, or even consonants versus vowels.

There still remain important questions about how the structure of the phonetic material of language (feature theory) is reflected in different kinds of linguistic performance. Just as in syntax, we cannot assume that the relationship between abstract linguistic description and actual performance is direct and invariant across tasks. Here again, there is significant evidence. For example, it is a fundamental assumption that phonetic features represent reciprocal relations: whatever the relation is between phone A and phone B in terms of a given feature, it is reciprocal. But Olmsted (1971) showed children's production errors are not necessarily or even generally reciprocal. The plausible interpretation is not that this fundamental principle of feature theory is wrong, but that production is influenced by peripheral factors as well as by the more abstract phonetic relations that are reciprocal.

Accordingly, it is not valid to conclude, as some studies have done, that a given feature theory is right or wrong, applicable or inapplicable, directly from an investigation of linguistic performance. Rather, we must bear in mind that performance is certainly the outcome of several interacting factors, one of which, we assume, is the basic phonetic structure of language. With this important provision, the study of children's categorizations may contribute evidence relevant to the development of a theory of phonetic features.

The evidence provided by children's categorizations may be more directly relevant to a theory of phonetic features than that provided by the study of speech production and recognition, insofar as it deals directly with categorization and with less influence of the peripheral factors that affect speech and hearing. The relevance of the present studies is two-fold. The first and most basic is simply the demonstration that children (and adults) do categorize speech sounds across phonemes; the phones of a language are not only divided into classes by functional contrast, but speakers treat the members of contrasting phonemes as related to each other in terms of specific phonetic properties. This demonstration provides significant confirmation for the fundamental assumption of phonetic feature theory: that phones are analyzable as bundles of properties, and that these properties are the basic phonetic units of language. Indeed the evidence from children helps to show that this structure is not merely an artifact of linguistic analysis, but is part of what we learn in acquiring a language.

The second area of relevance is more complex and less clear: the contribution of children's phonetic judgments to the choice and organization of features in phonetic feature theory. In general, this study makes no new proposals regarding phonetic features; the categorial judgments investigated here can be described adequately in terms of existing features. This fact is hardly surprising, considering that current feature theory has been developed to describe many aspects of general phonology, and considering the large number of classes that can be distinguished in terms of the 20 or so features currently proposed for English. In just one instance—the categorization of [æ] in relation to other front vowels—children's judgments provide evidence relevant to a recent development. Even in such a case, one must be cautious in drawing inferences from children's performance for a theory that has been developed on the basis of a great deal of other evidence, primarily from adult phonology. Nevertheless, children's (and adults') phonetic categorizations are potentially relevant data for the development of phonetic feature theory. The adequacy of current features for describing these categorizations gives some empirical support to the features themselves, as well as to the fundamental assumption discussed in the preceding paragraph.

In most instances, the issue in these studies is the relative salience of particular phonetic relationships, a psycholinguistic judgment not accounted for by phonetic feature theory itself. Typically, in the spelling and experimental judgments, children might categorize the phones involved in more than one way. When they consistently choose one of the possible classes, we conclude that the corresponding phonetic relationship is more prominent (or salient) to them than the other possibilities. Phonetic feature theory provides a matrix for the classification of speech sounds; the children's judgments indicate that across certain columns of the matrix (i.e. across certain phone-types), some rows (features) represent psychologically stronger relationships than others. This is the import of claiming that [s] is regarded as more similar to [z] than to [t], for instance. Phonetic feature description claims that [s] differs from [t] in one feature and from [z] in another, but no linguistic description ever claimed that these two differences must be of the same perceptual "size," or salience, and evidently they are not. Similarly, it is not necessarily the case that any two phonetic differences must be regarded as greater than any one other, and so forth. A particular feature relationship may hold across only some segments. In the example cited, voicing may be a relatively minor property among fricatives (such as [s] and [z]) but a more major one for other types of segments. The present studies measure the relative importance of certain phonetic properties in children's categorizations. In this primary respect, these studies deal with a psycholinguistic property that is not traditionally part of phonetic description itself.

1.3.2 Significance for a theory of language development. The fact that children can make reasonably consistent categorial judgments of speech sounds reveals a tacit and abstract linguistic performance that has not previously been studied as such. The judgments are tacit in that they are not evident on the surface of normal linguistic performance, such as listening and speaking, and one is usually not conscious of making them. They are abstract in that they usually involve children grouping together speech sounds which they can readily distinguish under normal listening conditions. We do not yet know whether these judgments precede or follow speech perception itself, either in speech processing ("real time") or developmentally. Also, the judgments are abstract in that they are not required by the phonetic facts themselves. These facts are often neutral between one categorization and another, so that the judgments indicate a specific contribution by the child: the use of one property rather than another as basis for categorization.

Thus the present studies deal with a set of phonetic categories more detailed than the phonemic distinctions that are most obviously required for the production and recognition of speech. These categories are evidently part of what one acquires in learning a native language. They constitute a further aspect of language development that must be explained. This particular development seems to have very little immediate basis in the data available to a child; adults rarely demonstrate in any direct way that two functionally distinct phones are to be regarded as similar, or "belonging together," in some way. One can conceive of possibly relevant evidence, such as similarities in spelling, in phonological processes, and in adult discrimination errors (to the extent that these actually correspond to children's categories), but these bases are not so systematic and compelling that they explain away the problem. Thus children's grouping of speech sounds poses the classic problem of language development at a rather concrete level: how does the child acquire linguistic knowledge on the basis of the deficient data given? Ultimately, we want to identify the child's contribution, the "map" imposed on the data of speech which allows him or her to derive the abstract categories.

The study of children's judgments provides new evidence about the availability of phonetic characteristics, and their relative salience, to children. These judgments are important precisely because they are abstract; they are not uniquely determined by the speech signal, or logically required for speech recognition, so they tell us something new about the processing of speech. When a child groups the rounded vowels together for spelling purposes, even though he or she can easily distinguish them in production and discrimination, we know that the qualities that these vowels share are available to the child, and more prominent than other qualities which might have been used to solve the spelling problem. The principle here is that the child's mental representation of speech sounds is not limited to a table of autonomous phonemes, related to each other only by functional contrast. Rather, in the studies reported here, children demonstrate that they can make use of phonetic properties in grouping speech sounds for various purposes. This insight is the central theme of this monograph.

Quite properly, a fair amount of psycholinguistic inquiry has been devoted to the development of phonemic distinctions, particularly in children's productions. We must not allow the traditional importance of this problem to imply that a set of independent phonemes is the limit of children's phonetic analysis, however. Evidently children can also recognize the phonetic properties that relate members of one phoneme to those of another through similarities of various types and degrees. As noted above, this observation poses the problem of acquisition, but it also shows one aspect of what children have available to them by the age at which they enter school.

The age of the children in the present studies—from four to eight overall—is important developmentally. Until recently, it has been assumed that most aspects of language learning were complete at age six or so; this assumption certainly seemed to apply to phonological development, except for the production of certain difficult sounds. Now there is evidence in syntax (C. Chomsky, 1969) and phonology (Moskowitz, 1973) of continuing development beyond the preschool years. One reason for the reversal is that the recent studies have dealt with linguistic knowledge that is ordinarily tacit, either because it is concealed by situational factors or simply because there is no reason for it to be evident in normal language use. Such is the case with the studies reported here. Phonetic categories are rarely made overt spontaneously, as in the invented spelling. Upon examination, however, it turns out that adults and children make different judgments in certain cases, indicating that the children will generally undergo further development. The course of this development is beyond the focus of the studies reported here, but some evidence of it appears in both the invented spelling and the experimental studies. In this development, there is a complex interaction between phonetic judgments and a knowledge of standard spelling; spelling does influence one's categorizations (and vice-versa), but the influence is not an absolute or necessary one.

1.3.3 Significance for the teaching of literacy. Although the children's phonetic categories are significant basically as an aspect of linguistic knowledge and language development, they are also related to the learning of reading and writing, particularly at the ages dealt with here. The relation is through the assumption that young children will find it easiest to learn an orthography that groups together those speech sounds that they regard as alike or similar. This is actually a traditional assumption, although its illustrations in the invented spelling are often surprising. However, the traditional assumption is specifically that children group speech sounds into autonomous phonemes, and that it is precisely this grouping that they expect to find reflected unambiguously in spelling. As noted in section 1.1, one pedagogical orthography (i.t.a.) is designed explicitly on this assumption (modified in practice by compromises with standard spelling and dialect differences), and the same assumption is made of adults in the application of phonemics to the design of orthographies (Pike 1947: 89, 208-209).

The evidence presented here suggests that this assumption may be incorrect in two respects. First, the [tr] study (chapter three) suggests that children's assignment of phones to phonemes is not always the same as that of adults or linguists, although this may be a minor, perhaps even negligible, phenomenon. Second, and more important, the grouping of the members of distinct phonemes into larger classes, both in the invented spelling and in the experimental studies, suggests that children may well find natural, or at least acceptable, a spelling system that is abstract, in the sense that it ignores phonetic or even phonemic distinctions. The study of the /s-z/ contrast (chapter six) is an example of this kind of abstraction on the part of children.

Assuming that the optimal spelling system for the fluent adult reader is a rather abstract one (Weir and Venezky, 1968; Chomsky and Halle, 1968; C. Chomsky, 1970; Klima, 1972), one would presumably not wish to emphasize phonetic and phonemic distinctions in initial instruction if these distinctions were (a) not maintained in the standard orthography and (b) not very salient to young children, and thus not likely to present an important learning problem. This seems to be precisely the case with certain distinctions which would be maintained in a "phonemic" spelling system, and which are maintained in i.t.a. These cases are not so numerous that one would argue that phonemic spelling is totally wrong for young children (although it may well be for adults); rather, the evidence suggests that it is not correct as a principle. We can no longer assume that children are best equipped to learn just a "one phoneme—one grapheme" orthography, or even that children's judgments of phonetic categories are uniform; the nature of these judgments must be studied in more detail. Meanwhile, the only distinctions not maintained in standard spelling that one might wish to emphasize in initial teaching are those that have been shown to be salient to children.

Conversely in the case of reading, we must recognize that when a child is asked to learn that in various contexts *e* may represent either [i] or [ɛ], that grouping is not merely an arbitrary one, whose difficulty is exactly the same as that of any other arbitrary 2-1 mapping of sounds into spellings. Rather, the difficulty of this aspect of English spelling may be measured in terms of its distance from a grouping of vowels that the child might have tacitly constructed. Chapter five attempts to do just this for a group of English vowels.

These applications of psycholinguistic studies to practical educational issues are to be taken in the context of other considerations, of course. The choice of an orthography for initial reading and spelling depends on many assumptions; for example, standard English spelling in effect demonstrates to children that *please* and *pleasant* are related words, and that some of the differences in pronunciation are to be regarded as automatic. On that view, one might well choose an orthography much more abstract than children's own phonetic categorizations, such as standard English spelling itself. The argument here is that one should at least not assume that children's judgments are less abstract than they actually are. Pedagogical decisions also involve assumptions that are outside the expertise of the psycholinguist. The study of children's phonetic categories is offered not as a simple solution to complex problems, but as a way of understanding one aspect of those problems.

CHAPTER TWO

THE INVENTED SPELLING

2.1 The phenomenon

The observations that stimulated the study of children's judgments of speech sounds were of spellings which some preschool children devised, and which turned out to represent groupings of sounds on phonetic bases. There is some educational and developmental significance in the ways in which the spellings began, the backgrounds of the children, the influence of adults, and how the spelling changed over time and interacted with learning to read and to spell in the standard orthography. These questions have been addressed in Read (1970, ch. IV) and C. Chomsky (1971); our primary concern here is with the spellings as an indication of phonetic categories. Nevertheless, it may be useful to indicate briefly how the spellings began and what sample of children was involved.

The spelling began under various circumstances and at various ages, but typically a child learned to recognize the letters and to name them by their traditional names in the third year of life (age two). At some point in the following months, the child learned that a letter usually spells a phone that occurs in the name of that letter. This step occurred when the child learned the first letter in his or her name, for example, or when the child began to recognize certain prominent words, such as those displayed on signs. At some point, the child began to apply this insight as a principle, using letters to spell new words according to the phones in the letter-names. Typically, these children asked their parents, "How do you spell X?" (where X represents some sound, rather than a whole word) only when they could find no approximation to X in the letter-names.

The children who provide the most interesting examples, least tainted by a knowledge of standard spelling, are those who began to spell quite early—as early as age three and a half. At this age, the children typically spelled by arranging movable letters of various sorts, or even plastic shapes that only accidentally and partially resembled certain letters (C. Chomsky, 1971). Only later did they develop the coordination necessary to manipulate a pencil on paper (or a crayon on wallpaper).

Thus started, some of the children spelled only on certain occasions, such as labeling a drawing, while others produced messages of many kinds in a more or less constant profusion. To some extent, a child's production depended on circumstances. One four-year-old boy who lived in England with his parents for a year, found himself confined much of the time with colds and sniffles. During the year he filled a blank book with his writings. All in all, the children produced every variety of writing from letters and stories to protests to parents to prayers. Some of it was instrumental, with a specific addressee, but most of it was creative work, apparently for the author's own enjoyment.

As the children developed, their growing knowledge of standard spelling did not necessarily influence their invented spelling immediately. Some of the children continued to create their own spellings even after they learned to read standard spelling. The characteristics of the invented spelling did change, however, under the influence of standard spelling, and some characteristics appear to have changed more rapidly than others. The overall rate of change seems to have depended in part on the demands of the child's first schooling. One child, who knew how to read, changed "almost overnight" to standard spelling, his mother said, when he entered a formal and rather traditional private school; a girl who continued in a Montessori school where her spelling was accepted, continued to show certain aspects of the invented spelling at age eight.

In interviews with parents and teachers, it appeared that none of these children had any special difficulty in adopting standard spelling. This is a remarkable fact only if one insists that their original spelling was a habit structure, which must have developed and changed through extensive practice. It seems more adequate to regard the spelling as based on a set of tacit hypotheses about phonetic relationships and sound-spelling correspondences, which the child was able to modify readily as he or she encountered new information about standard spelling.

The children who produced the spelling studied here were identified as original spellers in an unsystematic and informal manner. I happened to learn of two children who had created spellings which turned out to be rather similar. Having recognized an apparent phonetic basis for their spellings, I found other such children, primarily by talking with teachers in Montessori schools and public kindergartens. Parents sometimes told me of the performance of a child's siblings or of other children.

Obviously, one must be cautious in generalizing about this kind of informal and relatively small sample, but on the basis of interviews with the parents, two general aspects of the background seem fairly clear. Without exception the parents did not expect, or in any extraordinary way encourage, their children to construct their own spellings. They supplied the materials—which were quite ordinary, such as paper and crayon—but were generally surprised and somewhat puzzled by their child's spelling efforts. Possibly the most important parental contribution was that even though some of them worried about the development of bad spelling, all of the parents accepted the child's spelling as a creative production and offered adult spelling only when the child asked for it.

Perhaps this attitude, which attaches greater importance to the creative and independent nature of the child's spelling than to its correctness by adult standards, is more likely to be found in educated professional-class families in our society. At any rate, because of the role of personal acquaintance and private schools in the informal "sampling procedure," such families made up almost the entire sample. On this basis, it is impossible to estimate whether children in other kinds of homes might also produce original spelling.

In her description of the original *Casa dei Bambini,* located in the tenements of Rome, Maria Montessori points out that writing was a readily-acquired activity for four-year-olds (Montessori, 1964). It may be unwise to draw inferences from this to spontaneous spelling in the United States, however, because we are dealing with a different language and spelling system, and possibly with different prevailing attitudes toward correctness in spelling. We must also note that the original Montessori school offered preparatory exercises and lessons in writing, even though the activity became an independent one for most children.

This brief summary of the background of the invented spellings has indicated how it came about, the nature of the families represented, and what the children worked with, but it is not directly relevant to our primary concern: the phonetic basis of the spellings and their categorial nature. A more crucial issue is the uniformity of the spellings: to what extent does the invented spelling represent a single system, independently created by over 30 preschool children? As noted in chapter one, the primary sources of variation in the spelling are the age of the child, the amount that each child wrote (and the amount available for analysis), the influence of dialect variation, and, most important, the degree of influence of standard spelling. If one attempts to control these variations, however, by considering only nonstandard spellings from children for whom we have at least fifty examples, and by noting the age and the dialect of the child wherever these are relevant and known, one sees clearly that different children chose the same phonetically-motivated spellings to a degree that can hardly be explained as resulting from random choice or the influence of adults. The frequency of such choices will be presented in the discussion of particular spellings. It is revealing to study the phonetic bases of the children's performance, even though we do not know precisely what personal and situational factors made that performance possible.

2.2 The spelling of vowels

The representations of vowels present the categorial problem in its basic form: there are simply too many distinct vowels to be represented uniquely by the letters available, and there are English vowels that do not occur in the letter-names. The degree of classification required is made even greater by two striking facts: the children tended to represent the vowels by single letters, rather than using digraphs or other devices to increase the number of available symbols, and with few exceptions, they confined themselves to the letters A, E, I, O and U. Therefore, some 16 functionally distinct vowels were represented in large part by 5 symbols.

The restriction of the symbols used for vowels is itself an indication of a tacit categorization of vowels versus nonvowels. To illustrate the sharpness of the distinction, consider the spellings of /ɛ/. Phones of this type occur in several letter-names (F, L, M, N, S, and X), and yet of 450 spellings of this vowel, only one contains any letter other than A, E, I, O, U, or Y. (See Appendix A, Table 5.) Even though the phone-type /ɛ/ does not itself occur in the names of these letters, these letters are always employed in its spelling. (The children's solution will be illustrated below; it is based on phonetic relationships.)

Similar observations are true of the spelling of other vowels; Table 4 presents some examples.

The exceptions themselves are interesting. Three of the exceptions for /u/ contain W: KOSTWN (costume), PLLWL (pool), SPWN (spoon). When we consider that the letter-name of W contains /u/, indeed "double U," it seems clear how these spellings arose.

Table 4

Spellings of Vowels

Vowel	Total Spellings	Nonvowel Spellings
/i/	495	1 (plus 113 Y)
/a/	256	2
/u/	139	4
/ɪ/	509	5
/ɛ/	450	1

Note: "Nonvowel spellings" refers to spellings other than A, E, I, O or U; combinations of these with each other or with Y or W; or omissions.

There is also a large class of apparent exceptions for /i/ that seems to arise from standard spelling. Most children use Y as an occasional standard spelling for /i/, as in LADYS (lady's), or FAMLY (family).[1] Some children, not knowing that this spelling is restricted to word-final affixes in standard spelling, employed it more generally. (See Table 5.)

Table 5

Nonstandard Spellings of /i/ with Y

CRYM	cream	GRYN	green
MY	me	BYFR	before
WYC	week	SHY	she
ESYER	easier	SYT	seat

There are 113 such uses of Y to spell /i/, many of them nonstandard. Except for these and the few uses of W, it is clearly a valid generalization that the children represented vocalic nuclei with A, E, I, O, or U, combinations of these, or omissions. Only seven times in all the data do children represent true consonants with letters also used to spell vowels.

Like many other aspects of the invented spelling, this distinction may be the children's extension of a partial knowledge of standard spelling. Having learned the spellings of some vowels, they continued to use the same letters to represent other vowels. On the other hand, the distinction may arise in part from the children's own analysis of the letter-names; knowing that B spells /b/, C spells /s/, etc., they reserved for vowel-spellings those six letters whose names contain no obstruents, liquids, or nasals. The difference between these two explanations is only one of degree; in either case, the children learned something of standard spellings and extended that knowledge—in a phonetically consistent way—to new cases.

The interesting fact, and the evidence of tacit categorization, is that the children were able to maintain this consistent distinction between vowels and nonvowels even as they created their own, definitely nonstandard, spellings for vowels (see Table 6). When the

Table 6

Spellings for Tense Vowels

FAS	face	LADE	lady	TIGR	tiger
DA	day	EGLE	eagle	LIK	like
KAM	came	FEL	feel	MI	my
TABIL	table	PEBATE	Peabody	TIM	time
NACHR	nature	BREFCAS	briefcase	MISS	mice
GOWT	goat	U		you	
POWLEOW	polio	JUNUR		junior	
WENDOWS	windows	HUMIN		human	
KOK	Coke	FABUARE		February	
GOST	ghost	UNITDSATS		United States	

children sought to represent a vowel, they considered only the class of vowel-spellings, even when other letter-names actually contained the vowel they wished to represent, as in the case of /ɛ/. It is in this sense that the spellings reveal that vowels constitute a distinct category for children.

These vowel-spellings illustrate two general characteristics of the invented spelling. In the extension of the affix Y to nonaffixes, the invented spelling is clearly more "phonetic" than standard spelling; it does not maintain the morphophonemic distinctions that are important in adult spelling. (The spelling ESYER is an exception to this rule.) On the other hand, in distinguishing quite consistently between vowels and nonvowels, the spelling reveals underlying categorial distinctions of a different but also abstract sort. We will make similar observations in connection with other aspects of the spelling; they will tell us that certain types of distinctions are readily available to young children, while others are not.

2.2.1 *Tense vowels.* The conventional letter-names for *A, E, I, O,* and *U* suggest the use of these letters to represent /e/, /i/, /ay/, /o/, and /yu/. These are the predominant spellings, as shown in Appendix

A, Tables 27, 26, 36, 15, and 40, respectively. For example, Table 27 shows that 87% of the spellings of /e/ are based on A (A, AY, AE, etc.). Similar proportions hold for the other vowels that correspond to letter-names, except for the Y spellings of /i/, discussed earlier, and /yu/, which occurs much less frequently than the others. Table 6 presents some examples of these vowel spellings.

In many cases, these spellings are essentially the standard ones, and therefore we cannot assume that they are invented. In fact, even if they are based on the letter-names rather than on adult spellings, they do not tell us much about children's categorizations; their main significance is in helping to explain other vowel spellings. However, it is interesting to note that the spellings exemplified in Table 6 are a mixture of standard and original spelling. The use of CH for /č/ and of G for /g/, for instance, is evidently learned from adults, while the use of E in BREFCAS, or of R for /ɚ/ in NACHR, is clearly not given directly by adult spelling. These latter cases may be generalizations from adult spelling (E sometimes spells /i/) or may be based on the children's own judgments (that /ɚ/ is like /r/; see section 2.5).

2.2.2 Tense-lax pairs of vowels, unrounded.

Given that the children spell vowels with only those letters whose names do not contain consonants (plus W), and given that there are just five vowels that correspond directly to such letter-names, we see that the children must devise some less direct means of representing the remaining ten or so vowels and diphthongs of English. In this section we will examine their spelling of the lax unrounded vowels /ɪ/, /ɛ/, /æ/, /a/, and /ʌ/. We will take up schwa /ə/ in section 2.2.4.

Consider first the spelling of /ɪ/, summarized in Appendix A, Table 9. We see immediately that the distribution of spellings is essentially bimodal: at ages less than six years, 65% of the spellings are I (the standard spelling), 23% are E, and no other spelling constitutes more than 5% of the data. This general pattern holds in all three age groups.

Once again the standard spelling tells us nothing about the children's judgments; the interesting problem is to account for the relatively frequent occurrence of E, as in the examples in Table 7. Note that in no case in Table 7 is E the standard spelling of /ɪ/, nor is it ordinarily a standard spelling for /ɪ/. (The only significant exception is for those dialects that have [ɪ] before nasals in words such as *pen*, where other dialects have [ɛ]. Only one of the children in my sample spoke such a dialect, and he is not the source of the E spellings, for he used the standard I spelling exclusively.)

Table 7

Spellings of /ɪ/ with E

SEP	ship	SEK	sink	HEMM	him
FES	fish	WEL	will	DRENK	drink
EGLIOW	igloo	LETL	little	DOEG	doing
FLEPR	Flipper	PEL	pill	SOWEMEG	swimming

On the assumption that children categorize sounds solely as members of unit phonemes, these E spellings would be expected to occur only at chance level (the level of Y, OO, or U in Appendix A, Table 9, for example). If, on the contrary, one assumes that children can recognize phonetic relationships across members of different phonemes, there is a plausible explanation for the facts. Knowing that the spelling of /i/ is E, and facing the problem of representing /ɪ/, the children chose E because of the similarity between /ɪ/ and /i/, namely that of place of articulation: both are high front unrounded vowels. The children were able to ignore the difference in tenseness between these two vowels in order to construct a phonetically meaningful representation for /ɪ/. Subsequent sections, dealing with the spelling of other vowels, will present additional support for this interpretation.

First, let us consider the distribution of the E spelling. Is it the case that some children represented /ɪ/ as I exclusively, while others used E exclusively, or did some individuals use both of these spellings? Table 8 presents the relevant data for those who spelled the phone /ɪ/ five times or more.[2]

Clearly, some individuals (numbered 2, 5, and 27) did not use the E spelling at all, and two others (6 and 9) used it only once each at a frequency less than 10%; these children evidently knew the standard spelling for /ɪ/. Only one individual (33) used the E spelling exclusively, and then in only seven examples. The rest of the children represented /ɪ/ with E at frequencies varying widely from 14% to 80%. Of the 25 children who used any nonstandard spellings for /ɪ/, all but four used E at least as often as all other nonstandard spellings combined. It seems reasonable to conclude that the E spelling is a systematic invention, a spelling that occurs along with the standard spelling, perhaps when the child is unsure of the standard spelling, or when adults are not available to provide it.

These frequencies for individuals probably contain a developmental component; they are sums over the period of time during which each child created the spelling which I collected. The greater frequency of

Table 8

Distribution of *I* and *E* Spellings for /ɪ/

Child	I	E	%E	Total	Age
1	39	35	47.3	74	4-5.6
2	28	—	—	28	5.5-5.8
3	50	12	19.3	62	5.10-6.6
4	1	4	80.0	5	6
5	34	—	—	34	7.10-8.3
6	10	1	9.1	11	5.11-6.3
8	22	4	15.4	26	6-8
9	12	1	7.7	13	6.2
10	18	3	14.3	21	4.6-5.6
12	9	2	18.2	11	6.2
25	5	6	54.5	11	6
27	18	—	—	18	4.11-5.1
33	—	7	100.0	7	5
TOTAL	246	75	23.3%	321	

the *E* spelling below age 6 than above it (Appendix A, Table 9) suggests a developmental trend, but Table 8 does not indicate a strong correlation between age and the development of standard spelling. One would not expect to find such a correlation, since aspects of language development are not ordinarily linked directly to chronological age. For examining the course of development, longitudinal data would be more appropriate.

In hypothesizing a phonetic basis for the invented spelling, a crucial observation is that the frequency of that spelling is much greater overall than could be explained as a random choice in the representation of a unit phoneme. The average frequency of the *E* spelling among the children included in Table 8 who produced at least one such spelling is 23%—much greater than for any other nonstandard spelling.

Next consider the spellings of /ɛ/, summarized in Appendix A, Table 5. Here again we find a striking bimodal distribution, the two modes being *E*, the standard spelling, (42.7%) and *A* (42.4%). Analogous to the spelling *E* for /ɪ/, the high frequency of *A* for /ɛ/ cannot be accounted for in terms of standard spelling or as random error in the representation of unit phonemes. It *can* be explained as the letter whose name /e/ contains a vocalic nucleus which is similar to /ɛ/ in place of articulation and rounding, yet differing from it in tenseness and diphthongization. The spellings with no basis in standard spelling and no plausible phonetic motivation, such as *O* and *U*, occur at rates less than one percent—evidently the level of truly random error.

The one apparent exception to this generalization is the frequency of the spelling *I* (5.6%). It turns out, however, that 19 of the 25 *I* spellings occur before nasals where, as was noted earlier, some dialects have [ɪ] for /ɛ/,[3] and where, in any dialect, the nasalized [ɛ] tends to have a lower first formant, thus more closely resembling [ɪ]. The net result is that aside from omissions, every nonstandard spelling for /ɛ/ which occurs at a frequency greater than one percent has a plausible phonetic basis. Table 9 presents examples of the spellings in which

Table 9

Spellings of /ɛ/ with A

PAN	pen	TADDEBAR	teddy bear	SHALF	shelf
FALL	fell	PRTAND	pretend	DAVL	devil
LAFFT	left	RAKRD	record (N)	ANE	any
MAS	mess	ALLS	else	ALRVATA	elevator

/ɛ/ is represented by A. Of these, only ANE is actually a standard spelling with respect to the use of A for /ɛ/.

In the spellings for both /ɪ/ and /ɛ/, then, we find one nonstandard spelling that is much more frequent than any other, that letter whose name is similar in place of articulation to the vowel to be spelled: E for /ɪ/ and A for /ɛ/. The large difference in frequency between these and all other nonstandard spellings is difficult to explain, except on the assumption that children are capable of recognizing phonetic relationships between distinct speech sounds. They can treat these phonetic relationships differentially by grouping /i/ with /ɪ/ and /e/ with /ɛ/, despite differences in length, tenseness, and diphthongization. In particular, the frequency of these rather systematic spellings would be quite anomalous if we assumed that children treat phonemes as unanalyzable units. Furthermore, it appears that /e/, the more diphthongal and hence more readily analyzable of the two letter-names, is the one that is more frequently related to its lax counterpart. This difference is the focus of some experimental studies reported in chapter five.

Considering next the spellings for /a/ (Appendix A, Table 7), we find fewer nonstandard spellings than in the two preceding cases. Both *O* and *A* may be standard spellings for /a/, as in *not* and *father*, and these two spellings together make up 70% of the spellings for /a/.

Table 10

Spellings of /a/ with *I*

GIT	got	IR	are
CLIC, CLIK	clock	HIRT	heart
BICS, BIKS	box	RICET	rocket
DIKTR	doctor	UPIN	upon

SCICHTAP	Scotch tape
CIDEJCHES	cottage cheese
PIPS	pops
MIRSE	Marcie
BITUVMELC	bottle of milk

Except among the spellings created at age six or older, however, we do find the spelling *I* as the most frequent nonstandard spelling. Table 10 presents all 15 examples.[4]

Once again the plausible explanation appears to be that the children relate the vocalic nucleus of the letter-name /ay/ to the vowel /a/. Just as in the two previous cases, this invented spelling reflects a similarity in place of articulation between the letter-name and the vowel to be represented, ignoring differences in length, tenseness, and diphthongization.

Two considerations vitiate the force of this observation, however. One is, of course, the lower frequency of this invented spelling than of others, and its disappearance above age six. A second and related consideration is that almost all of the *I* for /a/ spellings (13 of 15) were created by a single child; unlike its counterparts, this spelling was not developed by several children.

The interpretation of the invented spellings for /ɪ/ and /ɛ/ was strengthened by the fact that both spellings reflected the same phonetic relationship and that the more diphthongal letter-name, /e/, was the one more consistently related to its lax counterpart, /ɛ/. Therefore, it is important to understand why the same analysis was applied *less* frequently to the letter-name /ay/, which is the most obviously diphthongal. The basic reason may be the somewhat exceptional nature of /a/ in English, a phonologically back but unrounded vowel. We will see that in the invented spelling, rounded back vowels are most frequently spelled *O*, and it may be that most children tend to treat /a/ like this group, especially if they know that *O* is one of its standard spellings. This tendency is reinforced by the dialects of the Boston area, where most of the invented spellings were collected. In this region, many vowels which are [a] in General American (and which were so coded in the tabulation of sound-spelling correspondences) are in fact rounded vowels of the type [ɒ] or [ɔ].[5] Both of these considerations suggest that /a/ may be spelled *O*, and in fact *O* is the most frequent spelling (58.6%). Sixty percent of these *O*-spellings are also standard spellings, so we cannot determine whether they may also have a phonetic basis.

In connection with the pairs of tense and lax vowels, there is one additional bit of evidence that nicely illustrates the systematic nature and phonetic basis of the invented spelling. After they knew the standard spelling for the lax vowels, /ɪ/, /ɛ/, and /a/, some children occasionally adopted that spelling for the corresponding tense vowel, thus writing *I* for /i/, *E* for /e/, and even *AY* or *AI* for /ay/. Having learned the prevailing spelling for the lax vowels, these children sometimes maintained the correspondence between tense and lax vowels, even at the cost of overthrowing the straightforward correspondence between tense vowels and letter-names with which they had typically begun.

Table 11

Spellings of /i/ with *I*

BRIF	brief	CLIN	clean	VERI	very
RILE	really	PUSI	pussy	REDI	ready
FILG	feeling	FILL	feel	SKINI	skinny
ISRIL	Israel	SHI	she	USLIP	asleep
SIKE	seek	CITI	city	GIMI	gimme

Spellings such as ISRIL, SKINI, and GIMI illustrate the use of *I* for /i/ and /ɪ/ at the same time. In some dialects, the final *I* of such words as CITI might merely represent [ɪ], but these spellings come from several children, none of whom spoke such a dialect.

Such spellings are not particularly numerous; they constitute 7.1% of the spellings of /i/, 5.3% of the spellings of /e/, and 4.8% of the

Table 12

Spellings of /e/ with *E*

JEN	Jane	ET	ate	TODE	today
BEC	bake	PLEY	play	TEC	take
CEME	came	THEE	they	PLEAR	player

Table 13

Spellings of /ay/ with $A\left\{\begin{matrix} I \\ Y \end{matrix}\right\}$

NAIYS	nice	NAT	night	TAYPRAYTR	typewriter
MAI	my	MAY	my	RAYT	right
BAY	buy	HAY	high	HAIDENS	Haydn's

spellings of /ay/. Even so, these spellings are the most frequent ones other than the *E, Y, A,* and *I* spellings (and digraphs) based on the letter-names or standard spelling. That they occur, and that they occur for all three of these letter-name vowels, illustrates two important points: the children attempted to maintain the pairing of tense and lax vowels, and were able to change even their spelling of the tense vowels, which was an obvious, basic, and well-practiced aspect of the spelling system. In those respects, the spellings tend to support the view that the invented spellings of the lax vowels represent a systematic categorization by place of articulation.

The spellings of /ʌ/ (not including the retroflex vowel /ɝ/) provide some additional support for the interpretation of the spellings of /a/. Both *U* and *O* are common standard spellings for /ʌ/, as in *putt* and *love,* and in the summary (Appendix A, Table 17), we find that these account for 41% and 34% respectively, of the children's spellings of /ʌ/. However, about two-thirds of the *U* spellings and about one-half of the *O* spellings were actually nonstandard for the word in which they occurred.[6] It may be that the frequent *O* spelling for both /ʌ/ and /a/ and for the back rounded vowels indicates an implicit grouping of central and back vowels (especially considering that many of these spellings are actually nonstandard for a particular word.) However, it seems more likely that the children learned that *U* and *O* represent /ʌ/ and that *O* spells /a/, and that they simply applied these generalizations too widely. If so, it is interesting that the children sought a standard spelling for these vowels, whereas they did not do so for most instances of /ɛ/, for example. This fact suggests that the phonetic relations between /a/ and /ʌ/ on the one hand, and vowels with a known spelling on the other, were simply not clear to the children, an interpretation which is consistent with the somewhat exceptional character of these phonologically back but unrounded vowels in English. The predominance of standard spellings sharply limits what we can learn from the children's spelling in these cases.

In a similar way, the spelling of /æ/ is uninformative, although the variety of spellings is very limited (Appendix A, Table 35); about 90% of the spellings of /æ/ are A. As in the case of the O spellings above, this choice might represent a coincidence between standard spellings and the children's grouping of /æ/ with /ɛ/ (and /e/), or it might simply be a standard spelling, used uniformly precisely because the children were unable to relate /æ/ to vowels of known spelling themselves. Here again the fact that the children's spelling was a standard one makes it impossible to resolve these conflicting poossibilities. We can draw no firm conclusion, therefore, about the perceived relations (or lack of perceived relations) between /ʌ/, /a/, /æ/ and other vowels.

Clearly, the frequent pairing of corresponding tense and lax vowels for spelling purposes is one of the most intriguing aspects of the invented spelling. It is likely to stimulate further research, especially considering the importance and complexity of relationships among English vowels and their standard spelling patterns. In 1974, two doctoral dissertations appeared which sought, among other goals, to examine the spelling of first-graders for indications of the nonstandard spellings of [ɪ], [ɛ], and [a] originally observed in the work of younger children. Kathleen Gerritz (Harvard University) worked as a first-grade teacher in Brookline, Massachusetts, and compiled and analyzed the spellings of her first-graders in the spontaneous writing which she encouraged during the school year. James Beers (University of Virginia) presented a list of 24 words selected for their vowel structure and frequency to first- and second-grade children in a Charlottesville school once each month for five months. He analyzed the spellings for indications of developing spelling strategies. Both studies revealed some influence of the judgments reported in this section.

Gerritz summarizes that eight of the twelve children in her sample "spelled the lax front vowels with the invented spellings Read reports" (p. 70), although she also notes that the children tended to use standardized spellings for these vowels at the same time or later (but not earlier). Beers concludes that the first-graders moved through a sequence of spelling strategies, of which the second, after "no attempt," was a "letter-name" strategy which leads to the spellings of [ɪ] and [ɛ] discussed in this section, as well as the letter-name spellings of tense vowels. If there is a difference in degree of confirmation between these two studies (and that is difficult to determine because of the very different methods of the two investigators), it may result from the fact that Beers included some low-frequency words in his spelling list, thus perhaps eliciting more invented spellings. The two dissertations do seem to indicate that relating lax vowels to corresponding tense vowels in order to spell the former is an important influence, particularly at an early stage. It is also notable that this support comes from two different dialect regions of the country.

Rystrom (1973-74) administered a Forced Vowel Selection Test to 63 Georgia children beginning the first grade, as soon as particular groups of children were able to write the letters *a, e*, and *i* upon request. The test consisted of a "spy" message in which each of the 23 words was printed with the vowel spelling replaced by a blank, e.g.:

B_l
_m tr_pt b_ sp_z.

The experimenter presented a simple story that served as context for the message, and then read the message to the children. (Part of the message, "Bill, am trapped by spies," is represented in the above sample.) The experimenter then said, "The first word on your page is *Bill*. Put an *a*, an *e*, or an *i* in this blank," and so on.

The 23 words that made up the test included three instances each of [e], [i], [ay], and [ɛ], [ɪ], [æ], as well as two instances of [a]. Rystrom analyzed the children's choices of letters for any evidence of the influence of letter-names and concluded that "the responses of primary age nonreaders to the FVST are random, while the responses of adult readers are patterned" (p. 179). From a second administration of the test at the end of the first-grade year, he concluded that the children were "only slightly inclined to associate letter names with letter sounds" (p. 181). Rather, the first-graders relied heavily on the sight vocabulary they had acquired during the year for their choices on the posttest. Rystrom concludes, "The strategies developed by the precocious children Read studied do not appear to be much used by ordinary children learning to read in a normal school setting," a conclusion which is in contrast with the evidence from the two dissertation studies reviewed above.

The problem posed by random performance is that before accepting negative evidence of children's knowledge at face value, we must be sure that the task was one that encouraged children to make use of whatever they knew. In this case, there is no indication, either in the instructions given or in the children's performance as reported, that the children actually understood their activity to be that of representing speech sounds orthographically. The key phrase in the instructions, for example, was "Dan wants you to help him by filling in the blanks on this page," an activity that could be construed without reference to orthography. The problem of what the children thought they were doing, and indeed whether they had any concept of using letters to represent speech sounds, is made all the more pertinent by the observation that about two-thirds of Rystrom's subjects were unable to write the letters *a, e,* and *i* upon request at the earliest testing session in the fall, and that these students were tested "as soon as they were able to write each of the three test letters on demand" (p. 177). Consequently, it does not seem at all implausible that these children either had little notion of alphabetic representation or that they did not take such representations to be their task at the time of the initial test. In terms of Beers' developmental sequence, Rystrom's children may well have been at the "no attempt" stage with respect to orthography, despite the fact that they filled in blanks with letters. It is not surprising that they made use of their sight vocabulary and their acquired knowledge of standard spelling on the end-of-year posttest. These observations do not tell us what intermediate strategies the children may have developed.

The difficulty of constructing tasks which elicit valid and reliable evidence of children's knowledge of linguistic relationships, and which help to identify any influence of that knowledge on their school performance, is indeed formidable. This researcher's experience, shared by many others, is that even seemingly minor modifications of experimental procedures can affect the character of the performance which children exhibit. A crucial problem is to make our questions accessible to young children, making it easy for them to draw upon their knowledge, and yet to pose a significant question. In this pursuit, my own research procedures have undergone several revisions. Chapter five reports some studies in which even kindergarten children displayed some knowledge of vowel relationships.

2.2.3 Rounded vowels. Because of the variety of standard spellings for the (back) rounded vowels of English and the interaction of these standard spellings with the children's spellings, it is not possible to discern the same degree of phonetic consistency in the invented spellings as was the case for front unrounded vowels. However, two generalizations are possible: *O* appears as a frequent spelling (both standard and nonstandard) for all the rounded vowels, and the nonstandard spellings are rarely anything other than *O* and various digraphs based on *O*, such as *OW, OU, OO,* etc. Table 14 lists the percentages of *O* and *OW* among the spellings of back rounded vowels and compares these with percentages for standard spelling. (The data on standard spelling were computed from an unpublished tabulation of sound-spelling and spelling-sound correspondences in English. Richard L. Venezky prepared this tabulation in 1963, based on the 20,000 most common words in the language, as indicated in the Thorndike Century Senior Dictionary.)

Table 14

O and OW Spellings for Back Rounded Vowels

Vowel	Children % O	Standard % O	Children % OW	Standard % OW
/u/	16.5	6.3	7.2	—
/ʊ/	25.0	7.2	—	—
/o/	69.5	81.3	11.8	8.3
/ɔ/	69.4	20.7	0.8	—
/aw/	21.2	0.3	10.6	33.4

Although the children actually use O for /o/ somewhat *less* frequently than does standard spelling (partly because they use OW somewhat more frequently), they clearly apply this spelling to each of the other rounded vowels more often than is characteristic of standard spelling. At the same time, spellings such as *I, E,* and *A* occur very infrequently. Together, these facts suggest that the back rounded vowels form a distinct category for the children, one which is clearly distinguished from the front unrounded vowels in spelling. Unfortunately, it is impossible to say whether backness or rounding is the more important defining feature of this class because of the unclear basis of the O-spellings for /a/ and /ʌ/, the only full vowels that differ in backness and rounding.

The spellings of /u/ (Appendix A, Table 21)[7] are quite varied, but the three most frequent, *OO, O,* and *U,* are all possible standard spellings, as in *school, move,* and *rude.* The only nonstandard spelling more frequent than 4% is *OW,* which is in fact a frequent child spelling of /u/, /o/, and /aw/ (*Cf.* Table 14). In the latter two cases, it is a standard spelling; evidently the children occasionally extend it to /u/. An interesting question is why *U* does not appear as a more frequent spelling for /u/, on the basis of the letter-name. Indeed, *U* is the most frequent spelling for /yu/ (Appendix A, Table 40), but it is rarely used to represent /u/ when this vowel occurs without the on-glide, so it appears that the children do not analyze this letter-name, identifying

/u/ in /yu/. This fact is somewhat surprising, considering how successful the children are in recognizing less direct relationships, such as
that between /ɛ/ and /e/.

At first, this comparison might even be taken to suggest, paradoxi-
cally, that children are better at recognizing relationships between
segments than they are at analyzing syllables into the segments that
constitute them. A study by D. J. Bruce (1964) makes this latter claim
that young children are not good at identifying what a word would
sound like if its first segment were removed. But generally children
who can spell in the way that has been illustrated have no difficulty
in analyzing words into segments. Furthermore, the ability of kindergarten children to recognize rhyme (Knafle, 1973, 1974) and even
create rhymes suggests that Bruce's results are not entirely representa-
tive and may be an artifact of the specific task in that study. Therefore,
the explanation of the low frequency of U spellings for /u/ may lie in
the children's knowledge of standard spelling or in a particular difficulty in separating this vowel from the on-glide in the letter-name
/yu/.

With regard to the spelling of /ʊ/ (Appendix A, Table 30), the first
question is whether the children represent /ʊ/ like /u/, just as in the
other tense-lax pairs discussed above. The answer is quite clearly
affirmative. The spellings that occur most frequently, and even their
approximate distribution, are the same for these two types of phones.
The significance of this fact is limited by the observation that two of
the three most frequent spellings of /ʊ/, OO and U, are also standard
spellings, as in *cookie* and *sugar*, so that most of the similarity between
/u/ and /ʊ/ in spelling might have arisen through a dependence on
standard spelling alone. However, the fact that O is a frequent spelling
of both /u/ and /ʊ/ (at about 20%) shows that the similarity is not
limited to standard spellings, for O is not a common standard spelling
of /ʊ/.[8] It is also interesting to note that the invented OW spellings of
/u/ (8%) do not occur at all for /ʊ/; apparently, the W represents the
length or diphthongization of /u/, /o/, and /aw/. (See below for
evidence that the feature represented is, in fact, diphthongization.)

The spellings of /o/ (Appendix A, Table 15) are exactly analogous
to the spellings of other tense vowels that correspond to letter-names;
O, OW, OO, and OE make up 89% of the spellings and all of those that
occur more frequently than 1%. Of these, OW is a standard spelling,
as in *bowl*, but the O spellings, which constitute 70% of the cases, may
be based on the letter-name, as well as on standard spelling. Table 15
provides examples of this type.

Table 15

Spellings of /o/ with O

BOT	boat	JOK	joke	OPN	open
CINTROLL	control	NOSIS	noses	UWOKIN	awoken
HOP	hope	ROD	road	OND	owned

There is a significant tendency for the *OW* spellings to occur in final position; they make up 29% of the spellings of final /o/, but only 14% of the total.[9] This might be taken as further evidence that the *W* is used to indicate length or diphthongization, although it is also true of standard spelling that *OW* for /o/ is most likely to occur finally (Venezky, 1970, pp. 118-119).

Sixty-nine percent of the children's spelling of /ɔ/ (Appendix A, Table 29) are *O;* this is a standard spelling (as in *off* and *long*) much less frequently (*Cf.* Table 14). Its frequency in children's spelling is another indication that children tend to generalize this spelling to all back rounded vowels. Of the other two spellings that occur more than 1% of the time, *A* is clearly a standard spelling (as in *ball* and *water*) and *UO* is the invention of three children in BRUOT (brought), FUOL (fall), and DUO (draw).

Finally among the spellings of rounded vowels, consider those of the diphthong /aw/ (Appendix A, Table 31). These are more varied than most—the most frequent spelling, *O*, occurs in only 21% of the instances—and they seem to represent diphthongization in that 67% of the spellings are made up of two or more letters. The spellings that occur 5% of the time or more are *O, AW, OW, OU, A, AOW, AOO,* and *OUE,* of which only *OW* and *OU* are standard (as in *now* and *about*). Of the invented spellings, about 60% have *O* as their first element and 40% have *A*. Since the spellings of /a/ were likewise divided between *O* and *A*, it seems that the children treat /aw/ as a diphthong whose nucleus is like /a/ and whose off-glide (spelled *W, U, OW, OO,* etc.) is like a back vowel. In this, the spellings are again quite accurate phonetically.

In summary, the rounded vowels appear to form a class, usually spelled *O, U, OO, OW, OU,* etc. Because these often coincide with standard spelling, it is not possible to infer the basis of this classification or its detailed internal structure. However, the spellings of pairs like /u/ and /ʊ/ is at least consistent with the relationships inferred from the spelling of pairs like /i/ and /ɪ/. At the same time, the fre-

Table 16

Multi-Letter Spellings for Back Rounded Vowels

Vowel	% multi-letter spellings—children	% multi-letter spellings—standard
/u/	51.2	49.5
/ʊ/	39.5	44.9
/o/	22.8	18.7
/ɔ/	16.1	53.1
/aw/	67.0	99.7

quency of spellings composed of more than one letter (including *OW*) gives some insight into the categorization of back vowels; Table 16 presents the percentages of such spellings.

The two most striking features of these data are the high frequency of multi-letter spellings for these vowels (the average percentage of such spellings by children for all other vowels is 8.3) and children's monotonic decrease in frequency of such spellings with vowel height. The data from children's spelling corresponds quite closely to that from standard spelling, except for the spellings of /ɔ/. This discrepancy is informative, for it indicates that when children use multi-letter spellings distinctively, it is on the basis of rounding and diphthongization rather than length (duration), since /ɔ/ is acoustically the longest vowel in this series (House, 1961, p. 1174). Duration increases, on the average, from high to low vowels (excluding the effects of tenseness and of context), so that data above are just the opposite of what one would expect if duration were the basis for the distinction.

The position of /o/ in the monotonic function in Table 16 is probably misleading, since the children represent /o/ with the letter *O* alone in 70% of the cases, no doubt partly because of the identity of the vowel and the letter-name. We can probably not compare the frequency of multi-letter spellings for /o/ with that for vowels which do not correspond directly to a letter-name. In fact, multi-letter spellings constitute 85% of the spellings of /o/ which are not *O* or omissions. Leaving /o/ aside, it seems that the use of multi-letter spellings corresponds rather well to rounding, which decreases with vowel height, and to diphthongization, in that /aw/ and /u/ are more frequently so represented than are /ʊ/ and /ɔ/. Note that the children use *OW* (Table 14) for just /u/, /o/, and /aw/—the class of diphthongal rounded vowels—even though it is not a standard spelling for /u/. Chapter five will present some experimental evidence of relationships among front vowels, as judged by children, in which it also appears that diphthongization is a more salient property than duration.

2.2.4 Reduced vowels. The reduced vowel /ə/ is the only vowel for which the most frequent spelling appears to be omission (Appendix A, Table 28); indeed, it is the only phone other than /y/ for which this is the case. However, it turns out that more than 80% of these omissions are in the contexts /ɚ/ (coded as /ər/), /əl/, /əm/, and /ən/, where children often do not represent a vowel (see section 2.5 on the spelling of syllabic sonorants). When the omissions in these contexts are disregarded, the percentage of omissions overall becomes 9.3, and the most frequent spellings of /ə/ become *I* (28.0%) and *E* (25.9%). Virtually any vowel spelling may be a standard spelling for /ə/, of course, and the predominance of these two may reflect the fact that in certain contexts /ə/ is qualitatively very similar to the other high or mid unrounded vowels. Here again the children are grouping vowels together for spelling purposes on the basis of a real phonetic similarity.

The spellings of reduced vowels contribute much to the distinctive character of children's spelling, not only because such vowels are very frequent, but also because the spellings ignore the lexical relationships that are important to adult readers. Table 17 illustrates these spellings (except for those before sonorants, which are discussed in Section 2.5).

Table 17

Spellings of /ə/

PLEMETH	Plymouth	PLATD	planted	SEPEKOL	Cepacol
BENANE	banana	PASINT	present (noun)	CIDEJCHES	cottage cheese
BCOZ	because	IGAN	again	BRAYSLIT	bracelet
RALTIVIS	relatives	ICSPANS	expense	DSID	decide
UKLOK	o'clock	MINETS	minutes	OPISITT	opposite
WATID	wanted	NOSIS	noses	LICWID	liquid
OPON	upon	AFISHILL	official	SRCIS	circus
MACSICO	Mexico	ROCIT	rocket	NOULICH	knowledge
CERIT	carrot	DAFADILS	daffodils	SATU	Santa

Aside from the invented spellings of full vowels, perhaps three things make these spellings striking to adults: the omissions, some of which may be close to phonetic accuracy (BCOZ, DSID), the loss of lexical relationships (no *relate* in RALTIVIS, no *office* in AFISHILL, no *oppose* in OPISITT), and the absence of distinctive representations for derivational units (the last syllables of WATID and LICWID, and of NOSIS and SRCIS, spelled alike). Young children's spelling is very hard to read silently, even when one knows what to expect.

2.2.5 Homography and relationships in spelling. One result of attempting to represent English with about 24 letters (*Q* and *X* were rarely employed) using primarily single-letter spellings, rather than distinctive digraphs, is a considerable degree of homography. This characteristic is amply illustrated in vowel spellings where, for example, *O* may represent any of the back vowels, rounded or unrounded, or where BAT might spell *bat, bet,* or *bait.* As was pointed out in chapter one, the existence of homography in children's early spelling by no means indicates that it is optimal for children. More plausibly, we may suppose that the children felt constrained to use only the standard alphabet, and limited their attention to the sound they wished to represent at any particular moment, without reflecting on the fact that they had used a chosen spelling for other sounds at other times. The children often wrote with no apparent addressee, and homography is a potential problem for the reader, not the writer. Nevertheless, the children did have other choices: they might have relied totally on adult spelling, or they might have invented new symbols. The fact that they did neither of these shows that they found homography tolerable, at least as writers.

It is the character of the homography which distinguishes children's early spelling from adult spelling, however, and which indicates what the children do and do not know. In standard spelling, *a* represents widely different vowels, as in *sane, sanity, father,* and *small,* but there are principles of at least two sorts which govern these correspondences. In morphologically related words like *sane–sanity,* the pronunciation of the vowel changes predictably while the spelling remains the same. The importance of this invariance for reading and its relationship to phonology has received renewed attention in recent years (Chomsky and Halle, 1968; C. Chomsky, 1970). In addition, there are generalizations tied to the spelling context, e.g., that *a* before final *ll* always represents /ɔ/ (Venezky, 1970, p. 112). In the children's spelling, too, *A* may represent several different vowels, as in TAK (take), PAN (pen), BAK (back), NAT (not), and even NAT (night) and WANS (once), but it is clear that these are not limited to particular contexts. The children's spellings are based on the letter-names (TAK), on phonetic similarity to the letter-names (PAN), on a knowledge, often imperfect, of standard spelling (BAK and NAT—not), and on a knowl-

edge of standard spelling together with perceived phonetic relationships (NAT—*night* and WANS). To a considerable degree, it is the
use of sound-spelling correspondences derived in these various ways,
without the contextual and morphological constraints on standard
spelling, that gives children's spelling its distinctive character.

As a result, there is little evidence of an attempt to represent meaning relationships in the invented spelling. Few pairs of words in which
meaning relationships are reflected in standard spelling occur in the
data from children. Words like *sign–signature, muscle–muscular, di-
vine–divinity, serene–serenity*, etc., where the spelling similarity reflects
a derivational relationship, simply do not occur, and it seems unlikely
that young children understand the meaning relationship in such pairs
(C. Chomsky, 1970, pp. 297, 306). When such words do occur, it
appears on the whole that children do not attempt to display meaning
relationships. For example, one finds such spellings as WETH (width–
cf. *wide*), CHOLDRN (*children*–cf. *child*), INSTROKSHINS (*instructions*–cf. *instruct*), SIGIRAT (*cigarette*–cf. *cigar*), RALTIVIS
(*relatives*–cf. *relate*).

The only evidence that suggests an attempt to reflect derivational
relationships comes from a Montessori class (all aged four or five).
These children appeared to use *-tion* endings only where there are
related verbs ending in /t/:

CONVENSHUN	convention
INFORMASHUN	information
COMFERMASHON	confirmation
CONGRAGRLATIONS	(cf. congratulate)
AGOOKATION	(cf. educate)

No comparable evidence exists from spellings done outside of school.

Given an imperfect knowledge of standard spelling, the children
were far more likely to fill in the gaps by spelling on the basis of (what
seemed to be) similar sounds than of similar words. Nor were they
likely to limit the resulting spellings to particular graphic contexts. It
is in these specific ways that the invented spellings are much more
"phonetic" than standard spelling. Learning about the morphophonemic and contextual influences on English spelling comes later, and
much of the phonology relevant to standard spelling may also develop
later.

2.3 The spelling of /tr/ clusters

Turning now to consonants, we find that in many instances the children adopted the standard spelling rather than grouping sounds together as they did for the vowels. Consider the spellings of /g,h,θ,/ and /ð/, none of which occurs in letter-names (Appendix A, Tables 7, 8, 32, and 33). For these sounds, the children used the standard spellings 90% of the time or more, so we can learn little about their phonetic judgments. In fact, the general tendency to adopt standard spellings for consonants but to create spellings for vowels by comparing one with another may be related to a phenomenon observed experimentally with adults, namely that synthetic consonants are more likely to be heard as falling into discrete categories, while synthetic vowels may be heard as lying along a continuum (Liberman, Cooper, Shankweiler & Studdert-Kennedy, 1967, pp. 442-443). Evidently, the children are more likely to find among vowels, rather than consonants, phonetic relationships that are strong enough to support a relationship in spelling.

Nevertheless, some such relationships are exemplified in spelling. Consider first the spelling of /tr/ clusters in Table 18. In these cases,

Table 18

Spellings of /tr/ with CHR

AS CHRAY	ashtray	CWNCHRE	country
CHRIBLS	troubles	CHRAC	truck
CHRIE	try	CHAC	track

the spelling of /tr/ is CH(R). This is a minority judgment; these six examples are the only ones among 36 spellings of words containing /tr/. They are interesting, however, because although they seem bizarre at first, they do have a reasonable phonetic basis. Furthermore, we have found similar judgments experimentally and in other spellings, including the spellings of first-graders (see chapter three).

The phonetic basis of these spellings is the affrication of /t/ when it occurs before /r/ in English; in a triple like *tick, trick* and *chick,* no two of the initial segments are actually identical; the "t" of *trick* is affricated, that is, released slowly, with the resulting turbulence characteristic of /č/. Typically, the [t] of *trick* (as opposed to that of *tick)* is palatal/alveolar, and to a moderate degree affricated and retroflex. In the first two of these properties, it is similar to the [č] of *chick;* the main difference is in the degree (i.e., the duration and intensity) of affrication. Table 19 presents the relevant articulatory features of these sounds.

Table 19

Articulation of [t], [tr], and [č] in English

Feature	[č]	[t(r)]	[t]	Interpretation
delayed release	+	+	−	(affrication)
anterior	−	−	+	(place of artic.)
distributed	+	−	−	(type of contact)
retroflex	−	+	−	(tongue shape)

Given this situation, with similarities in both directions, and assuming that only two distinct spellings are to be used for these three sounds, it is a question whether the initial sound of *trick* is to be grouped with /t/ or with /č/ in spelling. It is clear from the spellings of /č/ (Appendix A, Table 3) that most children knew the standard *ch* spelling, so we should not be surprised to find that spelling applied to /tr/ clusters.

The same phonological process applies to /d/ before /r/. Such /dr/ clusters (without an intervening syllable boundary) are less frequent in the words that the children spelled, but again we find spellings representing the corresponding (voiced) affricate, /ǰ/, as minority judgments among the 17 cases: GRADL and JRADL (dreidel), and JRAGIN (dragon).

The significance of these spellings is not in their numbers, obviously, but in what they show about children's knowledge. The spellings do not indicate, as a parent, a teacher, or even a therapist might at first suppose, a perceptual shortcoming. On the contrary, the underlying perception is accurate, and it may be more available (closer to awareness) than that of the child who simply asks, "How do you spell [drə]?" Naturally, when children have no basis for choosing between two phonetically justifiable spellings, they sometimes choose the one that is not standard. The effect is that they are representing a phonetic property (affrication) which is automatic in this context, and which is therefore ignored in standard spelling. This very general principle of spelling states that predictable aspects of pronunciation need not be represented. What such spellings as these really show is that the children who created them have yet to learn that /t/ is regarded as the underlying form or, in traditional terminology, that affricated [t] belongs to the phoneme /t/. Neither the spelling principle nor the somewhat arbitrary fact about the categorization of English has to do with "correct" perception.

Perhaps an anecdote will illustrate that two distinct aspects of knowledge are involved here. In a class of 27 first-grade children, I encountered 5 who consistently judged that /tr/ "sounds more like" /č/ than it does like /t/. Four of these children, interviewed individually, even showed that they could easily read the words *train, teddy bear*, and *chair* printed on cards and then asserted with equal certainty that it is *train* and *chair* that begin with the same sound, even while they looked at the printed forms. "But look," I said, pointing to the words, "*train* and *teddy bear* begin with the same letter." "Oh, yeah," one of them assured me, "but that's different." Clearly, this girl had learned that English spelling does not represent some phonetic relationships that she could hear. Even though she could read well, she had simply not yet accepted the prevailing adult view that an affricated /t/ is a kind of /t/.

Chapter three will report the test of children's judgments referred to here, as well as other tests of these judgments and their embodiment in spelling.

2.4 The spelling of nasals

Another interesting aspect of the children's spelling of consonants has to do with the spelling of the nasals /m/, /n/, and /ŋ/. Only /m/ and /n/ occur in the letter-names and not surprisingly, the children spell them with the conventional letters (see Appendix A, Tables 13 and 14). The velar nasal, /ŋ/, does not occur in a letter-name, and the children represent it either as N (categorizing it as a nasal) or as G (grouping it with the other voiced velar), with the N-spelling predominating. The standard spelling NG increases in frequency from 12% among those under 6 years to 60% among those older than 6 (Appendix A, Table 34).

We note, however, that compared with most other consonants, there is a rather high proportion of omissions of nasals—3% overall for /m/, 9% for /n/, and 18% for /ŋ/—with a higher proportion of omissions among the younger children. Most of these omissions occur in a particular environment, namely, when the nasal immediately precedes a stop or fricative. Table 20 compares the percentage of omissions of nasals preceding stops with that in all other contexts.

Obviously, most of the omitted nasals are in a preconsonantal environment, and the difference between this environment and all others in this respect is extremely unlikely to have occurred by chance. Furthermore, the omission of nasals in this environment continues beyond

Table 20

Percentage of Omissions of Nasals by Context, All Ages

			Context:		
Nasal	/^{C}stop	N	Other	N	Level of statistical significance (χ^2)
/m/	23.7	38	1.1	369	.001
/n/	24.0	242	3.7	644	.001
/ŋ/	63.0	54	0.7	143	.001

Table 21

Omissions of Preconsonantal Nasals

BOPY	bumpy	MOSTR	monster	HACC	Hanks
NUBRS	numbers	PLAT	plant	THEKCE	thinks
ATTEPT	attempt	AD	and	AGRE	angry
GRAPO	Grampa	WOTET	want it	SEK	sink
STAPS	stamps	CAT	can't	NOOIGLID	New England

age six, at least for /n/ and /ŋ/. Table 21 presents some examples of this rather large and durable phenomenon.

Given that the children use suitable representations for the nasals in all other environments, one assumes there is a reason for the frequent omission of just preconsonantal nasals. There are at least two possible explanations: the first has to do with the duration of nasals in this context, and the second has to do with the articulatory similarity of the nasal and the following consonant. The former suggests that children may regard the nasal of a word like *went* as primarily a feature of the preceding vowel; the latter suggests that they may collapse it with the following consonant.

Malécot (1960) reported that preconsonantal nasals tend to nasalize preceding lax vowels, and that when the following consonant is voiceless, the nasal segment itself tends to be very short. This result, Malécot claimed, holds for most dialects of American English, especially for the vowels /ɪ/, /ʌ/, and /æ/, and for the stops /t/, /p/, and /k/. Both lists are in descending order of the duration of the segmental nasal. The effect is also more extreme in polysyllables, such as *anchor* versus *anger*, than in monosyllables. In an extreme case, such as *anchor*, the purely nasal segment may be entirely absent, the perceived nasal being signaled only by the nasalization of the vowel and the place of articulation of the stop. In Malécot's terms, these observations meant, surprisingly, that vowel nasalization could be regarded as a distinctive feature in American English; in terms of children's spellings, they mean that a spelling such as BLAKET (blanket) or THAQ (thank you) is phonetically accurate, given that the children have no symbol for vowel nasalization. The omission of preconsonantal nasals may be another instance of grouping together distinct vowels for spelling purposes, in this case representing nasalized vowels like their non-nasalized counterparts.

The second explanation has to do with a restriction on the occurrence of preconsonantal nasals: within a morpheme in English a nasal must be articulated in the same place as a following stop: only /m/ may precede /p/ or /b/, only /n/ may precede /t/ or /d/, and only /ŋ/ may precede /g/ or /k/. The result is that there is no tongue-movement between a nasal and a following stop, only the closing of the velum. Possibly the children are spelling according to the articulatory gestures that they can feel, so that a word like *went* would seem to have three segments, not four, and the nasal might be regarded as the onset of the [t]. In this case, the children would be grouping /t/'s and "nasalized /t/'s" together for spelling purposes.

Even a third possible explanation develops from the observation that nasals are partially redundant in just the position in which children omit them: preconsonantally. "Partially" means that, given that a nasal occurs before a known stop within a syllable, one can predict which nasal it is. For this reason, English spelling (of monosyllables, anyway) would carry the same information if a single symbol, say *n*, represented any preconsonantal nasal. *Bump* would be spelled *bunp*, *bunt* and *bunk* would be spelled just as they are, and no ambiguity would be introduced. The children's spelling appears to ignore just this one piece of information, albeit a crucial one, for pairs like *set* and *sent*. In this respect, perhaps the children's spelling is an overabstraction.

Treating a partially redundant segment as wholly so is not unprecedented. In Old English and Germanic languages generally alliteration depends on the second segment of a word if the first is /s/ and the second is a true consonant. That is, /sp/ must alliterate with /sp/, not with /st/ or /sk/. In such a cluster, /s/ was (and is) partially redundant in essentially the same way that preconsonantal nasals are: given that a consonant occurs initially before a stop, it must be /s/. Similarly, in the folk-rhymes of Faroese **kvæði** (a narrative ballad tradition of the Faroe islands), and in folk-rhymes generally, imperfect rhymes are tolerated if the rhyming parts of the syllables differ by just one feature (O'Neil, 1970). At the lexical level, *wet* and *went* differ by a segment specified by just one feature. The third possible explanation is like the second, in that it predicts that the omission of nasals in spelling depends on their close relationship to a following stop, so that the spelling essentially treats the nasal as a feature of the stop.

The alternative explanations share a crucial assumption: that the children do indeed perceive the presence of nasalization, that they recognize a contrast between *set* and *sent*. Each explanation asserts that the nonrepresented nasals are collapsed with either the vowel or the consonant, for different reasons. In that respect, the explanations all suppose that the spelling constitutes an abstraction from what the children hear. The assumption that children of age four and older do hear a contrast between pairs like [sɛt] and [sɛnt] seems reasonable on the basis of common experience, and I have informally confirmed it by asking 21 kindergarten children (individually) such questions as, "If you have a little piece of paper that you can paste onto something else, is it a *stinker* or a *sticker*?" All of the children identified the correct word in each of seven such sentences, and they did not hesitate to tell me what I had already suspected—that the task was easy to the point of silliness. Accordingly, it does seem that the nonrepresentation of preconsonantal nasals is some kind of abstraction from what children hear.

The three alternative explanations differ fundamentally, however. Respectively, they assert:

1. that in spelling, unlike adults, children do not take a nasalized vowel, followed possibly by a brief nasal segment, to be equivalent to a vowel plus nasal sequence, and that this judgment may depend on the duration of the nasal segment. In this view, the spellings are essentially accurate as phonetic, but not phonemic, representations.

2. that children's spelling has an important kinesthetic component, that its segmentation corresponds to felt gestures, so that for children there can be a nasalized stop (a phonetic contradiction in most systems).

3. that young children's spelling actually anticipates the kind of abstraction found in standard English spelling, indeed excessively in this case. This claim contrasts most directly with the acoustic and articulatory narrowness put forth in 1 and 2 above.

Logically, it is possible that more than one of these claims may be correct. For example, children's spelling may be influenced both by the duration of preconsonantal nasals and by the fact that their place of articulation is predictable from their context. It is even possible that different children, or a single child at different times, may be influenced by different aspects of these nasals. However, there are clearly fundamental principles at issue here, and it is important to try to decide among them, as far as the evidence permits.

The alternative explanations do make empirically different predictions. The first "acoustic" explanation, based as it is on Malécot's analysis, claims that the omission of preconsonantal nasals in spelling may depend in part on the duration of the nasal segment, which varies according to the preceding vowel and the following stop. In particular, we should expect to find nasals omitted mainly in the context of certain lax vowels and voiceless stops. The latter two accounts, based on the assimilation of the nasal to the following stop, predict that the spelling will be independent of the quality of the preceding vowel or the voicing of the stop. The third explanation, in terms of redundancy, suggests that we might find omissions of other partly redundant segments, such as the /s/ of initial /s/ + stop clusters. The remainder of this section will present relevant evidence from the invented spellings, and chapter four will present a group of experiments designed to test the inferences drawn here.

In the invented spelling, preconsonantal nasals are omitted most frequently when they follow the vowels /ɪ/, /ʌ/, and /æ/ (in ascending order of frequency of omissions), exactly as Malécot's observations would suggest. However, it happens that these vowels, which typically precede short preconsonantal nasals, are among the most common overall in words of the relevant structure in the children's spelling. Accordingly, we must consider the proportion of omissions; Table 22 lists the overall percentage of omissions of all nasals, according to the preceding vowel.

The vowels /ɪ/, /æ/, and /ʌ/ are the contexts in which preconsonantal nasals are most frequently omitted, as suggested by Malécot's observations, although their relative ranking is not the same as in Malécot's study. The vocalic context, therefore, is at least partly consistent with the duration hypothesis and inconsistent with an explanation based solely on the similarity between nasals and following stops.

Similarly, the duration hypothesis predicts that the voicing of the following stop should affect the omission of nasals in spelling, whereas

Table 22

Preconsonantal Nasals Omitted Following Five Most Frequent Vowels

Preceding vowel	% of nasals omitted
/ɪ/	56.0
/æ/	42.4
/ʌ/	33.3
/ɛ/	26.8
/ə/	18.8

the explanations based on homorganic articulation suggest that voicing should not matter. In fact, we find that a greater percentage of each of the three nasals is omitted before the voiceless stop, as suggested by Malécot's observations. Table 23 presents the relevant figures.

Table 23

Nasals Omitted by Voicing of Following Stop, All Ages

Nasal	% Voiceless	% Voiced	% N	Statistical significance
/m/	38	14	38	NS (Fisher)
/n/	27	18	242	NS (χ^2)
/ŋ/	69	53	54	NS (χ^2)
All	35	23	334	@ .02 level, χ^2

The number of instances of preconsonantal nasals (N) in the various cells is large enough for a Chi-square test in the cases of /n/, /ŋ/, and all three nasals combined. Only in this last case, with the data for all nasals pooled, is the tendency toward omission in a voiceless environment statistically significant. We conclude that the voicing of the postnasal consonant is a significant factor overall, as the duration hypothesis predicts.

On the duration hypothesis alone one might suppose, however, that there should be very few omissions of nasals that precede voiced stops, since the duration of such nasals may be quite long compared to that of nasals preceding voiceless stops. In fact, 23% of the nasals in a voiced environment were omitted. Possibly both the duration of preconsonantal nasals and their articulatory similarity to following stops are factors in their frequent omissions from spelling.

There is little external support in the children's spelling for the third proposed explanation, that preconsonantal nasals are omitted because they are partially predictable. Although a few /s/'s are omitted, (1.8% overall), not one of these is in a syllable-initial /s/+ stop cluster, where the /s/ is analogous to a preconsonantal nasal in that it is partially predictable. The children's spelling is abstract chiefly in that it groups certain distinct phones together, rather than omitting partially redundant segments entirely.

Chapter four reports some experiments designed to investigate further the basis for the omission of preconsonantal nasals in spelling, and particularly to distinguish the importance of vowel nasalization, nasal duration, and homorganic articulation.

2.5 The spelling of retroflex vowels and sonorant consonants

By a wide margin, the most frequent spelling of the retroflex reduced vowel /ɚ/ and its stressed counterpart /ɝ/ is simply R (Appendix F, Tables 1 and 2). In standard spelling, these are represented as a vowel followed by r, but it is clear that the children usually treat them as a single segment, which is classified as /r/ rather than as a vowel. This implicit classification of the retroflex vowels with /r/ rather than with other vowels is consistent with adult similarity judgments (Singh and Woods, 1971), in which a retroflex vowel was categorized separately from 11 other American English vowels.

Only one vowel-plus-/r/ sequence is typically spelled R, namely [ar] (Appendix F, Table 5); presumably, it is so spelled because it is the name of the letter R, rather than because of a categorial judgment of the sort reflected in the spellings of /ɚ/ and /ɝ/, which do not correspond directly to any letter-name. The other vowel-plus-/r/ sequences (Appendix F, Tables 3, 4, 6, and 7) are spelled as a vowel followed by /r/. For these forms we do not have reliable information about the pronunciations of the children or their parents, so in coding we have collapsed the tense-lax distinctions between [ir] and [ɪr], [er] and [ɛr], and [or] and [ɔr]. Nevertheless, the vowel spellings do appear to reflect either these distinctions or the standard and invented spellings for the lax vowels; we find both ER and IR for[ir/ɪr] and AR and ER [er/ɛr]. In a study based on more detailed phonetic information, it would be interesting to know whether these spellings reflect the fine phonetic distinctions or the contrast between standard and invented spellings, or both. It is even possible that the tense-lax alternations found in vowels before /r/ (within and across dialects) form part of the basis for the children's recognition of tense-lax relationships in their spelling. The children may be able to use phonological as well as purely phonetic information in devising the classifications discussed in section 2.2.2.

In the spelling of other sonorants in unstressed syllables (i.e., /əl/, /əm/, and /ən/), we find that frequently no vowel is represented Appendix B, Tables 2, 3, and 4). In this respect, the spelling of these sequences contrasts with that of cases in which the reduced vowel is followed by obstruents; recall that sonorants and retroflex vowels account for over 80% of the apparent omissions of /ə/ in spelling. Table 24 presents examples of these spellings, which may be contrasted with

Table 24

Spelling of Syllabic Sonorants

LITL	little	OPN	open
CANDL	candle	WAGN	wagon
PEPLL	people	EVN	even
GOBL	gobble	CRAN	crayon
PESL	pencil	KITN	kitten
SPESHL	special	CHOLDRN	children
		DEDNT	didn't
		SATNS	sentence
TMORO	tomorrow	SODNLY	suddenly
FRM	from	LINE	lion
		IDEN	indian

the spellings of /ə/ before obstruents presented in Table 17 in section 2.2.4.

In most of these cases, the omission of a vowel in spelling is probably accurate phonetically. When a sonorant in an unstressed syllable follows an obstruent (a "true" consonant), the sonorant alone, without a vowel, may constitute the sonority peak of the syllable. Such a "syllabic" consonant is most likely to be homorganic with the preceding obstruent, but it may also occur in other cases in which the obstruent and the sonorant are close enough that it is possible to articulate them without an intervening (reduced) vowel (Kenyon, 1969, secs. 88-91). This condition is true for most cases in which the children do not represent a vowel preceding a sonorant, as illustrated in the examples above. Thus, these spellings show that the children make a rather fine phonetic distinction between the short reduced vowel that occurs before obstruents, as in BRAYSLIT, and the sonorant consonant that may occur in a similar environment, as in PESL. More important, the fact that children can make this distinction shows that the category "vowel" (as opposed to "syllable" only) is a part of their phonetic analysis. The children tacitly distinguish among syllabic segments, between vowels and syllabic sonorants. This evidence independently supports the assertion (in section 2.2) that vowels constitute a phonetic category for children.

There are some extensions of this "syllabic" spelling to environments in which it is not phonetically accurate. We find it in some cases where the preceding segment is not an obstruent, so that the sonorant could not be syllabic according to the customary definition, as in FRM, CRAN, CHOLDRN, LINE, IDEN in Table 24. Some of these apparent inaccuracies may be explained as the use of a letter to spell the syllable that is its name (perhaps the N in CHOLDRN) or the reversal of letters (perhaps NE for EN in LINE). In any case, most of the single letter spellings of sonorants in unstressed syllables appear to represent true syllabic consonants.

This observation, together with the spellings of /ɚ/ and /ɝ/, shows that children tend to distinguish between a VC sequence and a single syllabic segment. Furthermore, this aspect of children's spelling tends to persist over time, unlike the vowel categorizations, for instance. In Appendix B, Tables 2 and 4 show that children of age six and older are just as likely as younger children to represent /əl/ and /ən/ as L and N. We see the persistence of this spelling also in that it appears in words for which a child has learned some other aspects of standard spelling, such as the two T's in LITTL or the LY in SODNLY. On a spelling-dictation exercise with 47 first-graders, 21 produced:

BRATHR–brother   TABL–table   FETHR–feather

and some others produced one or two of these. These first-graders produced other invented spellings, such as the omissions of preconsonantal nasals, but none as frequently as these. It appears, then, that one of the aspects of standard spelling that children adopt least readily is one that adults are not usually aware of: the representation of a vowel in every syllable, even when no vowel occurs phonetically or when the vowel that occurs is retroflex.

2.6 The spelling of intervocalic flaps

Another instance in which the children's spellings are sometimes nonstandard but phonetically accurate is that of the voiced tongue-tap, or "flap," that occurs when an alveolar stop intervenes between two vowels if the preceding vowel carries a greater degree of stress than the following one.[10] (The following "vowel" may be one of the syllabic sonorants just discussed.) In this position, there is no contrast between /t/ and /d/; both of these (lexically) are realized as a short tap of the tongue at the alveolar ridge. Because this flap tends to be voiced, it is phonetically closer to /d/. Note, for instance, the phonetic difference between the /t/ of *let* and the /t/ of *letter* (or *let 'er*).

In just the intervocalic environments, the young children often spell the /t/ as *D*. Table 25 presents some examples. The *D* in these words

Table 25

Spellings of /t/ as *D*

PREDE	pretty	WOODR	water
FIDI	"fighted"	NODESEN	noticing
LADR	letter	BEDR	better
CIDEJCHES	cottage cheese	RIDEN	writing
BODOM	bottom	ADSAVIN	eighty-seven
AODOV	out of	GADICHANS	get a chance

is phonetically more accurate than the standard *t*. Even among children less than six years old, however, cases in which a phonetic voiced flap is spelled as *T* are far more numerous. Where *t* is the standard spelling, how the children learned it is an interesting question, but not one that we can answer definitely. They may have asked their parents or learned from their reading of standard spelling, or they may have noticed that an intervocalic voiced flap alternates with /t/ when the same segment occurs before a consonant, as in pairs such as "let them" and "let 'em."

Sometimes children evidently adopt a general rule that a voiced flap is to be spelled *T*, for in a few cases they apply that spelling to stops that are actually /d/ lexically and *d* in standard spelling. In these cases, the children are clearly applying what they have learned from

Table 26

Spellings of /d/ with *T*

NOBUTE ⎱ NOBTIEE ⎰	nobody
PEBATE	Peabody
MITL	middle

other words, rather than imitating the adult spelling of these particular words.

The other interesting observation is that the children use the (standard) *T* spelling even in words for which they have not yet learned other aspects of standard spelling. These standard spellings of the flap

Table 27

Spellings of /t/ with *T*

BITUVMELC	bottle of milk	WOTR	water
ETTENG	eating	SATRDY	Saturday
LATR	letter	INVITIG	inviting
LITL	little	WATD	waited

are actually much more numerous than the spellings with *D*, even among the younger children; all of the above examples come from children of ages four and five. They may well have learned this standard spelling from adults, but it is interesting that they adopted it earlier than other aspects of standard spelling, such as the spellings of syllabics or of preconsonantal nasals. Even though the children can *hear* the distinction between voiced and voiceless stops, as indicated by their consistent distinction between /t/ and /d/ in general (and between /k/ and /g/ and /p/ and /b/), they learn rather readily that some voiced flaps are to be spelled *T*. It seems that they learn the spelling of this sound, rather than of the whole words in which it occurs.

This is a case in which the children evidently hear a distinction and have the alphabetic means to represent it, but in which they learn rather early the standard, abstract, spelling. We may account for this fact in terms of phonetic categorization or in terms of the phonological regularity, the predictability of voicing in certain intervocalic contexts. In phonetic terms, it may be that the voicing contrast is a relatively minor one in children's categorization, so that given a slight acquaintance with standard spelling, they find it relatively easy to ignore the distinction orthographically. On the other hand, it is perhaps relevant that voicing in this context is predictable. Children's early use of *t* for voiced flaps may indicate not merely a phonetic grouping, but their recognition that regular phonetic alternation is not preserved in spelling. It may be that the low-level phonological rule that gives a voiced flap as the realization for a lexical /t/ or /d/ is a particularly "transparent" rule. Children may learn readily (from whatever source) that the flap is regarded as a /t/. Either way, the early development of this abstraction suggests that voicing is a less salient distinction in children's categorization than are other features discussed earlier, such as that between vowels and syllabic sonorants. The issue is whether the predictability of this distinction is important to children's orthography, as it is to standard spelling. Section 2.7 presents evidence concerning children's spelling of other predictable alternations in voicing, and chapter six reports an experiment designed to distinguish, at least partially, between the phonetic relationship and the phonological one.

2.7 Alternations involving voicing

One effect of not representing predictable phonetic variation in standard English spelling is that the alternant forms of certain affixes are spelled uniformly. The past tense ending is -*ed*, whether it occurs in its voiceless form as in *hopped* [hapt], voiced as in *lobbed* [labd], or with a vowel as in *wanted* [wantəd]. Exceptional spellings occur where some aspect of pronunciation is not predictable: completely irregular verb alternations, such as *go/went*, and subregularities, such as the tense/lax alternation in the vowels of verbs like *creep/crept* and *feel/felt*.

The same general principle carries over to the spellings of plurals, where the contrasts among the phonetic realizations /s/, /z/, and /əz/ are entirely predict. ble. English spelling represents the first two as -*s*, distinguishing the last as -*es*, as in *cups*, *cubs*, and *dishes*. For both inflections, the spelling system is abstract with respect to the voiceless/ voiced alternation, and except for the /əz/ plural form, preserves only lexical (unpredictable) variation in spelling.

With these facts in mind, we now consider how the children represent predictable alternations. There are really two questions, although only indirect evidence could allow us to separate them: do the children recognize the various occurrences of past tense or plural as belonging to the same morphological item, and do they recognize the predictability of the variation? Concerning spellings, we may ask, do they assign phonetic or morphophonemic spellings, and do they spell exceptional items in an exceptional manner?

2.7.1 The spelling of the past tense marker. The answer to these questions is that the children generally represent past tense phonetically. They spell /t/ as -*T*, /d/ as -*D*, and /əd/ as -*ID*. When the children develop from this three-way distinction, they often begin by using -*D* to represent both /t/ and /d/, still distinguishing these from /əd/.

Table 28

Spellings of Past Tense

LAFFT	left	COLD	called	STARTID	started
HALPT	helped	MARED	married	ADDID	added
SWOUPT	swooped	GLOWSD	closed	WATID	waited
GAST	guessed	KILD	killed	WOTID	wanted
LIKT	liked	STAD	stayed	HATID	hated

Table 29

Spellings of Past Tense [t] with *-D*

FIXD	fixed
WALKD	walked
FINISHD	finished
LOOKD	looked
PEKD	peeked

The first abstraction is from the voicing contrast. In this process the children sometimes extend the *-D* spelling to the /t/ in irregular verbs, but in general (judging from a few instances), the irregular verbs retain their more phonetic spelling.

For one child, Edith, there is a revealing month-by-month sequence from 5,10 to 6,3, during which time this development took place. At 5,10 she began to mark past tense endings: HOP-T (hopped), STOP-T (stopped). But she was unable to apply this diacritic orthography to past tense exclusively or consistently: HOPPED-T (apparently with adult dictation for HOPPED, since the double consonant and *-ed* do not otherwise occur), CAT-T (cat), WAT (went), WOCT (walked). The following month (5,11) showed more of the same; she had revised her notation slightly, and she treated an exceptional form as if it were regular: THA'T (that), JUS'T (just), WAN'T (went).

At 6,0 (really almost two months later) we have the first abstract treatment of regular past forms. The diacritics disappeared, along with any apparent confusion between verbal inflections and the inherent segments of other words: PEKD (peeked), FILLD (filled). The *-D* of PEKD was the only morphophonemic spelling in this month; it was also the only phonetic /t/ as an inflection. Otherwise, /t/ was spelled *T*. At 6,2 and 6,3 Edith continued to spell past tense /t/ as *-D*. She even overgeneralized this spelling to an irregular verb in one instance:

FINISHD (finished)   LAFT (left)
WALKD (walked), but also   WANT (went)
WAND (went)   SLAPT (slept)

But in general, at this age Edith distinguished regular from irregular cases (which means that she recognized the relation between *sleep* and *slept, leave* and *left,* and *go* and *went*), spelling irregular past forms *-T*, while she spelled regular past forms *-D* and *-ID.*

This girl's development in this respect is more fully and, with her diacritics, more explicitly illustrated than most, but it displays two quite common characteristics: the development from a phonetic to a more abstract representation of past tense /t/, using *-D,* and the separation of the irregular cases, which do not receive an abstract spelling.

It would be incorrect, I believe, to attribute these developments entirely to adult teaching. In that *-D* alone is not the standard spelling, and in the systematic errors in applying it, as well as in nonstandard spellings elsewhere in the words, we can see that the children are not simply copying these spellings from dictation, but are to some degree actively developing them for themselves.

There is also situational evidence of their relative independence. At the time she wrote these examples, Edith was attending a Montessori school, where the practice was to accept all the children's writing with a minimum of correction. Her mother, who had attended a Montessori school herself, followed much the same practice at home; she told her children spellings only when they asked, and she rarely corrected what they offered. Of course, the children used information from adults; at age six, most of them could learn from reading as well as from direct oral instruction, so that the occurrence of *-D* here is hardly to be regarded as spontaneous. But the adult information was evidently "filtered" through the child's own notions, which also influenced what he or she wrote.

The occurrence of *-D* as the first uniform spelling for [t] and [d] in regular endings might perhaps result from the ambiguity of the standard spelling when it is affixed to a word with a final *-e,* as in *named.* But together with the fact that at the same time children commonly represent /əd/ as *-ID,* the collapsing of the distinction between /d/ and /t/ in the spelling *-D* appears to be the first step in the development of an abstract representation for past tense endings. This spelling demonstrates that the development from a phonetic to an abstract spelling is not necessarily a development directly to standard spelling. It is important that such a spelling commonly precedes the appearance of both the standard *-ed* spelling and other aspects of standard spelling, such as those of /ɛ/, of preconsonantal nasals, and of /ɚ/. In this respect and in the fact that it is overgeneralized at first, it is analogous to the appearance of *T* for voiced flaps. It thus offers additional support for the suggestion that it is relatively easy for children to develop spellings that are abstract with respect to predictable contrasts in voicing.

2.7.2 The spelling of /z/. Another bit of evidence for this same conclusion comes from the observation that /z/ (in affixes and as an inherent segment) is usually spelled S; as Appendix A, Table 25 shows, about 91% of the occurrences of /z/ are spelled S or some combination of S with a vowel-spelling, while even in the youngest children only about 6% are spelled with Z or some combination containing Z. S is the usual standard spelling for /z/, except initially, and according to Venezky, *z* is "the least frequently used letter in Modern English orthography" (1970, p. 90), so we may assume that the children have been strongly influenced by standard spelling in this respect. Nevertheless, the failure to record the /s/–/z/ distinction is remarkable in children who in other ways have shown an attention to fine phonetic distinctions and a capacity for original spelling.

Furthermore, there are several kinds of evidence which suggest that the children's spelling of /z/ may be partly independent of standard spelling. Most obvious, perhaps, are the cases in which the children use the spelling Z, even though it is nonstandard; only one of these is for an affix. (See Table 30.)

Table 30

Spellings of /z/ with Z

IZ	is
DIZ	does
WOZ, WUZ, WAZ	was
BECOZ	because
BCOZ	because
OWSENZ	oceans

More striking, however, are the cases in which the children have adopted a nonstandard spelling, but one which is normally used for /s/. (See Table 31.)

Finally, in a great many cases the children employ a standard (*s*) spelling for /z/, but other aspects of the spelling are so obviously in-

Table 31

Invented Spellings of /z/

EC	is	DUSSINT	doesn't	COSE	cows
RAISIC	races	IRSS	ears	SASE	says
TETCHERC	teachers	SISE	size	ISE	eyes
EYECINSTIN	Eisenstein	SOO	zoo		

Table 32

Standard Spellings for /z/ in Nonstandard Contexts

SES, SAS	says	BKOS	because
CIDEJCHES	cottage cheese	TRCES	turkeys
SINDAS	Sundays	KUS, KOS	'cause
CHRIBLS	troubles	HARRS	hers
ES	is	KWOTRS	quarters
HES	his	POS	paws
PINTRES	pine trees	HWNTRS	hunters
ISE	eyes	POLES	please
TOWSE	toes	HAWULS	howls

vented that one wonders why (or whether) the child did not invent a spelling for /z/ as well.

Taken together, these three kinds of evidence show that the children sometimes invent a spelling for /z/, and that some of these inventions treat /z/ as if it were /s/. When the children do use a standard (s) spelling for /z/, it has been more readily adopted than many other aspects of standard spelling. Like the spellings of intervocalic flaps and of past tense affixes, the spellings of /z/, even though they are obviously influenced by standard spelling, suggest that a predictable contrast is one that children can easily ignore in spelling. Among the instances in which /z/ is represented like /s/, however, we observe several where the voicing of /z/ is not predictable. Words such as *is*, *size*, and *zoo*, represented in Table 31, include /z/ as an inherent segment (not an affix) in a position in which /s/ could also occur. Thus, although the spellings of intervocalic flaps, past tense affixes, and /z/ all suggest that children readily adopt an abstract spelling for predictable alternations in voicing, there remains a question as to whether predictability, in addition to the phonetic relationships involved, contributes to this early abstraction.

Since the children do not distinguish /s/ and /z/ in their spelling,

it is important to know that they do perceive the distinction between
the two sounds, and therefore, that the spelling is an abstraction. Informal sessions with nursery school and kindergarten children have
convinced me that children of even three and a half years can usually
answer questions involving minimal pairs, such as *sip/zip, racer/razor,*
and *bus/buzz.* This task was extremely easy for kindergarten children
and for the children who created the spellings (Read, 1970, p. 137-
144). The use of S to represent /z/ cannot even be explained mainly
as a visual reversal of the letter Z; some reasons are presented in Read
(1971, p. 29).

Taking the view that, influenced by standard spelling, young children readily adopt the spelling S for /z/, and similarly abstract spellings for /t/ and /d/, we find a plausible answer to a question raised by
Berko in her classic study of children's acquisition of morphology.
Having shown that preschool children can form the appropriate /s/
or /z/ plural of even nonsense words, and thus that they have acquired
knowledge of a rule that extends to new instances, Berko questions
whether the rule is morphological or phonological in nature, and notes,
"It would be interesting to find out what the child thinks he is saying—
if we could in some way ask him the general question, 'How do you
make the plural?'" (1958, p. 173). We might look on the children's
spelling as embodying one kind of answer, namely that children regard
the /s/–/z/ (and the /t/–/d/) alternants as a single form at the level
relevant to spelling, as do adults. However, since children generally
distinguish /s/ and /z/ plurals from /əz/ in spelling (and /t/ and /d/
past forms from /əd/), their initial basis for the abstraction appears
to be phonological, rather than morphological.

Accordingly, a pedagogical orthography, such as i.t.a., that employs
distinct symbols for the voiced and voiceless plurals may be introduc-
ing phonetic detail that a preschool child can readily, perhaps even
spontaneously, learn to ignore. Considering the early occurrence of
abstractions with respect to voicing in children's early spelling, phonemic accuracy in pedagogical spelling may be an inappropriate goal.
The question that is at least logically prior to the development of pedagogical proposals is: Which phonetic distinctions (and similarities) are
most important in a child's own phonological system as he or she begins
to read and write?

2.8 Conclusions

We have seen evidence that children represent certain phonetic relationships in their original spelling. In summarizing what this mass of evidence suggests about children's categorization of speech sounds, let us distinguish between the main features, which are numerically large and which are untainted by standard spelling, and the interesting but less clear indications, in which the children may be heavily influenced by standard spelling.

2.8.1 *Main conclusions.* First, there are two indications in spelling that vowels constitute a distinct category for children: among those speech sounds for which a spelling is not suggested by the letter-names, the vowels are far more likely than obstruents, nasals, or glides to receive an invented spelling in which one phone is paired with another that is phonetically similar; and the set of invented spellings for vowels is virtually disjoint from the set of spellings for nonvowels, even when the vowel in question occurs in letter-names, as in the case of /ɛ/.

Second, the pairs of tense-lax vowels that are similar in place of articulation tend to be spelled alike, especially /e/–/ɛ/ and /i/–/ɪ/. All four such classes are related in spelling to some degree, but /e/–/ɛ/ is the clearest and most widespread.

Third, nasals strongly tend to be omitted from spelling in just the cases in which they immediately precede consonants. The categorial significance of this fact is that children may regard the nasal as an aspect of the preceding vowel or of the following consonant. The nasal is not represented in spelling precisely because the children have no distinct representation for the nasalization of another segment. Chapter five reports an experimental study of the alternative hypotheses.

Finally, among the large effects in spelling that provide evidence of children's categorization is the fact that syllabic sonorants and /ɚ/ and /ɝ/ are spelled with the single letters *M, N, L,* and *R.* The categorial significance of these spellings is that the retroflex vowels are regarded as more /r/-like than vowel-like, and the syllabicity of the sonorants is distinguished from that of a syllable consisting of an unstressed vowel and an obstruent, another indication that vowels constitute a distinct phonetic category.

Each of the four judgments listed in this section is common to a considerable number of children, is reflected in first-grade spelling, and yet cannot plausibly be the direct result of standard spelling or adult influence. It seems reasonable to regard them as the categorial judgments of children confronted with the problem of representing English speech sounds with a restricted alphabet. The significance of these judgments is that the children were capable of grouping one speech sound with another in order to devise representations, and that the groupings all reflect genuine phonetic relationships, such as might be indicated more explicitly in a phonetic feature description. Although a relatively small number of children created the spellings, their accomplishment suggests that the analysis and classification of speech sounds may develop tacitly prior to formal instruction. Further inquiry into this process may provide important insights about phonological development in children and even about the phonetic material of language.

2.8.2 Less clear categorial inferences. In addition to those cases in which the children invent a nonstandard spelling, there are cases in which the children's spelling raises interesting questions but is so confounded with standard spelling that we can draw no clear conclusion. These cases may warrant further study.

One such question is the categorization of the back, rounded vowels. Even when nonstandard, the spellings of the rounded vowels are distinct from those of the front unrounded vowels. One cannot determine the actual basis of the distinction, however, because the spellings of most back vowels and of the unrounded vowels /a/ and /ʌ/, in particular, are too similar to standard spelling.

A second tantalizing bit of evidence is that /tr/ is sometimes spelled CHR, indicating that some children classify the first segment on the basis of its affrication. That much is clear, but so many spellings are standard that it is impossible to tell what proportion of children may make such a judgment at any given point. This is the only subphonemic categorization discussed.

Perhaps the most general of these unresolved issues is the possibility that children may abstract more readily from predictable contrasts in voicing, at least for alveolar obstruents, than from other contrasts. For intervocalic flaps, past tense affixes, and the segments /s/ and /z/, including plurals, the children rapidly develop spellings that ignore the voicing contrast, even though young children can readily distinguish /t/ from /d/ and /s/ from /z/ in speech reception. The development is in the direction of, and undoubtedly influenced by, standard spelling, but in each case there are nonstandard spellings of various sorts that indicate that the children are developing generalizations of their own.

Each of the invented spellings is an abstraction; indeed, in an extended sense all spellings are. The use of *A* to spell /e/, /ɛ/, /æ/, etc., and of *AT* to spell /et/, /ɛt/, and /ɛnt/, for example, are obviously abstractions from phonetic contrasts. The interesting character of the spellings of flaps, past tense affixes, and /z/ is that they are, or rapidly become, abstract from contrasts that the children have the alphabetic means to represent. The suggestion is that for alveolar obstruents, voicing may be a somewhat less salient basis of phonetic categorization than some of the other features which influence children's spelling. Except for some of the occurrences of /z/, each of these contrasts is phonologically predictable. We have not yet distinguished the contribution of this factor from that of the phonetic relationship. Chapter six reports a relevant experiment.

2.8.3 The children involved. It would be easy but, I believe, incorrect to disregard the evidence presented here as having been produced by exceptional children. They were exceptional in that they began to spell and, often, to read early. Some, but not all, appeared to be independent and creative beyond the average, but their creativity was sometimes a result of their spelling accomplishments. Most of them came from relatively privileged middle-class families with professional and academic parents, but this fact may have been a result of the informal procedure by which I located young spellers. Within this limitation, the families were quite diverse in beliefs and backgrounds. The one characteristic that all the parents had in common was a willingness to accept the child's own spelling efforts, to provide simple materials (first blocks and other elementary alphabet toys, then paper and pencil), and to answer questions. A cluster of unfortunate attitudes prevalent in our society may suppress this willingness in many parents: a fear that the child's own efforts will lead to "bad habits," a belief that English spelling is bizarre, and a corresponding reliance on the expertise of professional teachers or on sometimes complex educational devices that bear the stamp of expert approval. All of the parents provided just the information that any inexpert literate adult could provide: the names of the letters and answers to such questions as, "How do you spell 'chuh'?" They did not coax or expect their children to spell; most were surprised, in fact. There were no unusual educational devices relevant to spelling in any of the homes, and although the parents may have had inner qualms about "bad habits," their manner was relaxed and nondidactic. All of the children have by now readily mastered standard spelling, with none of the laborious retraining that the notion of "habits" implies. Learning to spell need not be a process of acquiring habits, apparently.

In any case, to attribute the children's accomplishment *a priori* to exceptional general intelligence or an exceptional environment merely begs the important question. The children had tacitly acquired a knowledge of phonetic relations of which their parents were themselves unaware. What the children had learned was not related in any obvious way to what they had heard or seen. The important theoretical question is how preschool children learn abstract relations of this sort. Until we have serious evidence bearing on this question, we cannot assume that general intelligence must be the major factor in acquiring the knowledge that makes spelling possible. Even if it were true that all young spellers are exceptionally intelligent, the statistical observation by itself would not account for the occurrence of the spelling, for its specific character. Despite individual variations in development, the crucial conclusion remains that children can (and to some degree, must) make categorial judgments about the sounds of their language before they learn to read and write.

2.8.4 *The strengths and weaknesses of the spelling evidence.* The use of children's spelling as a clue to their phonetic judgments is not a traditional kind of inquiry. As was indicated in section 1.1.2, there are other sources of relevant evidence. For example, one can study systematic errors in production (Olmsted, 1971) or perception (Graham and House, 1971); one can study children's knowledge of phonological rules (Morehead, 1971; Messer, 1967; or Menyuk, 1968); one can even study explicit judgments of rhyming (Knafle, 1973). Each of these can produce evidence of phonetic categorization, even though that may not be their main significance. Accordingly, it is appropriate to assess the status of evidence drawn from spelling, particularly since linguists and psychologists have generally eschewed evidence of this type, except in historical studies.

Perhaps the greatest strength of the spelling evidence is that it arises from a natural and spontaneous effort by children to represent their language. Almost all of the spelling reported in this chapter was created spontaneously; very little was elicited by adult requests. As the following chapters show, one may readily observe many of the same phenomena in children's spelling and other judgments during the early school years. In this way, the spelling evidence relates directly to the major educational task of those years, the acquisition of literacy. The spellings are apparently based on (conscious or unconscious) judgments of phonetic similarity, a level of processing which is distinct from perception itself. In these respects, the spelling evidence has both theoretical and a practical significance.

The weaknesses inherent in the use of spelling evidence are perhaps more obvious. A problem specific to the early invented spelling discussed here is that it is created by a minority of children; it remains an open question whether other children make similar judgments, or even whether one can devise ways of investigating the judgments of young children who do not create spellings.

A more general limitation of spelling evidence, and the one that has perhaps been most influential in restricting the use of spelling data to historical linguistic studies, is the simple fact that spelling is constrained by the alphabet chosen and undoubtedly confounded by the influence of standard orthography. Even given the children's imperfect knowledge, this latter influence makes it impossible to assess the salience of the relationships between /p/ and /b/, or between /i/ and /e/, since the letter-names and standard orthography provide a ready means for children to distinguish the members of these pairs. In addition, there are phonetically irrelevant errors in children's spelling, such as the well-known visual confusion between mirror-image characters such as *b* and *d*.

Finally, as in all naturalistic studies, there are presumably important influences on children's spontaneous spelling which are not subject to manipulation or control by the investigator. Among these is our inability to control or even to determine the precise phonetic "input" to the children's judgments. We also have no control over or knowledge of the alternatives which were effectively open to a child for a particular spelling. When a child represented /ɛ/ with A, was he or she conscious of the basis for doing so? Were other possibilities considered and rejected?

Despite these shortcomings, the evidence presented in this chapter clearly indicates some original spellings of great frequency which cannot be explained in terms of the influence of standard spelling, superficial confusions among letter-shapes, or unusual pronunciations, but which can be plausibly accounted for in terms of children's tacit categorization of speech sounds on the basis of certain phonetic similarities. This fact provides important insight into the nature of children's phonological knowledge at the age at which they enter school.

The use of spelling as an indication of children's phonetic judgments in no way conflicts with the priority now accorded to speech, as opposed to writing, in linguistics and psycholinguistics. Historically, linguists have found it necessary to argue that "language is speech and the linguistic competence underlying speech. Writing is no more than a secondary, graphic representation of language . . ." (Langacker,

1973, p. 59). The arguments for this view are well known, and by now the position of speech as the primary realization of language is so widely accepted that almost no serious linguistic and psycholinguistic evidence is drawn specifically from written language. Furthermore, the precise relationship between language and writing has been very little studied, although Chomsky and Halle (1968) sketch one view of this relationship. But it is precisely *because* writing is a secondary realization of language that one can use children's invented spelling as a clue to their phonetic categorizations. The apparent phonetic basis for children's invented spelling suggests that, for them at least, spelling is indeed a code upon the spoken language. It is possible, therefore, to study the categorial judgments implicit in the encoding. For adults, the written forms evidently correspond to a more abstract level of language, as Chomsky and Halle and others (Klima, 1972, and C. Chomsky, 1970) have argued.

Chapters three and four report experimental studies undertaken in an effort to check the inferences based on spelling evidence with children who have not created original early spelling. These studies attempt to reduce the direct influence of standard spelling and to exert greater control over the phonetic input to children's judgments. The experiments thus confront two kinds of problems; prior to the substantive problem of verifying the inferences based on spelling, there is the methodological one of devising manageable tasks which call for phonetic judgments analogous to those involved in spelling, but which are not subject to the limitations discussed above. In principle, one could attempt to investigate many aspects of children's phonetic judgments, but the studies reported here are all aimed at the judgments revealed in spelling. In various ways, each experiment was designed to answer two questions: Do children categorize speech sounds differently from adults? Do they do so in terms of certain phonetic features, and are some features especially prominent as bases for their categories? These are important questions in the study of language acquisition and have a plausible connection to learning to read and write.

2.8.5 The educational significance. The educational importance of invented spelling and phonetic categorization by children is that we cannot assume that a child must approach reading and writing as an untrained animal approaches a maze—with no discernible prior conception of its structure. Evidently, a child may come to school with a knowledge of some phonological categories and relations; without conscious awareness, the child may seek to relate English spelling to these relations in some generally systematic way. If this inference is correct, some long-neglected questions become crucial for understanding and facilitating the process of learning to read and write: What levels of phonological analysis do children tacitly control at various stages of development? How do these analyses relate to lexical representations and to standard spelling? How can literacy instruction build on this relationship while encouraging children to extend and deepen their notion of the sound system of the language? Detailed answers to these questions are not at all obvious; in fact, it is difficult to devise means of acquiring answers since children's phonological judgments are rarely explicit, as they are in the invented spellings.

The prevailing assumption has been that a first-grade child analyzes spoken English into discrete, contrasting phonemes. The vowels of *please* and *pleasant* differ distinctively, and for the first-grader there is no reason why they should be spelled alike. Likewise, according to this view, the vowels of *please* and *plays* are simply two different vowels; their acoustic and articulatory similarities are not perceptual facts for children, certainly not at a level that might influence their judgments of what is "natural" in a spelling system. Consequently, we have assumed that for children, an optimal spelling system is one which maintains a one-to-one correspondence between phonemes and graphemes, and that the difficulties of standard orthography may be identified and measured by this standard. This assumption has been made rather explicitly in the development of pedagogical spelling systems (Pitman and St. John, 1969) and in other applications of phonemic analysis to orthography (Pike, 1947, pp. 89, 208-209).

The invented spelling and our consequent experiments do not show precisely what constitutes an optimal orthography, nor do they resolve all the theoretical issues here. But they do suggest that the correct picture is more complex: children analyze and categorize phones according to certain phonetic characteristics, and in some circumstances they may assign spellings to these categories, rather than to individual phonemes.

In the classroom, an informed teacher should expect that seemingly bizarre spellings may represent a system of abstract phonological relations of which adults are quite unaware. Until we understand this system better, we can at least respect it and attempt to work with it, if only intuitively. A child who wants to spell *truck* with a *ch-* will not be enlightened by being told that *ch-* spells "chuh," as in *chicken*. The child already knows that; in fact, the relation between the first segments of *truck* and *chicken* is exactly what he or she wants to represent. Nor will exaggerated (or exasperated) pronunciation of *truck* help much, for monolingual adult speakers of English are usually limited to pronouncing the two possibilities that our phonology allows. We will either insert a false vowel after the [t], which does away with the affrication at the cost of distorting the word, or we will exaggerate that very quality which the child wishes to represent. Drill and memorization of words with *tr-* and *dr-* may help the child to learn such cases, but these techniques suggest that spelling is arbitrarily related to speech and can only be memorized. This suggestion is not true of either standard spelling or the child's own invention. Better, it would seem, to say something like, "Yes, *truck* sounds like *chicken* at the beginning, but it is also like the first sound of *toy*, and that's what we show by using a *t*." Similar tactics could be used for children who spell *pen* with an *a*, *dent* without an *n*, *brother* without an *e*, *liked* with a *t*, or *butter* with a *d*. Such children need to be told, in effect, that their phonological judgments are not wrong (though they may seem so to most adults), and that it is reasonable, indeed necessary, to categorize abstractly what they hear.

However, they must also learn that standard spelling reflects a system rather different from their own. They will have acquired the basis for this adult system only when they have tacitly learned not to represent the effects of regular phonological processes such as affrication and vowel shift, so that their spellings are phonologically abstract. Then they can learn to read and spell on the principle that the written form corresponds to lexical relationships, rather than to phonetic ones. They are on their way when they begin to abstract from phonetic variations, as the spontaneous spellers did in their preschool development. It may be particularly important to recognize when their own efforts are too abstract, or abstract in the wrong direction, and to suggest, at least implicitly, that they are using the right principle, even if in the wrong place. We cannot teach this principle if we ourselves believe that to learn to spell is to get in the "habit" of associating sounds with letters, or phonemes with graphemes. For at least some children, to learn standard spelling is to learn to broaden and deepen their preschool phonological analysis, which is already abstract enough that phoneme-grapheme correspondences are indirect outcomes of a more intricate system. In this sense, learning to read and write may be a matter of knowledge rather than habit.

CHAPTER THREE

EXPERIMENTAL STUDIES OF [tr] CLUSTERS

3.1 The goals

The evidence presented in the preceding chapter raises the question of whether children in general, especially those who do not create their own spelling, tacitly organize phonetic material in the ways that the invented spellings suggest. Most children, who apparently do not create spellings prior to entering school, may conceivably make different judgments, or may find it difficult or impossible to make any overt judgments of phonological relationships. This chapter and those following will report sets of experimental studies designed to elicit evidence of children's phonetic judgments primarily in kindergarten and first grade, and in some cases to inquire more specifically into the basis for these judgments.

Most children, like adults, rarely make overt judgments of phonetic categories; obviously normal language use hardly ever requires that we comment on how our phonetic material is organized. Therefore situations that elicit such judgments must be contrived and unnatural to some degree. In these experiments, we sacrifice the spontaneity of the spelling for a wider population and for some control over the choices presented and the phonetic input. Accordingly, the methodological question of whether and how judgments can be elicited is prior to the substantive questions and is of some importance in itself. If children can be brought to express meaningful judgments, we can investigate many aspects of their phonetic categorization, such as uniformity and development.

3.2 The same–different test

The first investigation, both in execution and in exposition, concerns the categorization of the affricated [t] and [d] which occur before [r] within formatives. (Note that the absence of affrication is one of the

79

differences between *night rate* and *nitrate*, even when the [t] of *night* is not replaced by glottal stop.) The children sometimes represent these [tr] and [dr] clusters as *CHR* and *JR*, as explained in section 2.3.

The importance of this minority judgment is that in these cases, the children evidently categorize the first segment of [tr] clusters with the corresponding affricate [č]. These spellings are interesting also because they are the only ones that may represent a different *phonemic* grouping among children and adults. One wonders how great the influence of standard spelling is on this classification.

Finally, an ambiguity of the invented spellings that may be resolved with further evidence is whether the children considered affricated [t] to be the *same* as [č], or merely closer to it than to other varieties of [t]. The young spellers always chose from among known spellings—in this case, between *t* and *ch* (*d* and *j*). The investigation reported here presented other children with a similar choice, but in terms of sounds, not spellings, and gave them an opportunity to indicate whether they regarded affricated [t] as different from both [t] and [č].

3.2.1 Design. For these purposes, I developed a test of children's judgments of these sounds and administered it individually to 80 kindergarten children drawn from seven classes in the schools of Brookline, Massachusetts, during May of 1970. For comparison, the test was also given to 28 preschool children in two nursery schools in Brookline and Boston, to 27 first-graders in one class in Brookline, and to 12 spontaneous spellers of various ages. Altogether 147 children took the test.

In each classroom, the teacher told the children that I had a "word game" to play with them. In most of the classrooms the children already knew me as a person who had been in the room earlier in the year to play other "word games," reported elsewhere (Read, 1970, Ch. III). Almost all the children in all the classes were eager to play the game, often boisterously so. No child who did not volunteer after, at most, a few words of encouragement from me or the teacher, was forced to participate. Even the shy children, after observing that others returned unharmed, usually volunteered. Almost all the children said, when asked, that they had enjoyed the game, and many asked, or looked in my briefcase, for more such games. When I returned to a class, some children tried to insist on playing again, even when I told them that I had only the game they had already played.

Each child chosen (the basis of selection is discussed below) went with me from the classroom to a fairly quiet location. Because of limited space available in the schools, the conditions were often far from ideal, but noise or distractions were never severe.

To each child I said, "This is a game about words that start with the same sound—that sound the same at the beginning." Then I showed the child a large card (pretest) with eleven small pictures attached. I asked the child to name each picture. The names (and the arrangement) were as follows:

racing car	telephone	skate	radio
dog(gie)	lamb	teddy bear	boat
book	(bunk) bed	drum	

If a child did not know a name, or offered one other than the above (such as *submarine* for *boat*), I suggested the expected name: "Let's call that a boat." Then I asked the child, "Can you find some things there that begin with the same sound as *baby*?" When a child had picked out *boat, bed, book,* and *bear*, or at least some of these, I asked, "How about *telephone*? How about *dog*?" and any words beginning with [b] that he may have overlooked.

This pretest taught the children the nature of the task and the procedure to be used (with some modifications) on the two tests that were to follow. Each child's performance was scored in one of three categories. The most competent children could pick out just the words beginning with [b], reject my incorrect suggestions, and even supply other words beginning with [b]. Some could name some of the initial letters.

The middle-level children sometimes offered a rhyming word instead: *maybe* for *baby*, for instance. In this case, I pointed out, "Those sound alike at the end; they rhyme. But I'm asking about words that *begin* with the same sound. For instance, *bike* begins with the same sound as *baby*." At most, these children were unsure of or wrong about one case, but in general, they could reject the incorrect suggestions and accept correct ones. With some help, the middle-level children could identify sameness of initial sounds.

The least competent children often picked at least as many wrong as right answers. They usually accepted any words that were suggested. A small amount of teaching was to no avail. Most children fell at the two extremes of this three-way categorization; they either clearly could or clearly could not identify first sounds.

In the case of a few children who were mystified and uncomfortable with the pretest exercise, I announced that that was the end of the game and did not question them further about initial sounds. Otherwise, I asked each child if he or she wanted to play some more; all did. Even those who had done poorly on the pretest were pleased to continue, although their performance was eventually disregarded in the analysis of results.

The first test dealt with words beginning with [tr], [čV], and [tV] (where V represents an arbitrary vowel). Again, each child first named the eleven pictures on a card; the expected names were:

train	teddy bear	chair	tracks	tie
			tree	chicken
turkey	church		turtle	cherries

These pictures had been selected from among others because in a pilot study children could usually provide the expected names. Still, on the average, each child came up with one name different from the above. Each such name was corrected before continuing. For instance, many children, influenced by the pretest perhaps, said just *bear;* I suggested, "Let's call him *teddy bear.*" The children always accepted these suggestions and almost always produced the desired name later. In any case, none of the unwanted names began with [t] or [č], so that their possible effect on the results was limited.

After the child had named each picture correctly, I uncovered a picture of a truck on a separate card. The children had no difficulty in naming that picture. Then I asked, "Can you find any things here [pointing vaguely to the large card] that begin with the same sound as that [pointing to the truck]?" I never had to pronounce "truck," and as far as possible, I avoided pronouncing any of the other names, especially those beginning with *tr-*, in order not to influence the results by the degree of affrication in my own pronunciation.

After the child had selected or rejected as many of the names as he or she would spontaneously, I asked questions about any that had not been judged. "What's that [pointing]? Does that begin with the same sound as that [pointing to the truck]?" In order to prevent this process from becoming too repetitious, for myself if not for the children, I sometimes pronounced the name of the item, or otherwise varied the form of the question. Except with very unspontaneous children, my pronunciation was limited to words beginning with [t] and occasionally [č], where degree of affrication is presumably not in question. A notation was made of each judgment by each child, distinguishing those that were relatively spontaneous from those that were elicited by a further question.

For a few children whose performance on the pretest was weak, and who were uneasy or tired, the "game" was declared finished. Otherwise, almost every child again declared that he or she would like to continue with the next (and last) card. This second test dealt with words whose initial sounds are [dr], [dV], and [jV], each compared to that of a *dragon*, depicted on a separate card.

drawers	jacks	dinosaur	drums	jar
	duck	drill	jump-rope	door
dress	jack-in-the-box	dog	jacket	doll

Note that the *dr*-card contains fourteen pictures, as compared with eleven on each of the others. Otherwise, the procedure corresponded to that described above.

At the end, I asked each child if he or she had enjoyed the game (all said they had), and asked that the words we had talked about be kept secret from the other children in the class. When they returned to their classroom, the children showed no inclination to discuss the content of the "game" with others.

3.2.2 Selection. The pretest results show that kindergarten children vary substantially in their ability to identify sameness of initial sounds. Just over half of those tested selected the words with initial [b] with zero or one error, but the other children could not identify sameness of initial sounds consistently. They participated confidently, but their judgments were inconsistent with each other and with any conceivable dimensions of phonetic similarity. In the first class visited, for instance, six of the fifteen children tested made more than one error on the pretest and went on to produce inconsistent answers on the other two tests. (See section 3.2.3 for a definition of "consistent.") In the next class eleven of nineteen failed the pretest, and again, each of these eleven gave inconsistent test answers.

An independent measure of the children's ability to identify the sameness of initial sounds confirmed the validity of this pretest. Two months earlier the "Pre-Reading Test of Scholastic Ability to Determine Reading Readiness"[1] had been administered in every Brookline kindergarten. Subtest 4, on initial sounds, consists of two practice items and twenty test items, each represented in the child's test booklet by line drawings of three common objects. The instructions to be read aloud by the tester for each item (after the practice) are like the following:

14. Move your finger down to the next box. Find a bus, a truck, and and a car. Listen—*bus, truck, car*. One of these begins with the

same sound as *train*. Put a mark on the picture whose name
begins with the same sound as *train*.[2]

For the two kindergartens (34 children) tested first, scores on this
standard subtest corresponded to performance on the pretest in the
following way: every child with a standard score of 15 or more made
competent judgments on the pretest, and every child who was in-
competent on the pretest had scored 13 or lower (none scored 14).
With three exceptions, the converse was also true: every child who
scored 13 or lower performed inconsistently on the pretest and the
two test cards.[3] The exceptions may well have resulted from children's
development during the weeks intervening between the two tests. On
the basis of this correspondence between two independent tests of
the children's general ability to judge sameness of initial sounds, it
appeared that little meaningful evidence would be lost if in the remaining kindergartens, we tested only those children with scores of 14 or
better on the standard subtest and any others recommended by the
teacher as possibly able to identify sameness of initial sounds. As a
result, about half of each class was chosen.

As this method of selection was applied in the five other kindergartens, the relationship between the independent measures held up;
every child who rated lowest on the pretest (eight in number) had
also scored 13 or lower on the standard subtest.[4] The converse was not
true; some children with low test scores (12 in the kindergarten sample
of 80) performed adequately on the pretest—again, probably the
effect of intervening development. In general, the selection criterion
corresponded to some large differences in performance, and was to that
degree natural.

3.2.3 Results. We are interested in the following questions:

1. Do those children who can recognize sameness of initial sounds
   categorize [tr]- with [tV]- or [čV]-, or do they identify the
   initial sound of *truck* only with other instances of [tr]-?

It is the possibility of making the narrower phonetic grouping, regarding the affricated [t] as different from *both* [t] and [č], which is
offered by this test and not offered by the set of spellings that the
young children chose from.

2. If those children who can recognize sameness of initial sounds
   group [tr]- with [tV]- or [čV]-, which of these judgments predominates, if either?

Any groupings of [tr]- with [čV]- are of particular interest, since they would indicate that the young original spellers are not unique in their categorization on the basis of affrication. Also, for those kindergarten children who make this judgment, one aspect of standard spelling will seem relatively unnatural, even though adults find it quite unremarkable. Exact counterparts of these questions arise for the [dr]- cases.

Since we are concerned with children's categorization, we must consider not merely the total number of times that all children chose words with initial [č], [t], and [tr] as having the "same first sound" as *truck*, but rather the pattern of judgments by individual children. Those patterns of judgments that appear to bear on the questions posed are as follows:

1. The [tr] judgments: those children who chose only *train, tree,* and *tracks* as having the same initial sound as *truck,* and who rejected all eight other words.

2. The [t] judgments: those children who chose the three [tr]-words *and* the four [tV]-words as all having the same initial sound as *truck,* but who rejected the four [čV]-words.

3. The [č] judgments: those children who chose the three [tr]-words and *church, chair, chicken,* and *cherries* as all having the same initial sound as *truck,* but who rejected the four [tV]-words.

These categories are defined in terms of the ideally consistent choices. As one might expect, some children approximated these patterns except for one or more inconsistencies; for example, a child might judge that *train, tracks, tree, teddy bear, tie,* and *turkey* all begin with the same sound as *truck,* but might reject *turtle* along with the four [čV]-words. The nature of the resulting pattern of judgments helps to justify a principle for how many such inconsistencies to accept in the data to be analyzed. A single inconsistency, as in the example given, still allows an unambiguous summary of the child's choices—in this case, as a [t] judgment. With even two inconsistencies, however, it is often not possible to summarize the choices unambiguously; in the example given, if the child has rejected both *turtle* and *turkey,* the choices would be as close to the [tr] as to the [t] category. Accordingly, such results are reported here, but no interpretation is based on them.

Table 33 presents the results of the [tr] test by category and level of consistency. The children included are just those who met the criterion for identifying sameness of initial sounds on the pretest, i.e.,

Table 33

Kindergarten Children Choosing Words
that "begin with the same sound" as *truck*
n = 49
mean age = 5, 10.6

Consistency	[j]	[dr]	[d]	All
−0	8	6	11	3
−1	7	2	2	2
Total	15	8	13	
−2	1	1 3	2	
−≧3		(1)		

who made zero or one error on the eleven pretest items. These were
49 of the 73 native speakers tested (=67%). The more consistent
judgments, in the inner table, constitute the basic data.

With the results divided in this way, the number of children in
each category is relatively small, but it is important that each child
represented above made eleven reasonably consistent judgments in an
individual testing situation. There is independent evidence that the
individuals represented here are just those who can reliably identify
sameness of initial sounds generally, from the pretest, from the standard test, and from the fact that altogether, these children made only
one judgment (of 159) that rejected exact correspondences (e.g.,
truck–train). Moreover, most of these children were quite confident
about their judgments, and some gave a coherent additional account
of which sounds they heard at the beginning of which words.

This confidence was just as characteristic of those in the [č] category
as of the others. Some children made it clear that they found the relationship between *truck* and *chicken*, for example, completely obvious,
and that they heard no such relationship between *truck* and *turtle*.

Table 34 presents the results of the [dr] test for the same children
in the same manner.

The results of these two tests are similar in essential respects. Inspection of the two tables suggests that:

a. most of these kindergarten children, who can identify sameness
   of initial sounds in general, regard the first segment of [tr] clusters
   as either [t] or [č], rather than categorizing it only with other
   affricated [t]'s. Similarly, they regard [dr] as beginning with
   either [d] or [j].

Table 34

Kindergarten Children Choosing Words "with the same first sound"
as *dragon*[5]
n = 49

Consistency	[č]	[tr]	[t]	All
−0	12	3	11	2
−1	1	2	1	0
Total	13	5	12	
−2	2	3	1	1	3
−≧3		(7)		

b. virtually equal numbers of these children regard the first sound
of *truck* as [č] and [t]; likewise they divide equally in regarding
dragon as beginning with [j] or [d].

3.2.4 Discussion. These results seem to indicate that most preschool
children categorize the affricated [t] of [tr] or [d] of [dr] clusters
with the corresponding stop or affricate, even when they are not required to group these with some other segment, as they are (in effect)
in spelling. Furthermore, just half of the children who make such a
categorization do so on the basis of affrication. It seems that the
judgment underlying an invented spelling such as CHRIE (try) is
fairly common—indeed, more common than one might have suspected
from the proportion of such spellings. Evidently a considerable number
of kindergarten children may find the categorization implicit in the
standard spelling *tr* to be the reverse of their own judgment.

For several reasons, we may have a fairly high degree of confidence
in these inferences. They are based on the performance of a rather
large number of children (as psycholinguistic studies go), selected
from seven different kindergartens in a reasonably diverse community.
In addition to the consistency of their judgments, there is independent evidence that the children represented in Tables 33 and 34 are
just those who could reliably identify sameness of initial sounds. The
children in the [č] ([j]) category do not differ significantly from those
in the [t] ([d]) category in this respect.[6] The children who judge the
first sound of *truck* to be the same as that of *chair* are otherwise just
as good at judging sameness of sounds as those who feel that *truck*
begins with the same sound as *turkey*. Finally, the close correspondence
between the results of the two tests provides some additional mutual

Table 35

Percentage of Consistent Judgments of [tr] and [dr], Kindergarten

Test	Affricate	[tr]/[dr] only	Stop
[tr] (n = 36)	42	22	36
[dr] (n = 30)	43	17	40

support. Table 35 summarizes the main results (the completely consistent and "-1" judgments in Tables 33 and 34) in terms of percentages.

The similarity in the results of the two tests appears not only in the combined performances of different children (Table 35), but also in the performances of individuals; a child who judged the first segment of *truck* to be an affricate ([č]) was very likely to make the corresponding judgment that *dragon* begins with an affricate ([ǰ]). In fact, no individual made an *affricate* judgment (of any degree of consistency) on one test but a *stop* judgment on the other.

Table 36 compares the judgments of individuals on the two tests, with completely consistent and "-1" judgments combined, and with those of lesser consistency omitted.[7] It is difficult to apply appropriate

Table 36

Judgments of Consistent Individuals on [tr] and [dr] Tests, Kindergarten
n = 31

	[č]	[tr] only	[t]	All
[ǰ]	12	1	0	0
[dr] only	1	3	0	0
[d]	0	0	12	0
All	0	0	0	2

statistical tests to a contingency table such as 36, where df > 1 and the frequencies in some cells are very low, but it is clear from inspection of the table that almost all of the children lie along the diagonal, i.e., are consistent in their categorization across the two tests. As a measure of the consistency of the main results, Fisher's exact probability test can be applied to the 2 × 2 contingency table formed from just those individuals in the [č], [t], [ǰ], and [d] categories. In this case, the probability of the obtained degree of consistency arising by chance is approximately 3.7×10^{-7}, or one in 2.7 million.

The importance of this large degree of individual consistency across the two tests is two-fold: it tends to increase one's confidence in the reliability of the two tests, and, of greater theoretical significance, it strongly supports the view that these categorizations are based on phonetic features, rather than on unanalyzed phonemes. If a child's categorization of [tr] were made without regard to the specific properties, such as affrication, that it shares with [dr], one would hardly expect to find the degree of consistency that actually occurred.

Although the meaning of the consistent [č] and [t] ([j] and [d]) categorizations seems quite clear, some problems arise in the interpretation of the more marginal results. With regard to the [tr] and [dr] categorizations, (i.e., those children who chose only *train, tracks,* and *tree* as having the same first sound as *truck*), an important question is whether these children considered "first sound" and "begin with" to refer to the entire consonant cluster [tr] rather than to the initial segment only. A child who made the former interpretation would presumably make [tr]/[dr] judgments, without regard to affrication.

This ambiguity might have been avoided if the pretest had included sets of words beginning with, say, [br] or [bl] in addition to [bV], and if the children had been trained to choose all of these as beginning with the same sound, or if those who rejected the clusters had been screened out of the group selected as capable of identifying sameness of initial sounds. In that case, any remaining children who made exclusively [tr] judgments would be just those who do not categorize the affricated [t] with either [t] or [č]. As it stands, however, the judgments in the [tr]/[dr] categories are ambiguous in this respect. We may infer at least that it is a minority of children who do not categorize affricated [t] with either [č] or [t], and it may in fact be a smaller minority than the results suggest. It seems reasonable to conclude that an extended pedagogical alphabet, with special symbols for affricated [t] and [d], would not seem more natural to most children and so would probably not facilitate learning to read and spell, even though a substantial proportion of children do perceive the affrication of these phones, as indicated by the [č]/[j] judgments.

Another problematic performance is that of the children who accepted *all* of the names as having the same first sound as the key word. Children who did so were often less spontaneous and less certain in their judgments, and commonly had failed on both the pretest and the standard test, so it is surprising to find some children who were successful in judging phonetic identity on these tests making judgments in the "all" category. Since these children presumably distinguish [t] from [č], the fact that they equated *both* of these with the initial segment of *truck* seems to indicate confusion about these particular sounds, or at least a shifting basis of categorization. Either way, these few results do not bear clearly on the questions posed here.

Considering the nearly equal frequency of stop and affricate judgments on both tests, one might suppose that the children are making this categorization as a group of taxonomists might; there being no contrasting [čr] or unaffricated [tr] sequences (within a syllable) in English, it is essentially indeterminate whether affricated [t] is to be categorized with /t/ or with /č/ in classical phonemics. No doubt phonemicists have been influenced by convention, including standard spelling, in categorizing it with /t/, so that one might even suggest that the children have demonstrated what a group of naive or unbiased taxonomists might do. It is entirely possible that the essence of this view is correct: that in this case, neither set of phonetic relationships naturally predominates over the other, and that children in general divide about evenly in their categorization of affricated [t].

There is, however, another possibility: that the categorizations with [t] ([d]) are learned from adults, via standard spelling, and that prior to this influence, children categorize [tr] on the basis of its affrication. It is not possible to decide this issue on the evidence at hand, but there are some interesting indications. Of the 49 kindergarten children represented here, just seven were able to read at a level at which they were likely to have encountered words beginning with *tr-* and *dr-*, according to their teachers. Of these, five made fairly consistent stop judgments, as one might expect, but two made consistent affricate judgments. (It is also true of the original spelling that some children could read standard spelling fluently but continued to indicate contrary categorizations in their own spelling.) It seems, therefore, that a knowledge of standard spelling is a possible influence, but if so, it is not a necessary or immediate one. Of course, a child's demonstrated ability to read is by no means the only avenue for adult influence; one very common source may be *Sesame Street* and other educational programs for children, which sometimes present lists of words that begin with the same letter (allegedly the same sound); such lists for *t* typically include both [tr]- and [tV]-words, for example. Accordingly, from the fact that some children who cannot read nevertheless categorize [tr] and [dr] as beginning with stops, we cannot conclude that this categorization is independent of adult influence.

One might suppose that those children who succeeded on the pretest for this study but who had failed on the corresponding standard test administered two months earlier, and who had therefore only recently developed the ability to identify phonetic similarity, might differ from others in their judgments. This possibility is supported by the (small) difference in the standard test scores of the [č] and [t] groups, mentioned in footnote 6. However, this comparison is inconclusive; three such children made generally affricate judgments, one made generally stop judgments, but all the rest (10) made judgments of the [tr]/[dr], *all*, or inconsistent varieties, reflecting the relative linguistic immaturity of these children and the fact that the pretest required easier judgments than the [tr]/[dr] tests. The following three sections present additional evidence about the role of learning and development in the phonetic categorizations revealed in this study.

Finally, it is interesting to note whether children's categorizations were related to their own pronunciations. The evidence on this point comes from transcriptions done by the experimenter as the children named the pictures. Only those pronunciations judged to be nonstandard were transcribed. Two children pronounced [tr] and [dr] clusters as [čr] and [ǰr], and these children did, in fact, make [č]/[ǰ] judgments. It is important to bear in mind, however, that even for these two children, we do not know whether their pronunciations influenced their judgments or the other way around. In any case, most [č]/[ǰ] categorizations were not directly reflected in the child's own pronunciation of [tr].[8] The dialects of the community in which the study was done do not differ substantially among themselves or from other dialects of American English in the degree of affrication given to these clusters. The differing categorizations apparently do not correspond to large differences in pronunciation by the children or others.

3.2.5 Development: first grade. I gave the same tests to smaller samples of children both younger and older than those in kindergarten. The purpose was to determine whether even younger children might be able to express consistent judgments, and to examine the development of children's judgments over the preschool to first-grade years. We particularly wanted to see whether the division among kindergarten children reflects a transition between categorizing by affrication ([tr]-[č]) and the adult judgment, which presumably corresponds to spelling ([tr]-[t]). We also wished to obtain more evidence about the relationship between these judgments and a knowledge of standard spelling.

Table 37

Judgments of First Sound of *truck*, First Grade
n = 25

Consistency	[č]	[tr]	[t]	All
−0	3	2	8	3
−1	2	−	2	2
−2	−	−	1	−	2	−

Table 38

Judgments of First Sound of *dragon*, First Grade
n = 25

Consistency	[j]	[dr]	[d]	All
−0	1	4	12	1
−1	3	−	1	−
−2	1	−	2	−

Accordingly, the same tests were given to 27 members of a first-grade class; all the same procedures applied, except that very little selection was necessary.[9] Tables 37 and 38 present the results.

To facilitate comparison with table 35, the consistent answers of each type are expressed as round percentages of the total consistent answers in Table 39.[10]

Table 39

Percentage of Consistent Judgments of [tr] and [dr], First Grade

	Affricate	[tr]/[dr] *only*	Stop
[tr] (n = 17)	29	12	59
[dr] (n = 21)	19	19	62

Again the two tests are quite reliable with respect to each other. Comparing tables 35 and 39, we see that there is a change between kindergarten and first grade toward judgments of the [t]/[d] type, as well as toward more consistent judgments; neither result is surprising.

More interesting is the fact that some first-graders still make the affricate judgments. We may compare these children with those who made stop judgments, in terms of their reading achievement as reported by the teacher.[11] At the lower levels of reading (pre-primer through 1-1), all three main types of judgments occur, but children at the 1-2 level of reading and above make only [t]/[d] and [tr]/[dr] categorizations.

One might assume from this relationship that words with the clusters *tr-* and *dr-* first appear in the readers at the 1-1 level, the last level at which children made [č]/[j] judgments. Such a simple connection does not hold. *Tr-* and *dr-* clusters were taught at the primer level, so most of the first-grade reading program (the 1-1 material) intervened between the first reading of these words and the complete disappearance of [č]/[j] judgments. In other words, there are children who know how to read *truck* and *chair*, *dragon* and *jacks*, but who still believe that these pairs begin with the same sounds. In fact, there were five such children (who made [č] and/or [j] categorizations) among the first-graders tested; one girl gave consistent [č]/[j] judgments, yet had mastered the entire first-grade reading material since she had first learned to read words with *tr-* and *dr-*.

To confirm this partial independence of phonetic judgments and reading knowledge, I tested these five children individually for their ability to read the key words (*truck* and *dragon*) and the first seven words depicted on each test card. All but one could read every word with relative ease; for three, it was a ridiculously easy task (as they did not hesitate to tell me).[12] I then showed each child a sub-sequence of three words (*train, teddy bear, chair*) and asked them to read each one aloud again. Then I asked if any of the three begin with the same sound; four children picked out *train* and *chair* (pointing to the printed words) and denied, when asked, that *train* and *teddy bear* begin with the same sound. (The other child believed that none begin with the same sound.) Some pointed out that these begin with the same *letter*— a quite different matter, evidently. With a *dragon—jacks—duck* sequence, these same children judged that none begin with the same sound, although one child pointed out that *duck* would begin with the same sound as *dragon* "if it had a r instead of the *u*."

The import of this observation is that children may categorize English segments in ways that are contrary to the categorization implicit in English spelling, and they may not change these categorizations immediately upon learning to read the relevant spellings. This phenomenon is parallel to the observation that the spontaneous spellers could often read words in standard spelling that they continued to spell in their own way. Furthermore, in the interview situation, the children's judgments were sufficiently stable to stand up against contrary spelling in their immediate attention. These children told me quite explicitly that similarity of sound and similarity of spelling are two different questions. That is in fact an appropriate attitude for learning to read English, in which many spelling relationships do not reflect similarities in contemporary pronunciation. For this reason, it would surely be wrong pedagogically to claim that *truck* and *toy* are spelled alike (at the beginning) *because* they sound alike. Even in first grade some children will not agree that these words sound more alike than *truck* and *chair*, and some children evidently know that sound similarity is not necessarily to be inferred from spelling.

The first-graders were quite able to express their judgments about sounds; when asked, most could say what letter they thought certain of the words began with. In general, these comments confirmed the interpretations of the tests; those who made [č]/[j] judgments believed that *ch* and *j* were the initial letters of *truck* and *dragon,* while those who made [t]/[d] judgments believed that *t* and *d* were. The effects of letter-names were apparent occasionally; one little girl (in the [j]-2 category) said that *dragon* begins with *g;* a boy who made [č]/[j] choices said that *truck* begins with *h.* Another boy thought that *chair* begins with *h;* his answers were of the [t]/[d] type. More important, some children's comments support the view that [tr]/[dr] choices depend on the ambiguity of the notion "same sound" with respect to clusters. One who gave such answers asked me whether I was "looking for *d* or *dr.*" Another commented that *jacks* "has a *g* [like *dragon*] but no *r.*" These children required identity of both segments of an initial consonant cluster; otherwise, one would have made [d] judgments and the other [j], evidently.[13]

3.2.6 Development: nursery school. For further evidence as to whether the kindergarten results indicate a period of transition in these judgments, the tests were given to children at two nursery schools. The procedures were the same in all relevant respects, but even fewer nursery-schoolers could make consistent judgments. Of the 36 children who tried, just 13 reached the criterion (no more than one wrong) on the pretest.[14] Tables 40 and 41 present the results.

Because of the relatively small number of children represented here and especially the small numbers in each cell, it is doubtful that one can test whether these results are significantly different from those of

Table 40

Judgments of First Sound of *truck*, Nursery School
n = 13
mean age = 5 yrs., 0 mos.

Consistency	[č]	[tr]	[t]	All
−0	4	2	2	1
−1	1	1	−	1
−2	1	−	−	−

Table 41

Judgments of First Sound of *dragon*, Nursery School
n = 13

Consistency	[ǰ]	[dr]	[d]	All
−0	3	2	2	1
−1	−	−	1	2
−2	−	−	−	1
−3	1			

kindergarten. The most that one can say is that if larger numbers of four-year-olds made judgments in these proportions, there would be good evidence of a development from *affricate* to *stop* judgments over the three years studied.[15]

This conditional conclusion is strengthened by the fact that the two children who gave consistent [t]/[d] judgments were second-oldest and oldest in their respective nursery classes (5,7 and 5,5 years), and were able to read quite fluently, unlike most of their schoolmates.

Among the nursery-school children, as among the first-graders, there were some who could read *truck, chair,* and *teddy bear* (and similar words), yet who testified consistently that only the first two types, definitely not the first and last, begin with the same sound. In fact, at least three of the five children in the [č] categories in Table 40 could read the relevant words.[16] Again we see that if there is a general developmental tendency, it is not directly affected by knowledge of standard spelling.

Like other aspects of linguistic development, this categorization is not directly linked to absolute age. As noted, the second-oldest child (5,7) in one of the nursery schools (the Montessori school) made consistent [t]/[d] judgments, but the oldest child in the same school (6,0) made completely consistent [č]/[j] choices. Similarly for the kindergartens, the average age of those in the [č]/[j] categories (Table 33) was 5,10, exactly the same as that of those choosing [t]/[d]. The [tr]/[dr] children averaged 5,11. In the first grade, none of those giving affricate judgments was among the youngest in the class, but three of the four youngest made completely consistent [t]/[d] judgments. Clearly neither reading experience nor age directly determines this categorization. This conclusion is parallel to what appears in other linguistic development.[17]

3.2.7 *Spontaneous spellers.* For comparison, the test was given to twelve original spellers, usually in their homes. Partly because of their ability to make explicit what they heard, these children provided additional clues about the nature of the judgments and the direction of development. Unfortunately, no spontaneous speller under five years of age was available at the time. The twelve ranged in age from 5,0 to 6,6, a slightly wider range, on the young end, than in the kindergarten sample. The average age was almost 5,9, however, exactly comparable to the kindergarten average. On the pretest, all the young spellers succeeded easily in identifying initial sounds. Tables 42 and 43 present the results.

Again the numbers are too small for statistical comparison with the kindergarten sample, but there are some interesting observations.

Table 42

Judgments of First Sound of *truck*, Spontaneous Spellers
n = 12

	[č]	[tr]	[t]	*All*
complete	2	1	6	2
−1	1	–	–	–

Table 43

Judgments of First Sound of *dragon*, Spontaneous Spellers
n = 12

	[j]	[dr]	[d]	*All*
complete	3	1	7	1
−1	–	–	–	–

First, corresponding to their superior performance on the pretest, is the great consistency of the spellers; no twelve successive kindergarten children performed with so few inconsistencies. The spellers were quite explicit; they could name the letters involved, write the words, or imitate the differences in sound. One girl ([t]/[d]) pointed out that there were three sounds, "[čə], [tə], and [tə]," emphasizing the affrication of the last, not indicating the [r]. A boy ([t]/[d]) kept repeating [jrægən], [dərægən] during the second test, as if trying to decide which of these two "extremes" each test word was closest to. Another boy ([č]/[j]) wrote CHRAC for *truck*. These children obviously were more aware of their judgments and better able to express them than most.

Second, the spellers were mainly in the [t]/[d] category, more like the first-graders than like their nonspelling age-mates. Possibly this difference suggests somewhat earlier development on the part of the spellers. Individually, however, the spellers were not necessarily more advanced. A boy and a girl who made [č]/[j] judgments were both six years, two months old; among the nonspellers, there were several who made the adult judgment as much as ten months younger.

Donald, who accepted all the words on both tests, may have been in a period of transition at 5,1. He made no judgment about two words, changed his mind about another, and generally seemed hesitant and confused. When asked to write some of the words, he wrote TRAN (train) and DRES (dress), but when his mother wrote some words both ways, asking which was better, he preferred JRAGON and JRESS.

Again, age was no predictor of categorization. The youngest child in the group, who had just celebrated his fifth birthday, made perfectly consistent [t]/[d] choices, and clearly distinguished the initial sounds of *tree* and *church*, for instance. He spelled TREE, TRACK, TRAN (train), and DURM (drum, which he pronounced slowly and in three parts [də-r-m], so the spelling is evidently not simply an interchange of the two middle letters).

Rody (5,5) had apparently made a recent development. In early March, he had written a story about a dragon, spelled JRAGIN. In late May, he made entirely consistent [t]/[d] judgments on the tests and wrote DRAGIN. He was the boy who pronounced [jrægən] and [dərægən] as he proceeded through the second test, so he evidently made his judgments in terms of sounds rather than spellings.

The girl who at 6,2 made consistent [č]/[j] choices provided an example of the stability of the judgments. She had made her [č]-type decisions on the first test, and was more than halfway through the second, when her mother intervened. "Karen, are you fooling us?" she asked, scoldingly. Karen immediately reversed herself and decided that *jack-in-the-box* does not begin with the same sound as *dragon*. But then, without a trace of humor and only a slight awareness of her mother's displeasure, she went on to finish the test, making entirely consistent [ǰ]-type judgments.

3.2.8 Conclusions. The main conclusions which seem justified on the basis of these studies may be summarized as follows:

1. A significant proportion of kindergarten children categorize the affricated [t] and [d] which occur in [tr] and [dr] clusters with the corresponding affricates [č] and [ǰ], rather than with the stops [t] and [d]. This is in contrast to the categorization implicit in standard spelling and presumably that of most adult speakers of English. Specifically, about 40% of the children who made consistent categorizations, or about 30% of all those who could judge sameness of initial sounds in general, made this nonstandard judgment; this group was about equal in size to those who categorized [tr] and [dr] with initial stops, and it is larger than one might have expected from the invented spellings alone.

2. Most children judged these affricated stops to be "the same as" either the stops or the affricates; only a minority made the narrower judgment, that [tr] and [dr] are the same as other [tr] and [dr] clusters only, and at least some of this latter group may have interpreted "first sound" to refer to the entire cluster.

3. The pretest of ability to judge sameness of initial sounds and the two "same–different" tests have proven reliable, as compared with a standard test and with each other, respectively. Furthermore, individuals are highly consistent in their judgments across the two tests; this was shown in Table 36 for the kindergarten children, and it is equally true of the nursery school and first-grade children, and the spontaneous spellers. Of the 99 children whose judgments have been discussed here, not one made *affricate* judgments on one test and *stop* judgements on the other, whatever their degree of consistency, even though for some of the children, a few days or more intervened between the first and second tests. These facts support the crucial claim that the children's judgments reflect relatively stable categorizations in terms of phonetic features.

4. Even some first-graders make the *affricate* judgments, despite

the fact that some of these children know the standard spelling of words with [tr]- and [dr]- and can easily read relevant words. With children of various ages, it was clear that knowing the standard spelling did not necessarily or immediately change a child's judgment that [tr] and [dr] begin with [č] and [j]. Neither were these judgments directly related to age. Nevertheless, there appeared to be a development from *affricate* to *stop* categorizations over the three age groups studied, although it is not possible to test this inference because of the small number of children in the extreme age groups.

5. The main difference between the spontaneous spellers and the other children was in the greater consistency of the speller's judgments.

It seems, in short, that some children do construct interesting categorizations of speech sounds such as are suggested in the invented spellings and that these judgments may be brought out, at least in those children who can make reliable judgments, by tasks such as those reported here. Although the phonetic basis of the [č]/[j] judgments, namely the affrication of [tr] and [dr] clusters, seems clear enough, there are deeper explanatory issues that we are not yet able to reach. Why do some children categorize these segments as stops, while others regard them as affricates? Is it indeed an arbitrary (but individually consistent) choice? Or if there is a developmental sequence, as is suggested by an informal comparison of the results from the three age groups, why does the affricate grouping predominate at the early stage? Undoubtedly the greatest development that one could make in this line of research would be in bringing it to bear on such questions as these, questions essentially concerned with the interaction of children's *faculté de langage* and the phonetic structure of their native language.

In the meantime, some suggestions towards the improvement of teaching and learning seem to derive naturally from these results. Consider, for example, the spelling CHRAC (truck) produced by Douglas (age 5,4) as a part of his performance on the [tr] test. Obviously he uses -c for final [k] because he does not yet know that final [k] after a short vowel is usually spelled -ck, and that -c represents [k] only in other positions and before spellings other than i, y, and e (Venezky, 1970: pp. 66, 75, 90). This is the kind of relatively superficial but intricate correspondence rule that teachers may make use of. The spelling A for [ʌ] is of another sort; it is fairly common in young children (see Appendix A, Table 17 on the invented spellings) and I believe it arises because they know that A spells the word a. In other words, this apparent error arises merely from Douglas's making use of his very limited knowledge of standard spelling, and it will surely disappear as his experience widens. His spelling CHR- for [tr] is of yet another kind, namely the tacit categorization that we have seen is quite common. Although this spelling may seem bizarre at first, it is definitely not an occasion for summoning the perceptual disabilities specialist. In this instance, what Douglas needs to learn is simple but very important: the affrication of this cluster is one of many predictable aspects of pronunciation which are not indicated in English spelling. He needs to be told that even though *truck* does sound a little like "chuh" at the beginning, it is regarded as a "tuh" sound, because all *t-r*'s sound like that.

In short, Douglas's three apparent "errors" in the spelling CHRAC each have different but quite reasonable explanations. The situation will be mystifying and frustrating for both teacher and child if teachers do not distinguish among these different kinds of errors, or do not know (and do not trust their "ear" to tell them) that there is indeed a similarity in the initial sounds of *truck* and *chicken*.

3.3 The more-like/less-like study

In addition to the picture studies, which elicited categorial judgments of sameness of initial [tr] versus [tV] and [čV], we have conducted studies in which first- and second-grade children made judgments of relative similarity (more-like/less-like) between the pairs [tr]-[čV] and [tr]-[tV]. The children were asked to judge which of two real English words (e.g., *toes* and *chose*) "sounds more like" a nonce word (e.g., [trowz]) "at the beginning." These pairs were presented in an X: XA, XB pattern; the experimenter first introduced the nonce word and then the children heard the two pairs ([trowz]—*toes*, [trowz]—*chose*). The children, tested individually, heard the pairs on a tape recording, presented as two Sesame Street puppets asking the child to decide "which real word sounds more like the made-up word at the beginning." Those who made at least five out of six such judgments in one direction were considered to indicate a consistent categorization. We gave the same test to 13 university undergraduates in order to check our assumptions about adult judgments, and we used a modified design which called for judgments of sameness of first sounds from kindergarten children.

With the wisdom conferred by hindsight, we now believe the more-like/less-like procedure was inferior to that of the picture studies reported above; there was a smaller proportion of consistent individuals among the first-graders, for example. For this reason, and because the experiments have been reported elsewhere (Read, 1973, pp. 26-37), we will not discuss them in detail here.

Even though they were methodologically less clear, however, these studies do provide additional support for some of the main conclusions from the picture studies, as well as a basis for some new related inferences. In accord with our previous conclusions, some first-graders did chose the [tr]–[čV] similarity; 55% of the judgments overall and 6 of the 11 consistent individuals were in this direction. The kindergarten children made their judgments of sameness within a different (and apparently better) experimental design, so that the results are not directly comparable to those from first grade, but again, 29% of the judgments overall and 6 of 21 consistent individuals indicated that words with initial [tr] have the same first sound as words with initial [čV]. Therefore, taking these studies together with the picture studies, it seems that while the proportion of children varies somewhat with the experimental design, there can be little doubt that a substantial proportion of kindergarten and first-grade children regard the affricated /t/ and /d/ that occur in /tr/ and /dr/ clusters to be the same as, or more similar to, affricates than stops.

In addition, these studies allowed us to check some potential influences on these judgments. For one thing, we saw again that a child might choose the similarity in affrication, even though he or she knew the standard spelling of [tr]-clusters. For example, four of the six first-graders who consistently judged similarity in terms of affrication then spelled the last nonce word [trap] with an initial *t*, as did all of those who chose the [tr]–/t/ similarity. Also, since the children were asked to repeat each nonce ([tr]) word, we had another opportunity to listen to children's pronunciation; only four of the 168 first-grade pronunciations were [čr]. A large independent study of children's articulation errors has also found that this substitution is very infrequent (Venezky, 1971). The occurrence of an affricate in children's pronunciation of [tr] is evidently not nearly frequent enough to correspond directly to their categorization, whether as cause or effect. Similarly, we found no direct relation between the intensity and duration of affrication in the [tr] clusters on the recording used, as measured spectrographically, and the frequency with which the children chose the [tr]–/č/ similarity. Finally, we asked whether the relative familiarity of the real words (e.g., of *toes* vs. *chose*) could account for any tendency to choose those beginning with affricates. Using an adult word frequency list as an approximate measure of familiarity to children, we found that the [č]-words are actually less frequent than their counterparts beginning with [t]. Therefore if the children resorted to familiarity when they could not choose on the basis of sound similarity, their bias would have been to choose the [tr]–/t/ pairs.

3.3.1 New conclusions. In addition to giving independent support to some of our previous conclusions, the more-like/less-like study provided some new insights. Testing 24 second-graders (mean age: 7,10) at the end of January, we found that even some second-graders apparently judge similarity according to affrication; a nonsignificant majority (51%) of all judgments and three of seven consistent individuals chose the [tr]–/č/ similarity. One may question whether even the consistent individuals are a valid indication of categorization, however. The total number of consistent individuals (7) is not much greater than the number one might expect if the children were choosing randomly, i.e., the number determined by the binomial probability function (5.2). The small proportion of consistent individuals, even among second-graders, indicates the methodological inferiority of this design, as compared with the more categorial tests.

With our adult subjects, the evidence is clearer. Of the 13 university undergraduates, 11 were consistent in their choices and 9 of these chose the [tr]–/t/ similarity, as one might expect. In a general way, this result confirms our assumptions about adult judgments; it also means that first-graders and adults made significantly different judgments of the same recorded words ($\chi^2 = 32.7$, p < .001). The fact that two adults chose the tr–/č/ similarity in five of six instances, though, indicates that even some adults make this judgment when asked to attend to sound similarity.

In these studies, we also considered evidence of the relationship between these categorizations and spelling and reading. In the first grade, for example, there was an apparent interaction between children's judgments on these tests and their scores on a test of reading readiness: the children scoring highest in reading readiness made /t/ categorizations most frequently while those scoring lowest made /č/ judgments most frequently. Similarly, those children using a reading program in which *tr-* spellings had already been taught and those of highest reading achievement made predominantly /t/ judgments, while those children of lower reading achievement, using a reading program in which *tr-* spellings had not occurred, made predominantly /č/ judgments.

Finally, the categorization of [tr] as beginning with an affricate appeared to influence spelling when we presented a spelling list to 100 first-graders in their classes. Six words with initial [tr], two real and four nonce words, were mixed in with an equal number of other words. Of the 600 resulting spellings of [tr], 244 (40.7%) were other than *tr.* Thirty-two percent of these apparent errors (11% of all responses) reflected the frication of the [t]. For example, the nonce word [trif] is found to be spelled *chreef, jef, fefe,* etc. This type of spelling was more frequent than any other class of error, except for the omission of *r* in representing the [tr] clusters. Such spellings are almost twice as frequent for the nonce words as for the real words, suggesting that some children knew the standard spellings for the real words but did not extend these to the unfamiliar nonce words. With respect to spelling, then, we may conclude that the tacit categorization of [tr] as an affricate appears even in first-grade spelling, particularly of unfamiliar words, and that this judgment may be generally related to reading experience, even though knowing the standard spelling does not necessarily or immediately cause a child to categorize affricated [t] as a stop.

3.3.2 *Methodological conclusions.* In the more-like/less-like study, we tested each child on two consecutive days, using three [tr]- words and four other words (included to reduce tedium and response bias) on each day. Half of the children heard one such list first, and half heard the other list first. Testing on two consecutive days seemed desirable because performance on auditory discrimination tests can improve dramatically after the first day, presumably because of increased familiarity with the task (Kamil and Rudegeair, 1972). In this case, however, there were no significant differences by day or by list. This result lends some support to the view that these categorial tasks are not equivalent to auditory discrimination tests, methodologically or conceptually.

Finally, comparing these studies with the more categorial picture studies, we feel that while one can elicit judgments of relative similarity from first-graders, a judgment of sameness is likely to produce greater consistency in individual judgments, at least for the level of phonetic detail involved in the [t] comparisons. This difference was even greater in the kindergartens, where pilot testing showed that a test of sameness of initial sounds was much more reliable. In studies of relationships among vowels, we have elicited judgments of similarity from kindergarten children (see chapter five), but only after painstaking modification of the research design in extensive pilot testing. Evidently a judgment of sameness of sounds is much easier for young children and thus more reliable when the phonetic comparisons involve fine enough details to be plausibly regarded as "the same" at a low level of categorization.

CHAPTER FOUR

EXPERIMENTAL STUDIES OF PRECONSONANTAL NASALS

4.1 The goal

The present series of experiments with first-grade children was directed primarily toward finding out why children frequently omit any representation of a nasal when it immediately precedes a consonant within a word, as in the spelling BET for *bent*. As we saw in section 2.4, this spelling pattern is extremely frequent in the spelling of preschool children. Among children younger than six years, preconsonantal [m] (as in *bump*) is omitted from approximately 45% of the spellings, preconsonantal [n] (as in *bent*) is omitted in 27% of the cases, and preconsonantal [ŋ] (as in *sink*) is omitted in 70% of the spellings. What makes these spellings of special interest is that children do represent these nasals when they occur in other positions within a word—as the first sound in *make* or *night* or the final one in *sing*, for example. The same children who frequently omit preconsonantal nasals omit nasals in other positions less than 1% of the time.

Naturally, one supposes that there must be some explanation for the children's frequent omission of nasals in a specific position. In fact, there are at least two quite plausible reasons for this spelling pattern. Both of these possible explanations have to do with the phonetic structure of words such as *bump*, but they involve quite different principles. In attempting to discover which, if either, of these explanations is correct, we hoped not only to account for a common pattern in children's spelling, but also to distinguish between these two principles. In this way, the study of the preconsonantal nasals has an even more general importance in revealing something of the basic nature of children's phonetic judgments.

4.2 Test of first-grade spelling

We first asked whether the omission of preconsonantal nasals is a frequent pattern, even in first grade. In young children's invented spelling, typically done at home, we find a decline in the frequency of this pattern with older children. For [Vnt], for example (V represents any vowel), the [n] was omitted in 34.4% of the spellings by children younger than six years, but in just 15.4% by those older than six. (The total number of such sequences in our sample was 154.) Even among older children, the omission of such nasals is by far the most frequent nonstandard spelling.

We tested the frequency of this spelling pattern among the first-graders who were to participate in our study (from the Franklin School in Lexington, Massachusetts) with a simple spelling pretest. We took 32 children, in small groups, from their classroom to a quiet room, where we simply asked them to spell a series of words. We told them that they probably wouldn't know how to spell every word, but that they should attempt to spell each word "as you think it should be spelled." The experimenter then pronounced nine words, such as *rink*, *pump*, and *plant*. (The three nasals were each followed by the corresponding voiceless stop and preceded by each of the vowels [ɪ], [ʌ], and [æ].) We then scored each spelling as either "nasal represented," "nasal omitted," or "undecidable" (in case the child's spelling was ambiguous or incomplete).

This rough pretest should not be interpreted too seriously, since the results might be influenced by the experimenter's pronunciation, by response bias, or by other uncontrolled factors, but it was sufficient to indicate that the omission of preconsonantal nasals is a robust phenomenon in first grade. Of the 275 decidable spellings, 151 or 55% represented all of the word except the nasal. (The fact that this error rate is higher than that found overall among the young children's spellings is not necessarily significant because, not knowing the magnitude of the phenomenon, we deliberately chose those VNC sequences that were most likely to produce the error in the spelling test.) Furthermore, it is clear that this spelling is largely an "all-or-nothing" pattern. Of the 32 children, 25 ranked near the two extremes (0, 1, 7, 8, or 9) in number of nasals omitted; the distribution is clearly bimodal. The fact that first-grade children tend to treat all preconsonantal nasals alike, whether or not they know the standard spellings, reinforces the notion that something common to all such sequences must be the basis for the frequent nonrepresentation.

4.3 Possible explanations

As indicated in section 2.4, there are two properties of nasal plus obstruent sequences that might explain the spelling. The essential problem is that the children who omit the [n] of *bent*, for instance, *do* know how to spell the [n] of *night*, or for that matter, the [n] of *Ben*. That is, these children apparently do not categorize preconsonantal nasals with nasals in other positions. One special property of VNC sequences is that the nasal tends to be very short, much shorter than the "same" nasal in other positions. The longest difference between *bet* and *bent* is actually in the nasalization of the vowel of *bent*. In fact in certain contexts (depending on the vowel and the consonant and the number of syllables), the vowel nasalization is the *only* difference between such pairs (Malécot, 1960). Therefore, if a child tacitly regarded the vowel nasalization as the most prominent and most reliable indicator of a preconsonantal nasal, and then categorized the nasalized vowel with the corresponding non-nasalized vowel (not having any special symbol for [$\tilde{\varepsilon}$], as opposed to [ε], for instance), then BET would be an essentially accurate representation of *bent*. This interpretation suggests that children may categorize the nasality in *bent* as an aspect of the vowel, surprising as this may seem to adults. In fact, as the next chapter will illustrate, children readily categorize vowels and reflect these categorizations in their spelling.

There is, however, a second kind of categorization that may account for the spellings. It is a general property of English that when a nasal precedes a stop consonant (within a formative) that the nasal and the stop must be homorganic (articulated at the same position in the mouth). That is, only [n] may precede [t] or [d], only [m] may precede [p] or [b], and only [ŋ] may precede [k] or [g]; there could not be an English word *bunp*. In articulating a word such as *bent*, we produce the vowel, raise the tip of the tongue to the position for [n] and [t], and then raise the velum at the back of the mouth to close off the nasal passage, ending the nasality and thus producing the complete momentary closure that forms the [t]. Because we cannot readily feel the action of the velum, there is only one felt articulatory gesture (that of the tongue tip) in producing both the [n] and the [t].

We might hypothesize, in contrast to the "nasalized vowel" explanation, that there is a kinesthetic component to children's spelling, such that they group together two contiguous segments produced by a single (felt) gesture. In other words, they regard [nt], for example, as a single unit for spelling purposes and consistently represent it with the symbol for the stop. There is very little support for this possibility in other apparent omissions in children's spelling of clusters, but no other clusters are precisely analogous to those containing nasals. In only three of 36 [ld] clusters, for instance, is the [l] omitted in our sample of spellings.

These two putative explanations differ crucially in the principle which they suggest underlies this and possibly other aspects of children's spelling. One suggests that children regard the nasality as an aspect of the vowel, being influenced by its greater duration and consistency. (Vowel nasalization is always present, even when there is virtually no nasal segment.) The other suggests a partially kinesthetic basis for children's judgments. Both explanations assume that children normally discriminate *bet* from *bent, sick* from *sink*, and *pup* from *pump* (confirmed by a later experiment), but that they categorize the distinction as an aspect of either the vowel or the consonant. The first of our experiments was designed to test just this question: Where do children think the distinction occurs in such pairs?

4.4 The "pointer" experiment

In this experiment, first-grade children (in late February and early March of the school year) were interviewed individually in a quiet room in the school. The child sat at a long desk, on which were two magnetic boards, each having more than a full alphabet of plastic capital letters arranged at its edges. With this arrangement a child can readily spell words with the magnetic letters, without the labor and ambiguity introduced by handwriting. The experimenter sat on the other side of the desk facing the child.

The experimenter first produced a Sesame Street hand puppet (Ernie), whom all the children recognized immediately, and said that Ernie wanted to learn "how you spell some words." The children readily agreed to spell some words of Ernie's choosing. First Ernie scratched his head and said (in the experimenter's best imitation of the Sesame Street character), "Aw, gee, I bent my arm. How about *bent?*" The child then spelled *bent*. The experimenter asked the child to leave those letters in place, and to spell Ernie's next word on the other board. Then Ernie said, "I bet you can spell another word. How about *bet?*" The child then spelled *bet* on the second board. Note that the words were presented in a sentence context so that their identification would be unambiguous.

Eighteen of the twenty-eight children who participated in this study had not represented most of the preconsonantal nasals in a previous spelling task, and in fact, most children represented the paired words in this study exactly alike: both *bet* and *bent* as BET, for example.

(These children had, however, spelled pre-vocalic nasals in the standard ways.) Ernie then looked at the two spellings, and pointed to each as he "read" them: bet . . . bent. He then said, "Gee, that's interesting. They look alike, but they sound different, don't they? Bet . . . bent." In almost all cases, the child readily agreed that indeed they looked alike but they sounded different. (It is an interesting fact in itself that the children almost never indicated the slightest puzzlement or discomfort in acknowledging this obvious homography.)

Then the experimenter displayed a plastic triangle which, like the letters, contained a magnet and would adhere either to the board or to the letters themselves. In a conspiratorial voice intended to be distinct from that of Ernie, the experimenter said, "Now here's a special symbol that you can use to show Ernie where the difference in sound is, between *bet* and *bent*. You can put it anywhere you want—between the letters or over the letters—to show Ernie where the difference is. Why don't you show Ernie where the difference in sound comes in *bent*?"

After the *bet–bent* comparison, the child spelled a word of his or her own choosing for Ernie. Then in the same manner as above, the child spelled the pair *sick–sink* and marked the difference in sound, then another word of the child's choosing, and finally the pair *pup–pump*. An assistant unobtrusively transcribed all of the child's spellings and the positions of the pointer (the special symbol), along with any relevant pronunciations and comments.

If the child placed the pointer on the vowel letter, or above it, we regarded that as evidence of a categorization of the nasalization with the vowel; if the child placed the pointer on or above the final consonant spelling, we took that as evidence in favor of a nasal-consonant categorization; if the child placed the pointer between the vowel and the final consonant, we took that as evidence that the child did not categorize the nasal with either the vowel or the consonant. If these last cases predominated, one would presumably have to explain the nonrepresentation of preconsonantal nasals in other, noncategorial, terms. If the child placed the pointer in other positions, we regarded that response as indeterminate. These possibilities are summarized in Figure 1. We interpreted a child's performance on this task in terms of the position of the pointer and the consistency across the three trials.

Essentially, the twenty-eight children fell into three distinct groups. One group is made up of those children who apparently could not perform the task consistently (n = 7). The critical characteristic of these children was that they did not make two scorable responses of

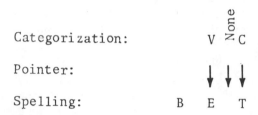

Figure 1. Possible positions of a pointer to the location of nasalization in a frequent spelling of *bent*: first grade

the same type. They made many indeterminate responses, including placing the pointer on or before the initial consonant, and a few non-responses. It is not surprising to find that some first-graders cannot consistently identify the position of a segment within a word. The remaining two groups were informative, however. The children in the second group (n = 10) placed the marker between the vowel and the final consonant in at least two of the three trials; these were also the children who represented the nasal in at least two of the three trials (three children omitted only the velar nasal of *sink*). The striking fact is that it was *only* these children, who knew the standard spelling, who placed the marker between the vowel and the consonant. All the rest of the children (n = 10) omitted the nasal and placed the pointer on or over the vowel, and they did so in all three trials. Only one child indicated the opposite categorization, placing the marker above the final consonant, and she did so on just two trials.

In short, the children who made consistent and scorable responses divided equally into just two groups: those who knew the standard spelling and who indicated that the difference in sound fell between the vowel and the consonant, and those who did not represent the nasal and who located the phonetic difference in the same position as the vowel spelling. We interpret this as strong evidence in favor of the view that children categorize preconsonantal nasals with the preceding vowels prior to learning the standard spelling, which in effect categorizes such nasals with pre-vocalic and final nasals.

There are, of course, other conceivable interpretations. It is possible that there is some general response bias under which children tend to locate the pointer near the middle of the word. However, the children who located the pointer at the vowel spelling were not only consistent but were also quite specific in indicating that they felt the vowel carried the difference in sound. They often placed the pointer directly on top of the vowel letter, or even displaced the vowel letter with the

pointer. One girl spelled BAT for both *bet* and *bent,* then placed the
pointer over the A, and explained "that (Ǎ) says [ɛ] and that (A)
says [ɛ]. Two other children changed the vowel spelling, e.g., to
SEEK (sink) and SIK (sick).

Despite this anecdotal evidence provided by the children, one might
still wonder whether placing the pointer over the vowel was not often
a vague gesture toward the middle of the word. We know that many
first-graders cannot identify the precise location of a phonetic segment, and since many of their spellings for *bent, sink,* and *pump* represented only consonant-vowel-consonant, might not the children have
placed the pointer over the vowel only to indicate that the "difference
in sound" occurs somewhere *between* the beginning and the end?

To further test this possibility, we replicated the pointer experiment,
using exactly the same techniques, except that the paired words were
disyllabic: *capper–camper, ticker–tinker,* and *crutches–crunches.* The
effect of using disyllabic spelling items is to shift the nasalized vowel
away from the precise orthographic center of the word, even in the
children's parsimonious representations. Since we elicited a great many
spellings like KAPR for *camper* and TEKR for *tinker,* any tendency to
point at the center of the letters shoulᴅ place the pointer between the
vowel and the consonant, or at least as frequently on the latter as on
the former.

The other effect of using longer words is to make the task more
difficult. Consequently we chose subjects who were at the beginning of
second grade, and we presented the words in sentences and illustrated
their meaings. Even with an additional four or so months of schooling,
as compared with our former subjects, the children found these words
somewhat difficult and unfamiliar, and, as we expected, they frequently
omitted the nasals. With twenty subjects, the nasal of *camper* was
represented seven times, that of *tinker* only five times, and that of
crunches six times. Scoring the results of this replication in the same
way as those of the original experiment, i.e. classifying the children's
efforts in terms of two or more scorable and similar responses, we find
that of the twenty children, five were inconsistent (no two similar
responses), five pointed to the nasal, and five pointed to the vowel.
The remaining five children were diverse; two pointed to the homorganic consonant (but on just two items each), one consistently pointed
to the initial consonant, one to the final consonant, and one seemed to
identify both the vowel and the nasal. Four of the five children who
pointed to the nasal were the children who consistently represented
the nasal; the fifth child did not represent any of the nasals but

consistently placed the pointer between the vowel and the consonant.

These results provide some additional, although not overwhelming, support for the view that children who do not represent the nasal tend to categorize it with the vowel. The relatively low consistency in the children's judgments may well reflect the greater difficulty of the task with less familiar and longer words. Precisely because of the difficulty, however, one would expect any response bias toward placing the pointer merely in the visual center of the word to emerge clearly. But on only five of sixty trials was the pointer directly in the orthographic center of the word, and no child placed it there consistently. Nor did the children place the pointer as often on the homorganic consonant as on the nasalized vowel; those who were consistent placed it on the vowel three times as often. Accordingly, it seems implausible to attribute the results of this or the first pointer experiment merely to a bias toward the center of the word.

It is important to recognize that the hypothesis that children categorize preconsonantal nasals with the preceding vowels really has three kinds of support: the phonetic structure of such words, in which vowel nasalization is the primary acoustic cue to the presence of a perceived nasal, as shown by Malécot; the children's spellings, from both preschool years and first grade; and now the performance on the pointer experiment. Perhaps it is not difficult to imagine other explanations for either the spelling or the experimental evidence separately, but it is hard to think of alternative ways of explaining both and uniting them with the phonetic facts.

4.5 The extended nasals experiment

In a further investigation of the nature of this categorization, we studied whether varying the duration of the nasal might affect children's identifications or spelling. In order to vary the duration of the nasal resonance while leaving other phonetic characteristics unchanged, it was necessary to make use of a program for editing recorded speech, designed by A. W. F. Huggins and implemented on a PDP-9 computer in the Speech Communication Group of the Research Laboratory of Electronics at M.I.T. This program samples (20 kHz), digitizes, and stores short stretches of speech. The stored waveform, or any part of it, can then be displayed, measured, and modified in various ways, including the possibility of replacing any sample by any other.

We first measured the duration of the preconsonantal nasal resonance in a variety of words in the author's speech, i.e., the speech of the experimenter in the pointer experiment. The duration of the nasals (as a percentage of the interval between the vowel and the release of the stop) was just slightly longer in general than that reported by Malécot; as in Malécot's study, the nasal resonance never exceeded 50% of the interval.

Next, we conducted an identification test, using words in which the preconsonantal nasal resonance had been replaced by an equal interval of silence. For example, the word *trunk* had 55 msec. of nasal resonance replaced by silence, so that its actual phonetic structure was [trʌ_k], in which vowel duration and vowel nasalization were the only cues to discriminating *trunk* from *truck*. We then played six recorded words of this type to 29 first-graders and to an equal number of adults (M.I.T. undergraduates). The adults responded by marking either *truck* or *trunk*, for example, on an answer sheet; the children responded by marking either a picture of a truck or one of an elephant's trunk on a pictorial answer sheet. As in Malécot's earlier experiment with different techniques and with adults only, the words were identified as containing nasals most of the time (from 62% to 100%, approximately in inverse relation to the duration of the replaced nasal resonance). Thus vowel length and nasalization are sufficient cues to the perception of a preconsonantal nasal. The more important result for our purposes was that adults and children are not different in this respect; indeed, in every instance in which the overall scores differed, more children than adults heard the word as containing a nasal, although the differences for individual words were not statistically significant. Therefore, the children's omission of preconsonantal nasals in spelling cannot be explained as resulting from a difference between their identification and that of adults, just as we had assumed at the outset.

Finally, we tested whether varying the duration of the preconsonantal nasal might affect children's spelling of it. Extensive pilot testing with the six words that had formed the basis for the identification study revealed that only the words with the longest nasal resonances in their natural form might elicit more representations of nasals in spelling when the nasals had been lengthened, again by using the AUDITS computer program. Accordingly, for this test we chose recorded pronunciations of three words which had rather long preconsonantal nasal resonances: *can't*, *hunt*, and *mint*, each with about 60 msec. of nasal resonance. (The recorded pronunciation of *can't* was somewhat exceptional in having a nasal this long, but it was included in order to have a variety of vowels.) We then produced versions with extended nasals by doubling the nasal resonance of the original in each case by repeating each glottal period. The quality of the resulting utterance might be suggested by a spelling such as *minnt;* the nasal was long (about 120 msec.) for the preconsonantal context, but not so long as to sound completely unnatural.

We then presented (via headphones) both the original and the extended version of each word to 30 first-graders. The six words were in two lists, with the two versions of each word in different lists. Each list had three other words included to reduce tedium and response bias. The two lists were presented to each child on consecutive days, with the order of presentation of the two lists alternated across children.

The result was that there was no significant difference between the original and the extended-nasal versions in the frequency of the first-graders' representation of the nasals. Table 44 presents the essential results.

Table 44

Percentage of Original and Extended Nasals Represented

	Version	
Word	*[n]*	*[nn]*
can't	58.6	75.0
hunt	60.0	51.6
mint	50.0	48.4

A χ^2 test of the largest of these differences, and the only one in the expected direction, shows that the difference is not statistically significant, even at the .30 level. Our conclusion is that children's non-representation of preconsonantal nasals is insensitive to the actual duration of the nasal, at least with durations up to about 120 msec., which we feel is near the limit of what sounds like reasonably normal speech.

As an indication of the degree to which this omission is specific to the preconsonantal context, we may compare the results in Table 44 with the same children's spellings of *game* and *fine,* which were among the six extraneous items in the two word lists. The nasal was represented 100% of the time in *game* and 92.6% in *fine.* (One of the two children who omitted the nasal of *fine* may have thought the word was *find* or *fond,* for she wrote FAD.)

There are two plausible explanations, we think, for the lack of relation between the children's spellings and the actual duration of the nasal. The first is simply that this omission is a truly categorial phenomenon, as we have assumed all along. That is, when a child hears a word such as *mint* or *pump* or *sank*, with the phonic structure $C\tilde{V}(N)C$, in which the vowel nasalization is always present and the duration of the nasal varies considerably (even in normal speech), he or she identifies the word and categorizes it as $C\tilde{V}C$ for spelling purposes, with little regard for the actual nasal duration. On this view, children might construct a different categorization if English were a different language, in which preconsonantal nasals had the duration of pre-vocalic nasals in general. But once having acquired this categorization, a child does not change it merely upon the presentation of a few examples of words with long preconsonantal nasals. The nature of categorial judgments, after all, is that physically different stimuli are treated alike.

The second explanation, suggested by S. Jay Keyser, is also categorial, but introduces the interesting empirical hypothesis that it is the predictability of preconsonantal nasals, not their short duration, that leads to their omission from spelling. Given a nasalized vowel and a following stop consonant in English, one has all the information needed to identify the intervening perceived nasal segment; indeed this is precisely what both children and adults did in the identification experiment, where the nasal resonances were replaced by silence. On this view, when children spell SAK for *sank* they are categorizing the nasalized vowel with the corresponding purely oral vowel, having no representation for nasalization. Then they simply omit the redundant information, namely the representation of the nasal segment. One difference between this explanation and the one outlined above is that it suggests that children do regard *sank*, for example, as having four segments, even when they represent just three. The other empirical difference is the prediction that in the few instances in English where (because of a formative boundary) the nasal and the consonant are not homorganic, such as *hummed* or *banged*, children may represent the nasal. Words of this type are so infrequent that we have no examples in the collection of children's invented spelling. This explanation deserves further study, because once again an important hypothesis about the principle underlying children's spelling is at issue.

4.6 Recommendations to teachers

We have seen that first-graders frequently omit the nasal in representing words such as *pump, hint,* and *sank,* where the nasal precedes a consonant. This apparent error must certainly be among the most frequent spelling errors in first grade. Through our studies, we found that children do indeed "hear" the nasal in such words—they distinguish them from *pup*, *hit*, or *sack*—but that they regard the main difference between these pairs as being carried by the vowel. This is, in fact, phonetically correct. Consequently, when children spell PUP (or POP, or whatever) for *pump*, there is probably nothing wrong with their hearing; they simply have no special symbol for the nasalized vowel that is the largest difference between *pump* and *pup*. They do not regard the "missing" sound as being the same as that at the beginning of *my*. Furthermore, they do not immediately alter their spelling when you pronounce the word as "pummp." Regarding the nasality as part of the vowel is a truly categorial judgment, and it is largely an "all-or-nothing" phenomenon. Children are quite consistent in their spellings of such words, one way or the other.

Accordingly, we suggest that teachers should *not* say something like, "No, what you wrote was HUT; what I said was *hunt*. Listen—Hunnnnt!" Although our extended nasals experiment was not designed to evaluate pedagogical techniques directly, it strongly suggests that this particular one is not likely to elicit the spelling that the teacher wants, at least not in the first few trials. The child probably knows what the teacher said, so these instructions are probably not useful. It would seem better to compare words like *Ben* and *bent*, and to point out that we *regard* them as containing the same sound. The emphasis on "regard" is intended to be a tacit acknowledgment of the child's categorization and its phonetic justification, so that the child will not come away with the feeling that neither the teacher nor the spelling system shows any appreciation for similarities and differences that are perfectly clear to him or her. This feeling, extended over many instances, may be a component of the despair that many adults and older children feel about English spelling. If this kind of comparison doesn't work, wait until the next opportunity and try again; the all-or-nothing categorial nature of the spellings suggests that once children learn the standard form, they apply the principle to many instances at once.

CHAPTER FIVE

THE VOWEL STUDIES

5.1 The problem

The present investigations have to do with children's judgments of the vowel [ɛ], as in *bet*. When young children create their own spellings, they strongly tend to spell this vowel *A*; in the corpus of spellings we have collected, for example, this one occurs in 50% of the examples from children less than six years old, and it is actually more frequent than the standard spelling, *E*. Among children older than six, this spelling occurs 39% of the time, far more often than any other non-standard spelling; no other spelling occurs in more than 5% of the instances.

Because of the large difference in frequency between this spelling and all other nonstandard spellings, one again supposes that there must be some reason why children choose *A* to represent the vowel of *bet*, and again there are at least two phonetically plausible explanations. In searching for a reasonable way to represent [ɛ], children may be grouping this vowel with either that of *late* (or the name of the letter *A*) or with that of *lad*. Both of these vowels are closely related to that of *let*, but in phonetically different ways, so that again in testing the basis for this spelling, we have an opportunity to find out which of two kinds of phonetic relationships is more prominent for children.

Our assumption is that children do hear the difference between these pairs of vowels, i.e., that at age six they can reliably discriminate *let* from *late* or *led* from *lad*, but that they also recognize the relationships between these vowels. When they do not know the standard spelling of a sound, they devise a spelling that reflects its phonetic similarity to a sound that they do know how to spell.[1] The important assumption here is that children do (tacitly) recognize relationships among functionally distinct speech sounds. This is the assumption which we tested.

5.2 First-grade spelling

We first asked whether children in school also produce this spelling, although our data on spellings by children older than six years would seem to be indicative. In the course of the pilot testing for the experiment with extended nasals, we had occasion to ask first-graders to spell some words not containing nasals, so we included the words *left*, *pest*, and *rest*. As usual the instructions were simply for the children to print the words as they thought they should be spelled. Table 45 presents the results.

Table 45

Spellings of [ɛ], First Grade

Spelling	left	pest	rest
E	17	21	18
A	9	7	7
other	1	1	0
%A	33.3	24.1	28.0

Here again the spelling A occurs in one-fourth to one-third of the instances, and it constitutes virtually all of the nonstandard spellings. Although this preliminary test was limited to a few similar examples, it gives additional evidence that this apparent error is a significant one, even for first-graders in February and March of the school year.

5.3 An explanation and a problem

If one examines the spellings of the front vowels in our data on young children's spellings, one finds the general picture shown in Table 46.

Children adopt essentially the standard spellings for the vowels of *bead*, *bayed*, and *bad* (or rather, spellings based on the letter-names in the first two cases), but they produce some extremely frequent nonstandard spellings for the vowels of *bid* and *bed*. In each case, this nonstandard spelling is the spelling of the corresponding tense ("long") vowel, the vowels of *bead* and *bayed*, respectively. We have suggested (Read, 1971, 1973) that when children do not know the standard spellings of the vowels of *bid* and *bed*, they tend to group together the two high vowels, or the two mid vowels, in order to assign a spelling to the lax ("short") member of each pair. This explanation

Table 46
Children's Spellings of Front Vowels

	Example	Symbol	Children's spelling at <6 years
high	bead	i	E
	bid	ɪ	I, E (23%)
mid	bayed	e	A
	bed	ɛ	E, A (50%)
low	bad	æ	A

predicts that other tense-lax pairs should be spelled alike, and indeed this is the case.

One problem, given this explanation, is to explain why the spelling A for [ɛ] is so much more frequent than the spelling E for [ɪ] (see Table 46). In the previous publications, we have suggested that of the two "long" vowels (the names of the letters E and A), the latter has a longer glide, and is easier to analyze. Intuitively, it is easier to hear that [e] begins like [ɛ] than it is to hear that [i] begins like [ɪ]. This explanation is reasonable as far as it goes, and it suggests that [ay] (the name of the letter I), which is most obviously diphthongal, should therefore be related to [a] in spelling even more often than the cases we have just described. One should find the spelling I for the first vowel of father most often of all. In fact, this spelling does occur, as in CLIK (clock), and it is the most frequent of the nonstandard spellings for this vowel, but it is less, not more, frequent than the other examples (about 11% among children younger than six).

A second explanation, which avoids this difficulty, comes from considering the low and mid vowels in Table 46. There we see that the vowel of bed is flanked (in terms of height) by two vowels, both of which are spelled A. The children who spell A for [ɛ] may be grouping [ɛ] with both [e] and [æ]; in effect, they may feel that if [e] is spelled A (or is the name of the letter), and [æ] is spelled A, then [ɛ] must surely be spelled A. This hypothesis is interesting, particularly because it suggests that children may recognize both of two phonetically justified relationships among these three vowels (and these relationships are qualitatively different), and that these categorizations may be additive in their influence on children's spelling. Accordingly, we designed experiments to measure the salience of these relationships for kindergarten children.

5.4 The [ε-e] and [ε-æ] experiments

We devised a test which indirectly asks children to judge the similarity of [ε] and [e], and of [ε] and [æ] (as opposed to pairings of [ε] and [e] with other vowels, which are not particularly close to it phonetically). If the vowels of English are simply discrete units for children, then they will perform randomly on these tests, and we will conclude that the phonetic relationships could not be the basis of the spelling pattern. If children recognize one or both of these relationships, we may conclude that the salient relationship(s) may be the source of the spelling.

In the test, the experimenter sits facing one kindergarten child in a quiet room. The experimenter introduces a hand puppet whose name is Ed, and indicates that Ed would like to play a word game. The child then puts Ed on his or her hand and the experimenter explains the game. Ed, it seems, likes to find "words that sound like Ed," like *Ted, Jed, fled, sled,* etc. At this point the child has a chance to suggest words that Ed might like. Then the experimenter presents pairs of words and asks which one Ed would like. "Would Ed like *bed* or *bead?*" "Would Ed like *food* or *fed?*" (Again, an assistant transcribes the child's choices, along with any relevant comments and nonstandard pronunciations.) The experimenter corrects any incorrect choices and announces "Right!" for the correct choices before continuing. When the child has identified the rhyming word in five out of six of these examples, we assume that he or she is able to identify rhymes with *Ed,* and we go on to the experiment itself.

To begin, the experimenter says, "Now I'll tell you some words that don't sound *exactly* like *Ed,* and you listen and see if you can tell me which one Ed would like—which word sounds more like *Ed.* Would Ed like *aid* or *owed?* Would Ed like *showed* or *shade?*" There are six test items of this type. The child's individual choices and those of all children are used to measure whether children judge [ε] and [e] to be more closely related than [ε] and [o], which do not share the relevant phonetic properties.

Some controls were included in this basic schema. In the pretest which establishes the rhyming class, we varied both order and the alternative vowel ([i] or [u]), so that the child could not succeed merely with a position preference, and so that the alternative vowel would not bias the experiment. In the experiment, more "control" items of this type ("Would Ed like *bread* or *brood?* Would Ed like *speed* or *sped?*") were alternated with the six test items in order to remind the child that he was to find a word that "sounds like Ed," and to provide a check on whether children were indeed listening for this target throughout the experiment. We could then use scores on these control items as a measure of the validity of each child's judgment of the test items.

The experiment testing the [æ-ɔ] relationship was the same except, of course, for the experimental items, which were of the type, "Would Ed like *add* or *awed?* Would Ed like *pawed* or *pad?*"

After the pilot testing and refinement which led to this experimental design, we tested kindergarten children in Nahant, Massachusetts, during April of the school year. With few exceptions, each child participated in both tests, always at least one day apart. Order of presentation alternated from child to child. About 82% of the children who participated achieved the criterion in identifying rhymes (5 of 6 correct), although about 25% required more than 6 trials to do so. Almost all children participated with evident enjoyment; in general, the experimental design was clearly successful.

Only when a child achieved the criterion in identifying the true rhymes did we go on to the experiment itself. We can have greatest confidence in the judgments of those children who correctly identified the true rhymes with *Ed* on the control items as well, i.e., those who clearly continued to seek words that "sounded like Ed" during the experiment. For this reason we will present the results from those children who made at least 5 of 6 correct identifications of rhyme both in establishing the class and during the experimental list itself. In fact, the results of the experiments do not differ greatly if we adopt a less stringent criterion for correctness on these latter control items.

We may test the results with an appropriate nonparametric statistical test (the Kolmogorov-Smirnov one-sample test), so that we need not assume that the underlying population is distributed normally in performance on this task. With the Kolmogorov-Smirnov test, we compare the obtained results with those predicted by the binomial probability function for six trials on the assumption that $p = \frac{1}{2}$ on each trial.

The essential result is that the kindergarten children made the phonetically justifiable choices on both tests to a statistically significant degree. On the [ɛ]: [e, o] test (n = 20), the children chose the [ɛ]: [e] relationship to a degree that is statistically significant at the .05

level. On the [ɛ]: [æ, ɔ] test (n = 21), the children chose the [ɛ]: [æ] relationship to a degree that is statistically significant at the .01 level. The clear inference from these results is that English vowels are not discrete contrasting items for kindergarten children; rather, children recognize phonetic relationships among them. The phonetic relationships in this case are of two types, such that individually or jointly they may explain the common pattern in the children's spelling of [ɛ].

We also tested whether adults recognize one of these relationships by administering the [ɛ]-[e, o] test to 22 adult volunteers, undergraduates who were paid ($2.00) for their participation in this and other experiments reported below. (The subjects were native speakers of English with no training in linguistics or phonetics and no gross speech or hearing disorders.) This replication with adults may also be construed as a measure of the validity of the test, for if adults did not make essentially the same judgments as children, we might suppose either that adults can no longer recognize the phonetic relationships, perhaps because of their knowledge of standard spelling, or that the test was not really a valid measure of phonetic categorization. In introducing the experiment, we told each adult that the test had been designed for use with children, and we asked them not to feel insulted if they found parts of the test rather easy. The puppet stood on the table (over a suitable support), and we did not invite the adults to put it on their hands; otherwise, the methods were the same as with children.

As one might hope and expect, the adults readily chose the words that rhyme with *Ed*, both prior to the experiment and on the control items interspersed with the experimental items. All 22 adult subjects chose the true rhyme in six of six items on the initial part of the test, and again on the control items (except for one subject who "missed" one control item). This success is hardly remarkable, but it does at least suggest that the adults were attending to sounds, rather than spellings, since there were three items (*said-seed, tread-treed,* and *bread-brood*) in which the spelling of the true rhyme did not include *-ed*.

On the experimental items, such as "Would Ed like *aid* or *owed?*" the adults clearly tended to choose the [ɛ]-[e] relationship, just as the children did. Fourteen of the 22 adults did so on six of six items; the distribution is tabulated in Table 47.

A Kolmogorov-Smirnov test of this distribution, as compared with that predicted by the binomial probability function if p = ½, shows

Table 47

Adult Subjects Choosing [ɛ]-[e] Relationship on Six Trials (n = 22)

Number of [ɛ]-[e] choices	0	1	2	3	4	5	6
Number of subjects	3	2	0	0	2	1	14

that the distributions are significantly different beyond the .01 confidence level. Furthermore, if we compare the first 20 adults tested with the 20 kindergarten children, using the same statistical test, the distributions are also different at the .01 level.

Both of these statistics may be misleading, however, since the adults clearly tend to cluster at the extremes, i.e., they tend to be consistent in their judgments across the six test items. Our impression in conducting the test was that some adults were aware of this consistency. Accordingly, we should not treat the six test items as independent trials, an assumption that is necessary for this statistical test. A safe solution is to consider only the judgments on the first test item, even though we are thus disregarding five-sixths of our data. The adults' and children's choices on the first item only are presented in Table 48.

Table 48

Judgments of [ɛ]-[e, o], First Item Only

	aid	*owed*	*Statistical significance (binomial test)*
all adults	17	5	
1st 20 adults	17	3	.001
kindergarten	15	5	.02

With the consistency across items removed, it is still clear that these results would be extremely unlikely if the choice presented were a random one for adults or children, and there is no significant difference between the two age groups. Our conclusion is that both adults and kindergarten children recognize the relationship between [ɛ] and [e] as stronger than that between [ɛ] and [o], although it is interesting that a minority of adults (5 of 22) did consistently choose the latter, phonetically distant, relationship.[2] The only significant difference between the two age groups that we can see is the adults' greater (probably conscious) consistency across items. These results also tend to confirm the validity of the test used, in that most adults clearly retain the ability which we are attributing to children.

5.5 The [ɛ]:[e, æ] experiment

The fact that we obtained results of greater statistical significance with the [ɛ]: [æ] relationship suggests that perhaps it is more salient to children than that between [ɛ] and [e]. However, we cannot directly compare the results of the two tests in this way, despite the similarity of the tests, because the alternative items were different. The choices on one test (e.g., *laid–load*) might be less clear than those on the other test (e.g., *sad–sawed*) for reasons, phonetic or otherwise, that have to do with the alternatives *load* and *sawed*.

Accordingly, we designed another test to compare [e] and [æ] directly with each other in terms of their relationship to [ɛ]. This test was like the previous ones, in that we first established that the puppet Ed likes words that rhyme with *Ed*. Then we introduced test items of the form, "Would Ed like *aid* or *add*? Would Ed like *fad* or *fade*?" etc., alternating with control items containing true rhymes. The same kinds of controls on position effects applied; in this case, the comparison vowels in the true rhyme trials were of the type, "Would Ed like *bed* or *bowed*? Would Ed like *fraud* or *Fred*?" with the comparison vowels [o] and [ɔ] chosen to minimize any bias they might introduce into the experiment itself.

We gave this test to 29 kindergarten children, generally the same children as in our previous tests, two weeks later in April. The children were generally spontaneous in playing the game and successful in identifying rhyme. Again, we consider the results from only those children (n = 21) who identified correctly at least 5 out of 6 of both the original rhymes and the control items during the experiment. Sixty-seven percent of the children's choices on the test items were for [æ]. The distribution of individual subjects according to the number of times they chose [æ] is presented in Table 49.

The difference in this distribution from that predicted by the bi-

Table 49

Kindergarten Judgments of [ɛ]-[æ] versus [ɛ]-[e] (n = 21)

Number of [æ] choices	0	1	2	3	4	5	6
Number of subjects	–	–	3	5	5	5	3

nomial probability function for p = ½ is marginally significant, as measured by the Kolmogorov-Smirnov goodness of fit test; it is significant at the .05 level for a one-tailed test only. Our conclusion from this test, together with those that tested the relationships separately, is that kindergarten children recognize both relationships, between [ɛ] and [æ] as well as between [ɛ] and [e], but of these two the former is more salient.

Again, to test whether adults make the same judgment (and indeed whether adults recognize the [ɛ]–[æ] relationship), and as a check on the reasonableness of attributing these phonetic categorizations to children, we replicated this experiment with paid undergraduate volunteers. Aside from not manipulating the puppet, the experiment was conducted in the same way as with children. Again, all the adults could identify the exact rhymes.[3]

Like the children, the adults clearly preferred the [ɛ]–[æ] relationship. The distribution of their choices on the six experimental items is shown in Table 50.

Table 50

Adult Judgments of [ɛ]-[æ] versus [ɛ]-[e] on Six Trials (n = 23)

Number of [æ] choices	0	1	2	3	4	5	6
Number of subjects	3	0	2	1	2	6	9

A Kolmogorov-Smirnov test of this distribution versus that predicted by the binomial probability function with p = ½ indicates a statistically significant difference beyond the .01 level. By the same test, however, the judgments of the first 21 adults tested and the 21 kindergarten children are not significantly different.

As in the [ɛ]-[e,o] experiment, we question whether these were six independent trials for adults, given their tendency to cluster near the (0,6) extremes and the likelihood that some adults were aware of their consistency on experimental items. Accordingly, we may consider judgments on the first item ("Would Ed like *aid* or *add*?") only.

The probability of observing the adult choices (or a result more extreme) if the choice is really random is .0018 (binomial test). To test the reliability of this result and whether order of presentation mattered, we repeated this single item one week later (at the beginning of another experiment) with the order (*aid-add*) reversed. With the same subjects (aside from one who did not return), the results were virtually identical (see Table 51).

Table 51

Judgments of [ɛ]-[e, æ], First Item Only

	aid	add
Kindergarten	7	14
Adults	4	19
Adults	3	19 (retest)

We conclude that adults, like kindergarten children, tend to regard [ɛ] and [æ] as more closely related than [ɛ] and [e]. This choice appears to be reliable, independent of order of presentation, and statistically significant. It seems plausible that this same judgment of phonetic relatedness is part of the basis for children's use of A to represent [ɛ], and that most people retain the phonetic categorization, although not the spellings, in adulthood.

5.6 Interpretation

These conclusions fit together with those from a previously published study to produce a picture of children's judgments of vowel relationships and an explanation for the spellings that is fairly specific, coherent, and phonetically reasonable. In an earlier study (Read, 1973) we tested four possible relationships among the four high and mid front vowels of English. The relationships were those of height and tenseness

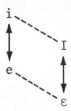

Figure 2. Relationships of front vowels tested in Read, 1973

(or length), as illustrated in Figure 2. In this study, it turned out that for six-year-olds (children entering first grade), the relationships that were strongest (and statistically significant) were those between vowels that are alike in tenseness (solid arrows).

Putting together the results of all the studies and the data on children's spellings suggests the picture of vowel relationships shown in Figure 3, where the stronger relationships are indicated by solid lines

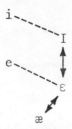

Figure 3. Composite representation of children's judgments of relationships among front vowels in English

and the weaker by dotted lines. The stronger relationships are those between [ɪ] and [ɛ] and between [ɛ] and [æ], as revealed in the experimental studies. The weaker relationships are those of height, between [ɪ] and [i], and between [ɛ] and [e], as revealed in the characteristic spellings and, in the latter case, in the experimental study.

We can now understand two properties of the characteristic spellings. The reason that the weaker relationship between [i] and [ɪ] influences children's spellings is simply that the children involved generally employ standard or letter-name spellings for [i], [e], and [æ]. They devise spellings for [ɪ] and [ɛ] by relating these to vowels that they do know how to spell. In the case of [ɪ], the related vowel of *known* spelling must be [i], even though this is the weaker relationship—thus the common spelling *E* for the vowel of *bit*. The reason that the spelling *A* for [ɛ] is much more frequent is, we hypothesize, that it is influenced by both kinds of similarity relationships, of which the more salient is that between [ɛ] and [æ].

The phonetic nature of the weaker relationships is one of height: the two high vowels and the two mid vowels are grouped together. We can also be fairly specific about the phonetic nature of the stronger relationships. Traditionally, these are described alternatively as the three short vowels, or in articulatory terms, the three lax vowels. It is now well established, however, that [æ] is actually the longest vowel of this series when context is held constant (House and Fairbanks, 1953; Peterson and Lehiste, 1960; House, 1961). Since [ɛ], to which [æ] is strongly related, is relatively short, it cannot be duration that children base their judgments on. This conclusion makes sense in terms of English phonology as well, since actual acoustic duration is a nondistinctive and quite variable property of vowels. Therefore, *if* we are to describe the two stronger relationships in a homogeneous way (and this is explicitly an assumption here), we must suppose that they are

128 VOWEL STUDIES

based on the fact that they are all monophthongs or that they are [−advanced tongue root], in the most recent development of Halle's proposed features.

The stronger relationships are also reflected indirectly in English spelling patterns, in that the three monophthongs are usually represented by a single letter, whereas the diphthongs [+a.t.r.] are subject to more complex spellings. This fact, however, could not be the basis of our experimental results with kindergarten children, since almost none of the children knew how to spell any of these vowels, a fact which we established in our pilot testing and in a subsequent experiment. Rather, we suggest that the facts are the other way around; children find this aspect of English spelling relatively natural because it reflects a categorization that they recognize prior to beginning formal instruction.

One hardly needs to emphasize that Figure 3 represents an empirical hypothesis; a good deal of research could be done on inferences from this hypothesis, and it may certainly turn out to be wrong. For example, it may be incorrect to describe both of the stronger relationships as arising from the same phonetic properties. However, at the moment the hypothesis provides a simple and coherent explanation for quite a range of facts—an extensive body of data on children's spellings and three experimental studies done with children in two different areas of the United States—and it explains these facts in a way that corresponds to phonetic descriptions which are themselves necessary to explain aspects of (adult) English phonology.

At the very least the studies indicate that children enter school with more than the ability to discriminate English vowels merely as a list of discrete units. It seems that children can detect relationships among these vowels. In effect, they can categorize them in terms of certain phonetic properties. It is a further hypothesis that children expect to find these relationships reflected in English spelling when distinct vowels are represented in the same way. Adopting this hypothesis, at least tentatively, let us compare the actual standard spelling system with what children may expect.

Figure 4 presents again the phonetic relationships represented in Figure 3, with the actual correspondences in standard English spelling also indicated (dotted lines). It is the vowels of *please* and *pleasant*, *sane* and *sanity*, and *wide* and *width* that are spelled alike.

Obviously these vowels are not closely related phonetically. They are related historically and phonologically in such a way that the vowels of word stems that are related in meaning tend to be spelled

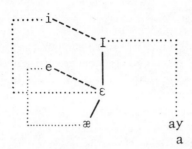

Figure 4. Vowel relationships in standard spelling vs. those that children recognize

alike, particularly in the polysyllabic words that derive, in one way or another, from Latin. It is not surprising that kindergarten and first-grade children are not familiar with similarities in spelling and in meaning in most of these sets of related words. What is interesting is that if we have correctly interpreted our research, relationships much closer to the phonetic ground *are* reflected in children's spelling, with the result, for example, that the three mid and low front vowels are often spelled alike.

The two kinds of relationships represented in Figure 4 may characterize the difference between what children know when they enter first grade and what they have to learn about the standard spelling of these vowels. The difference is not the notion that related vowels may be spelled alike, the notion of an abstract spelling, but the principle by which vowels are grouped together for spelling purposes—in the one case, phonetic similarities of two types, and in the other case, indirect derivational and morphological relationships. Knowing that children recognize vowel relationships of specific kinds suggests a different starting point for this process than if one assumes that children treat vowels as unanalyzed units. Section 5.8 will present some pedagogical inferences from this point of view.

5.7 The study of duration with synthetic speech

So far we have no independent evidence that we should describe the [i]-[ɛ] and the [ɛ]-[æ] categories as having the same phonetic basis, (specifically that the former is not based on duration, as the latter clearly is not). We have adopted that hypothesis merely because it makes the entire description more coherent. As noted earlier, in our 1973 study the strongest relationship was that between [ɪ] and [ɛ].

In that experiment, we asked children to identify which of two real words "sounds more like" a made-up word in an X: XAXB design. That is, we presented a nonce word such as [stɪp], asked the child to repeat it, and then presented the nonce word paired with each of two real words: [stɪp]-*step*, [stɪp]-*steep*. The child then judged which real word sounded more like the made-up word. With three examples of the type illustrated, six-year-olds chose [stɪp]-*step* to a degree that was statistically significant at the .01 level.

We reasoned that if this choice is based on the similarity in duration, both vowels being short, then children's judgments might tend toward randomness, if we artificially controlled duration, making the vowels of all three words of such a set equal in duration. (This reasoning ignores the likelihood, as argued in the previous section, that truly categorial judgments may not be much affected by changes in the phonetic input within a wide range.)

In order to control duration without varying other phonetic properties, it was necessary to use synthetic speech. We prepared two tape recordings of the stimuli that were used in the earlier experiment, using the synthesis-by-rule program developed by Dennis Klatt of the Speech Communication Group at M.I.T. This program rapidly synthesizes intelligible speech and allows considerable control over various parameters, in this case mainly vowel duration. One recording presented the entire experiment, including introductory material and practice items, in synthetic speech with vowel duration varying according to the rules built into the program; the other recording was identical to it, except that the duration of all stimulus vowels was fixed at 150 msec.

We then conducted these two experiments with 18 first-graders, each child hearing the two recordings on different days and with order of presentation varied. All other controls that were present in the original experiment were present in this case. The surprising result was that the children made absolutely random choices on *both* tapes; the preference for the [ɪ]: [ɛ] relationship that was prominent in the experiment with natural speech was completely absent, as were any other significant effects.

The differences between the two experiments, aside from that of natural versus synthetic speech, were extremely limited and presumably irrelevant: loudspeakers vs. headphones, Madison, Wisconsin, vs. Nahant, Massachusetts, one first grade vs. another. By far the most likely possibility is that the synthetic speech, which is intelligible but far from natural, is the crucial difference between the two experiments. In its present state of analysis, unfortunately, this particular experiment adds absolutely nothing to our knowledge about children's categorizations of speech sounds. It might be informative if we could identify a specific characteristic of the synthetic speech which accounts for the random results, but we have not been able to do so.

We replicated part of this experiment with 22 adult subjects (paid undergraduate volunteers) in order to discover whether the difficulty with synthetic speech was unique to children. Our earlier experiment using natural speech was also conducted with adults, and as reported in Read (1973), 19 adults chose the [ɪ]:[ɛ] relationship to a statistically significant degree (70%), just as the first-graders did. In this replication, we used only the recording in which vowel duration varied, in order to focus on the effect of synthetic speech alone.

Essentially, the adults made the same judgments of vowels in synthetic speech that other adults had made of natural speech. With three test items of the [stɪp]: *step, steep* variety, adults chose the [ɪ]: [ɛ] relationship in just over 80% of the trials (53 of 66 trials). The distribution of subjects according to the number of times they chose [ɛ] is presented in Table 52.

Table 52

Adult Judgments of [ɪ]-[ɛ] versus [ɪ]-[i] with Synthetic Speech (n = 22)

Number of [ɛ] choices	0	1	2	3
Number of subjects	0	4	5	13

This distribution is significantly different from what one would expect if the judgment were a random one (p = ½) at well beyond a .01 level of confidence (Kolmogorov-Smirnov goodness of fit test, two-sided). We conclude that adults regard the [ɪ]:[ɛ] relationship as closer than [ɪ]:[i] with synthetic speech as well as with natural speech.

Looking at the specific errors adults and children made in repeating the synthesized nonce words gives more information about the children's difficulty. The first general observation is that almost all the errors were in repeating consonants; just 4% of adult errors (4/105) and 3% of children's errors (2/62) were in the repetition of vowels. This fact is not surprising; synthetic vowels are usually more identifiable than synthetic consonants. The more interesting observation is that adults actually made significantly *more* errors in repeating the nonce words than did children, even though their performance of the task was evidently much *less* disrupted by the synthetic speech. On the seven nonce words, adults made a mean of 4.8 errors in repetition (with each sound scored individually), whereas children made a mean of 3.4 errors. In the comparable experiment with natural speech, children made a mean of only 0.2 errors per child on the same seven words. Adults likewise made few repetition errors. We have also examined the specific sound substitutions in adults and children's repetition errors on this task. Both groups made several kinds of errors, and in general, the pattern of errors is similar. There were one or two interesting differences, but these relate to the identification of consonants, rather than to the categorization of vowels.

It seems reasonable to conclude that the synthetic vowels were identifiable, and that enough information was present in the synthetic speech for adults to perform the categorial task. It is quite possible that the children's performance was disrupted rather globally by the distractions involved in identifying the synthetic consonants, rather than by any specific phonetic property of the synthetic vowels.

5.8 Recommendations to teachers

We see that spelling the vowel of *let* with an *A* is another very common error, far more frequent than other, similar errors, evidently. We concluded from our studies that children regard this vowel as being similar to that of *late* and that of *rat*, and again, they are phonetically quite correct. They reason, in effect, that if *late* is spelled with an *A* and *rat* is spelled with an *A*, then *let* must be spelled with an *A*. This reasoning is perfectly sensible, even though it is wrong. The children are simply much too close to the phonetic relationships. *Eventually* what they have to learn is that the vowels that are spelled alike are those that occur in related words like *please-pleasant*, and *wide-width*. Most of the examples of this point are probably not in a first-grader's vocabulary, however. Perhaps the best we can do is to point out the actual spelling of the vowel of *let* without seeming to deny the validity of the relationships the child recognizes or to question his "hearing."

We do not, of course, wish to deny that some children suffer from hearing losses and other basic difficulties, and that teachers should be alert for these, but most minor hearing losses would not affect speech sounds of this type. For most first-grade children who make the specific "errors" we have discussed here, the correct assumption is that they distinguish words as you do, but that they also recognize certain relationships among speech sounds. When they do not know the standard spelling, they suppose that it might reflect these relationships. In the case of the vowel of *let*, two types of relationships, one weak and one strong, intersect, so that the spelling *A* seems especially reasonable. Adults, too, can recognize these relationships (in our test situation, at least), but of course they do not usually connect them with spelling.

CHAPTER SIX

STUDIES OF THE RELATION BETWEEN [s] AND [z]

6.1 The problem

Our final set of experimental studies is different from the preceding ones in that it has to do with a grouping of speech sounds which may actually lead children toward standard spelling in most cases, namely, the relationship between [s] and [z] and the tendency to spell phonetic [z] as S. In our sample of young children's spelling, [z] is spelled S about 80% of the time, while the spelling Z occurs in only 4.5% of the examples at ages less than six years.

The representation of phonetic [z] with s is also characteristic of standard spelling, where the phonetic [z] in words such as *was, is, as, easy,* and in plurals and verb inflections such as *cubs* and *finds* are all spelled s. In fact, the letter z is used very rarely in standard spelling, usually only in initial position in words such as *zip* and *zoo*. One difference between these cases, which is relevant to standard spelling, is that the [z] at the end of *cubs* is predictable; that is, there could not be an English word with phonetic [s] in this position after [b], whereas the [z] of *zip* is not predictable, since there could be (and there is) a word such as *sip*. It is only some unpredictable [z]'s which are actually spelled z in standard spelling.

In a series of experiments we studied whether children do indeed categorize [s] with [z], especially as compared with two other phonetically plausible groupings. We also asked whether these categorizations are related to knowledge of standard spelling and/or to the predictability of the segments in particular contexts. Finally, we obtained evidence of children's spellings, including examples of their overgeneralization of the spelling of [z] with S.

The relevant phonetic facts are summarized in Table 53.

The symbol [š] represents the sound that is usually spelled *SH*, as in *ship*, which is a single sound, not a combination of two, as the spelling may suggest. The significance of this table is that the three

Table 53

The Phonetic Relationships among [s], [z], [t], and [š]

	nonanterior	anterior
noncontinuant		t
continuant, voiceless	š	s
continuant, voiced		z

speech sounds surrounding [s] are each different from it in one phonetic property (feature). If these speech sounds are all independent
unanalyzed units, or if children recognize relationships among them
but no one relationship is psychologically "closer" than any other,
then children should perform randomly in experiments designed to
elicit evidence of categorization. On the other hand, if children recognize the phonetic relationships and one of these is psychologically
closer than the others, then there should be a significant asymmetry in
the experimental results. The question is whether children recognize
an especially close relationship between [s] and [z] prior to learning
the spellings, which may actually make the frequent identity in the
spelling of these sounds seem relatively natural. We carried out a set
of experiments designed to test this hypothesis and to control the
influence of phonological predictability and knowledge of standard
spelling. These were conducted in Nahant, Massachusetts, in May of
the school year in both first grade and kindergarten.

All of the experiments were similar in design to our studies with
vowels, in that we first establish that a puppet likes a particular sound,
then test whether a child is able to identify that sound, and finally test
whether that child can judge which of two other sounds the puppet
would like better. We used two hand puppets, one named *Sid* and the
other named *Gus*, in order to test relationships to the sound [s] in
either initial or final position. As in all our other studies of this type,
we tested each child individually in a quiet room in the school, and
we controlled factors such as order of presentation and familiarity of
words.

6.2 The relation between [s] and [z] versus [s] and [t]

Our first experiment dealt with the vertical relationships in Table 53
between [s] and [z] and between [s] and [t], in both initial and
final position. In the experiment on final position, we establish that
Gus likes words like *dice, case, chess*, etc., and then we test the child's

identification of final [s] with questions like, "Would Gus like *race* or *raid*? Would Gus like *need* or *niece*?" When a child has correctly chosen the word with final [s] in at least 5 of 6 such cases, the experimenter announces that we will now try some words "that don't sound exactly like *Gus* at the end." The experimental trials consist of six items like, "Would Gus like *bills* or *built*? Would Gus like *right* or *rise*?" Note that these items are of two types: the final [z] of *bills* is predictable phonologically; because it is an affix, it must be [z], following a voiced sound. The final [z] of *rise*, on the other hand, is not predictable; there could be, and in fact there is, a word with final [s], *rice*. There were three test trials of each of these two types, and after every two trials there was a control item such as, "Would Gus like *louse* or *loud*," comparing [s] with [d] again, as a test of whether the child continued to seek sounds "like" [s].

This comparison turned out to be extremely easy for the children. Their responses were very rapid and certain. In establishing the original [s] class, fifteen of the eighteen children tested chose all of the first six items correctly; they chose correctly 51 of 54 control items during the experimental trials. Furthermore, the results were about as one-sided as those of an experiment with human beings could ever be: 102 of 108 choices were for the [s]-[z] relationship, as opposed to [s]-[t]. It is obvious that the difference between this result and random behavior is statistically significant at a confidence level which is beyond the range of readily available statistical tables. Given this one-sided overall result, there could not have been a statistically significant difference between the experimental trials in which the final [z] was phonologically predictable and those in which it was not. The results for these two types of items are exactly identical: 51 of 54 choices for [s]-[z].

Twelve adult subjects (paid volunteer undergraduates) made completely uniform judgments on this task. All twelve subjects correctly chose final [s] (versus final [d]) on six trials in establishing the original class and on the three control items presented at intervals in the experimental list. On the experimental items themselves, all subjects also chose final [z] (versus final [t]) on all six items. We note that this result is statistically significant (beyond the .001 level, by a two-tailed binomial test), even if we assume that the six trials were not independent for adults, and treat each subject as making one judgment rather than six.

Obviously, adults and children make the same judgment of this comparison, and they do so with great certainty. Accordingly, it may be important to note that the results are not as unremarkable as they may seem. For one thing, there is no purely phonetic reason why the judgments should be in the direction of [s]-[z]. The difference between the two categorizations, strong as it is, is psychological, in the sense that there is no necessary phonetic reason why one of these relationships should be more salient than the other. A second consideration is that the results could not be solely attributable to a knowledge of spelling. Among the test items of the "nonpredictable" type were *fizz-fit* and *maze-mate*, where the actual spelling (as well as the nonpredictability) of [z] does not indicate that it is related to [s]. Actually, there are two phonetic similarities between final [s] and [t], as opposed to [z]; they are voiceless, and therefore the preceding vowel is not lengthened, as it is in the case of [z].

If a knowledge of standard spelling influenced the judgments, it did so only indirectly. When we asked the children to spell certain words, 14 of 17 spelled the [z] at the end of *bills* as S (or SS); 14 of 17 children also spelled the sound at the end of *fizz* as Z. Yet the experimental judgments for these two words were identical, so that the children's knowledge of the actual spellings was clearly not a critical factor in the judgments.

We also tested these same relationships in initial position, where [z] is never predictable and where, in standard spelling, it is not spelled S. In this case, we used the puppet named Sid, who liked words that begin with [s]. Aside from the change in position, the design was the same as in the preceding case. The items that established the initial class were of the type, "Would Sid like *say* or *day?*" and the test items were of the type, "Would Sid like *zip* or *tip?*" There was, of course, only one type of test item, with respect to predictability.

The task turned out to be easy for first-graders, as one would expect, and the judgments were quite uniform: 57 of 66 judgments were for [s]-[z]. Again, this result is statistically significant beyond the .001 level (approximation to two-tailed binomial test). Because the results clearly tended to confirm those of the same test for final position, we tested a smaller number of first-graders (n = 11).

We take the results of these tests to mean that first-graders do regard [s] and [z] as much more closely related than [s] and [t]. This judgment may well arise from the phonological relationship or from a knowledge of the standard spelling, but these factors do not influence the children's judgments of individual examples. If one or both of these factors is the basis of the categorization, the children then generalize it to [s] and [z] in both of the positions we studied, without regard for actual spelling or predictability.

6.3 The relation between [s] and [z] versus [s] and [š]

Next, we designed and conducted comparisons of the [s]-[z] relationship with the other relationship illustrated in Table 53, namely, that between [s] and [š] in both initial and final position. The tests were analogous to those described above, with [š] substituted for [t] and [t] substituted for [d]. For example, in the test dealing with final position, we established that Gus liked words that end in [s], and we tested the child's ability to recognize words with this property using items such as, "Would Gus like *ace* or *ate?*" "Would Gus like *hit* or *hiss?*" We then introduced test items of the types illustrated by, "Would Gus like *fish* or *fizz?*" "Would Gus like *wells* or *Welsh?*" in which the comparison is between [z] and [š]. Again, in final position, but not in initial position, there are two types of [z]: those that are predictable and are spelled S, and those that are not predictable and are spelled ZZ.

We conducted this test with first-graders in early May of the school year. The children's judgments in this case were not as uniform as in the comparison with [t], and we were able to detect an influence which we did not see in the previous studies. The results for the test of final position are given in Table 54.

Table 54

Choices of [s]-[š] versus [s]-[z] in Final Position, First Grade
(n = 16)

	[s] *more like*	
	[š]	[z]
predictable	10	38
nonpredictable	18	30
Total	28	68

The overall preference for the [s]-[z] relationship is statistically significant at the .02 level (Kolmogorov-Smirnov goodness of fit test, two-sided), but we also see a tendency for this difference to be greater in the case of predictable [z]'s (spelled S) than for nonpredictable [z]. The difference between the predictable and the nonpredictable cases is not statistically significant at the .05 level, but it is nearly so.

We see further evidence of this effect in the results of the same comparison in initial position, where none of the [z]'s are phonologically predictable and all are spelled Z. In this test, there were only five test trials because of a shortage of familiar words in the language with initial [z]. We used test items such as, "Would Sid like *shoe* or *zoo?*" (See Table 55.)

Table 55

Judgments of whether [s] Is More Like [š] or [z] in Initial Position: First Grade (n = 18)

[s] *more like*	
[š]	57
[z]	33

In these results, we see the preference for the [s]-[z] relationship disappear for the first time. The preference for [š] here is not statistically significant at the .05 level, but the difference between the results of this test and of the same test for final position *is* significant at the .05 level.[1] The test is conservative, in that we are comparing the first five trials on the test in final position with the five trials in initial position. The sixth and final trial, which is omitted for this comparison in order to have the same number of trials on each test, was one of those with a predictable [z], so that in effect, the true difference between the two tests is reduced. It seems reasonable to assume that there really is an effect attributable to the predictability of [z] or to spelling, and to attempt to find out which is the correct explanation.

We knew, from testing the first-graders' spelling, that all of them knew the standard spelling SH for [š], and almost all (15 of 17 tested) spelled initial [z] as Z and final, predictable [z] *(bills)* as S. Therefore, one could explain the first-grade results by assuming: (1) that there is a weak underlying tendency to group [s] with [z], rather than with [š], (2) that this tendency is strengthened in the case of final [z]'s which are spelled S, but (3) that it is weakened by the effect of spelling when initial [z], spelled Z, is compared with initial [š], spelled *SH*. In other words, since most first-graders knew the standard spellings, one could account for the results by assuming an underlying tendency to group [s] with [z]. This interacts with a tendency to choose, as a counterpart to [s], whichever sound most obviously contains S in its spelling.

However, it is also possible that the children tend to choose predictable (or at any rate, final) [z]'s as counterparts to [s]. We can assume that they have acquired the rule of plural formation, which renders phonetic [z] predictable in plurals, because Berko (1958) showed that even five-year-olds use this rule productively, at least for the forms that are relevant here.

In order to distinguish these two possibilities, at least partially, we replicated the test of [s]-[z] versus [s]-[š] in initial position (only) with kindergarten children. We tested the children's knowledge of spelling by asking them (after the test of the relationship) to spell *ship, zip,* and *cabs,* or at least the first or last sounds of these, with the magnetic letters. Only one of the 20 kindergarten children spelled [š] as *SH,* four more spelled it *S,* and all the rest gave some other spelling or no response. Four spelled it *H.* (Recall that the name of the letter contains [č], i.e., [tš].) Three quarters of the kindergarten sample would have no basis in spelling, therefore, for a choice one way or the other.

On the categorial test, the kindergarten children as a whole displayed a slight preference for [s]-[z]. But when we separate the two groups on the basis of the spellings, there is a distinct difference. The fifteen children who did *not* spell [š] with an *S* tended to choose [s]-[z], while those five who spelled [š] as *S* or *SH* tended to choose [s]-[š]. Neither of these results, tested separately with our usual nonparametric test, is statistically significant (although both are significant at the .05 level as measured by the t-test).

A test of the difference between these two samples of kindergarten children reveals significance at the .02 level (Mann-Whitney U test, two-sided). If we compare the first-graders, who did know the spellings, with those kindergarteners who did not, in their performance on the same test (initial position), the difference is also statistically significant ($p = .033$, Mann-Whitney U test, two-sided, corrected for ties).

The apparent effect of standard spelling suggests the question of what judgment adults would make in this case, and intuitively at least, the answer is not obvious. Therefore, we replicated the test (initial position) with our paid undergraduates. As in the other studies, the adults dealt with the preliminary items and controls very easily; all 23 subjects chose [s] (versus [t]) on six consecutive items in establishing the initial class and on the three control items in the experimental list. On the experimental [s]:[š,z] comparison, the adults tended to choose [š], but the subjects were sharply divided on this point. (See Table

Table 56

Adult Judgments of [s]-[š] versus [s]-[z] in Initial Position (n = 23)

Number of [š] choices	0	1	2	3	4	5
Number of subjects	7	–	–	1	5	10

56.) Again, if we make the conservative but reasonable assumption that the six experimental trials were not independent for adults, we may consider just their choices on the first such item: 14 for [š] and 9 for [z]. By a binomial test, this difference is not significant, so we cannot regard adults as a group as having a clear preference in this case.

However, if we compare the adults with the kindergarten children who did not know the spelling of [š], there is a significant difference, just as there is between the same kindergarten children and first-graders. (See Table 57.)

Table 57

Choices of [s]-[š] versus [s]-[z], First Item Only, Adults and Nonspelling Kindergarten Subjects

	[š]	[z]
Adults	14	9
Kindergarten	2	13

By a Fisher test, the probability of this result or one more extreme is .004. We conclude that adults and kindergarten children who do not use S in spelling [š] are significantly different in judging this relationship. The results suggest that a knowledge of standard spelling influences the choice. There is, on the other hand, no real difference between first-graders and adults: 61% of both groups chose [s]-[š] on the first test item.

We therefore have quite clear evidence that the underlying tendency is to group [s] with [z], as compared with [š], but that this grouping tends to change when a child learns that [š] is spelled *SH*—certainly in first grade, and perhaps even in kindergarten. The underlying categorization *may* still arise from the fact that [s] and [z] are often predictable alternants; nothing in these results rules out the possibility of an earlier effect of learning part of the phonology of English. Our general conclusion, then, is that the relationship between [s] and [z] is much stronger for children than that between [s] and [t], and it remains so, since learning English spelling could only strengthen it. This relationship is also more basic than that between [s] and [š], but in this case it is heavily affected by learning to spell [š].

The influence of standard spelling on these judgments, best illustrated in the contrast between the first-grade and kindergarten results, is perhaps surprising, especially considering that the spelling of [š] is *SH*, not just *S*. First-graders evidently do not regard this digraph as merely an arbitrary addition to the set of available symbols. From one point of view, this influence merely reflects a potential source of bias in studying children's categorizations of speech sounds. More interesting, though, is the suggestion that children may almost immediately regard standard spelling as indicating phonetic relationships. The notion that the sound spelled *SH* "is a kind of [s]" appears to be a real one in first grade, as it may be in adulthood. In this case, the usefulness of the conclusion is questionable, since it is [s] and [z] that are more commonly related, phonologically and in spelling; an [s]-[š] relationship shows up more rarely, as in *race-racial*, and in these cases [š] is never spelled *SH*. But the principle that standard spellings indicate some kind of relationship is not, on the whole, a bad one (some notorious exceptions notwithstanding).

What the children have to learn is that the relationships preserved in spelling are not so close to the phonetic level, but are essentially meaning relations. This is illustrated in the example *please-pleasant* cited in chapter five on vowel relations, and in the fact that the plural is spelled *-s* (as well as *-es*), whether it is [s] or [z] phonetically. If our results suggest that children are quick to draw inferences about the language from spelling, we should not regret this willingness, but we should direct it toward those genuine relationships that are indicated in spelling.

6.4 Recommendations to teachers

We have seen that children do indeed regard [s] and [z] as related and that they strongly tend to spell them both *S*. This judgment therefore leads children toward standard spellings in most cases. It does, however, occasionally lead to nonstandard spellings; of the 17 first-graders that we tested on spelling, two spelled *zip* as SIP and three spelled *fizz* as FIS. In this case, it would seem especially important not to insist too strongly on the distinction between [s] and [z], for it is one that English spelling rarely honors. The important principle here is that only certain [z] sounds are actually spelled z. We can probably not explain the principle satisfactorily to a first-grader, but we can provide examples that may give a child a "feeling" for it. In these studies we also saw that children quickly assume that spellings must reflect some phonetic relationship—that the sound spelled *SH* must be closely related to [s]. Here again, our ultimate goal is for children to learn that spelling does reflect some genuine relationships, but that these are usually in meaning rather than sound.

The reader may recall that near the beginning of this monograph we encountered the question of whether an orthography which consistently marks all and only the functional distinctions is necessarily an optimal one for teaching literacy, as is widely assumed. We noted that the initial teaching alphabet (i.t.a.) even marks the distinction between [θ] and [ð], and we questioned whether children might not actually regard these sounds as so closely related that it is natural to spell them alike *(th)*. We can now evaluate another instance of the phonemic spelling assumption in i.t.a., namely, the practice of distinguishing [s] and [z]. In a compromise with standard spelling, i.t.a. represents these as *s* and *z* but employs a third symbol, ⤳, for phonetic [z] that is spelled *s*, as in *is* or *was*. On the basis of the research, we can see that it is doubtful that the distinction between ⤳ and *s* is needed; since children know that [s] and [z] are closely related, and since they readily represent [z] with *s*, the efficiency of i.t.a. and similar proposals might be improved by adopting standard spelling in this respect.

The insight that emerges from all of our investigations is that children enter school with not only the ability to speak and understand, but also the ability to detect phonetic relationships. These relationships sometimes affect their spelling, leading to some characteristic patterns that may seem bizarre. For example, the combination of the nasal and vowel spelling patterns gives the spelling BAT for *bent*. Our basic suggestion is, first, that teachers attempt to distinguish different kinds of spelling errors: those that are based on phonetic relationships from those that are based on visual confusions (such as the left-right inversion of *b* and *d*), from those that are based on overgeneralization of otherwise valid sound-spelling correspondences (such as the spelling SED for *said*). In the first and last cases, the child is actually using a principle that has some validity and will be useful later on. The principle in the first case is that related sounds may be spelled alike; this notion must be qualified and deepened quite considerably in order to be applicable to English spelling. In the meantime, a teacher should try to recognize when there is a phonetic relationship underlying an apparent error, and give the child credit for a correct judgment and a reasonable attempt at constructing a spelling.

After all, a child who tends to spell related sounds in the same way is actually closer to English spelling than a child who believes that every sound must have a unique spelling (or, of course, one who has no idea how sounds might be represented). While the second child has to develop a concept of abstract spelling, the first child has to learn that it is related words (or parts of words) that are often spelled alike, so that the sounds involved are often *not* closely related. Learning this principle as it applies to English spelling is certainly no simple task, and it is made more difficult by many real and apparent exceptions. No mere psycholinguist can adequately describe how children learn such a principle, but we can at least try to recognize the nature and the validity of what the child starts with, so that he or she can build on that.

FOOTNOTES CHAPTER ONE

[1] Chapter six will present evidence for this assertion for both children and adults. Except where otherwise indicated, "phoneme" refers to autonomous, rather than systematic, phonemes.

[2] [ɛ] occurs in the names of letters such as f and l, and [ʌ] is in the name of w. Section 2.2. discusses children's use (and nonuse) of this information.

[3] There are two tabulations, both according to the phone represented (where the 39 phones are at a broad level of transcription). One tabulation lists each spelling of each phone (in its whole-word context), with an identification of the speller, the speller's age, and a phonetic representation of the word spelled. It also indicates the number of exact repetitions (of a given word by a given child at a given age). The second tabulation, represented by the tables in Appendices A-I, lists each spelling of each phone in three groups according to the age of the speller, presents the number and percentage of each spelling in the three age groups, and the totals. In addition, there are subtabulations of the spelling of some phones according to their phonetic context. Both tabulations exclude the spellings of words that were entirely standard.

FOOTNOTES CHAPTER TWO

[1] Almost all of these children had final /i/ rather than /ɪ/ in these words.

[2] This criterion excludes the spellings done by various members of a Montessori kindergarten, as well as others. The reason for this limitation is that no reliable estimate of an individual's system can be based on so few examples.

[3] Seven of the I spellings came from the one child whose dialect was of this type. Note that the other frequent spelling for [ɪ], the invented spelling E, would appear as a standard spelling for phonemic /ɛ/, thus perhaps contributing a slight bias in favor of the standard spelling here.

[4] The figures in Appendix A, Table 1 include three repetitions.

[5] I do not have information about this aspect of each child's dialect, or that of his or her parents.

[6] The only other nonstandard spellings more frequent than 1% are A (10%) and I (4%). Most of the I spellings are from the child who produced most of the I spellings for /a/, so it seems that he grouped both of the central unrounded vowels with the letter-name /ay/. This child produced other standard and nonstandard spellings for /ʌ/, however. The A spellings come from nine different children, most of them from two children who also used other spellings. Possibly,

the *A* spellings represent a grouping of /ʌ/ with the other unrounded mid vowels /e/ and /ɛ/; they are, however, distinctly minority judgments, even for the children who produced them. A more plausible speculation is that the *A* spellings arise from children's learning that *A* spells the word *a*. They thus represent a grouping of /ʌ/ with /ə/.

⁷These are spellings of /u/, whether or not preceded by [y]; for spellings of /yu/, see Appendix A, Table 40.

⁸Exceptions listed in Venezky (1963) are *wolf, woman,* and *bosom*.

⁹In a Chi-square test of the frequency of *OW* versus other spellings of /o/ in final and nonfinal positions, $\chi^2 = 6.83$ (df = 1), which is significant at the .01 level.

¹⁰For example, note the difference between the flap in *fatal* and the [t] in *fatality*.

FOOTNOTES CHAPTER THREE

¹New York: Harper and Row, 1966. The test was administered in accordance with the published directions to half of each kindergarten (approximately ten children) at a time, by a competent tester and the regular teacher. The administration of the Brookline Public Schools made available the scores for each child involved in the present study.

²Teacher's Guidebook, "Pre-Reading Test of Scholastic Ability," p. 8. As in this example, [tr-] and [dr-] were each used once as the initial sounds of key words, but each was compared only with (unaffricated) labial or velar stops.

³The published national mean for the standardizing population of 772 first-graders (in the first two weeks of school) on this subtest was 13.1, S.D. = 4.3, reliability coefficient = .70, S.E. = 2.1. For all Brookline kindergartens the mean was 12, the S.D. was 4.9, and the median was also 12. A score above 15 is one of the characteristics of a child ready to begin reading instruction immediately, according to the test publisher.

⁴These were, of course, children nominated by the teachers, rather than chosen for their test scores. The actual test scores for such children were looked up only after the testing and rating.

⁵As noted above, each performance here includes fourteen, rather than eleven, separate judgments. As a result, there was more opportunity for inconsistency, and two inconsistent judgments could not make a child's answers as a whole indeterminate. Nevertheless, to facilitate comparison with Table 33, these (-2) judgements are not included among the central results. They do not affect the general conclusion, in any case.

⁶We may use the children's mean score on the standard test as a measure of their ability to judge sameness of sounds. The mean raw scores (of a possible 20

correct) are: [č] category: 16.7; [t] category: 18.5. This difference is not statistically significant (Mann-Whitney "U" test: U = 72, which is above the critical value [nonsignificant] even at ∝ = .10, two-tailed). With the correction for scores tied in rank, z = −1.21, p = .1131. The text discusses a possible explanation for the small difference in the means.

[7] Eighteen children were inconsistent on one test or both, and so are not included in Table 36. Ten of these were inconsistent on the [dr]-test only, no doubt partly because of the greater length of that test, and hence more stringent consistency requirement, as noted above.

[8] There were a few other nonstandard pronunciations, including one of *church* as [t͡sɚč].

[9] The class was in the same school as two of the kindergartens, and the test was given in the same weeks. No independent test of ability to identify first sounds was available, but all but two first-graders succeeded on the pretest.

[10] Percentages based on such small numbers may have greater apparent precision than is really justified.

[11] The teacher reported the level of difficulty of the books that each child was then able to read. In order, the levels are: pre-primer, 1-1, 1-2, 2-1, and so forth, where 1-1 means "first grade, first book." There are two levels to each grade; the highest achieved in this class was 3-2 (third grade, second book).

[12] Each word was printed on an index card. The children picked the cards up one at a time; there were no other cues. This test was conducted one month after the original ones. The exceptionally poor reader was merely guessing at some of the words; he also did not know that *ch* spells [č]. With coaching, he was able to read every word, but his attention wandered.

[13] One girl noted that *dragon* begins with *dr*, "but *door* begins with *do*." Her test answers, however, were [č]/[j] (-1), illustrating again the potential independence of phonological judgments from knowledge of spelling.

[14] Nine children who failed the pretest nevertheless took one or both tests (because they wanted to). All of these made inconsistent or *all* judgments, so apparently the pretest and the criterion were appropriate.

[15] Obtaining large numbers of consistent judgments from four-year-olds might be facilitated by minor improvements in the test. In the absence of a dramatically more effective test, however, approximately three children will be tested for every one who can make reliable judgments at age four.

[16] It was not possible to test reading ability directly in this case; the estimates are those of the teachers, who were not aware of the purpose of the question. Only those about whom the teachers had no doubt at all were considered to be able to read the words in question.

[17] To judge from the informal reactions of the teachers, this development is also

not directly related to general ability; the teachers were all surprised to find that some of their "best students" gave the unexpected answers.

FOOTNOTES CHAPTER FIVE

[1] Children know the name of the letter *A*, and they evidently know that the vowel of *lad* is spelled *A*, perhaps from common words like *cat* and *man*. However they learn it, they use the standard spelling for this vowel about 90% of the time, even at ages less than six years.

[2] One such subject commented after the experiment that he had chosen [o] "because it's softer sounding." It is interesting that he was evidently thinking of phonic quality, although it is hard to imagine what actual phonetic relationship between [ɛ] and [o] he may have had in mind. Only one kindergarten child chose [o] on 5 or 6 of the six trials, whereas five adults did.

[3] One adult tested did fail to choose the true rhymes consistently, and his choices on experimental and control items revealed an obvious position preference. He is not included in the sample here or for any other experiment.

FOOTNOTE CHAPTER SIX

[1] The statistical test is the Kolmogorov-Smirnov two-sample test, using only the first 16 subjects on the test of initial position, in order to have equal numbers of subjects on the two tests. The statistical test assumes that the two samples are independent, but in fact essentially the same subjects were tested, two or more days apart. Both this difference and the fact that the variable is discrete, rather than continuous, make this test conservative.

SELECTED REFERENCES

Beers, J. W. *First and second grade children's developing orthographic concepts of tense and lax vowels*. (Doctoral dissertation, University of Virginia, 1974) Charlottesville, Virginia: University Microfilms, 1975. No. 75-4694.

Bellugi, U., & Brown, R. The acquisition of language. *Monographs of the Society for Research in Child Development*, 1964, 29 (1, Serial No. 92).

Berko, J. The child's learning of English morphology. *Word*, 1958, 14, 150-177.

Borgström, C. Hj. Language analysis as a child's game. In C. A. Ferguson and D. I. Slobin (Eds.), *Studies of child language development*. New York: Holt, Rinehart and Winston, 1973.

Bruce, D. J. The analysis of word sounds by young children. *British Journal of Educational Psychology*, 1964, 34, 158-170.

Chomsky, C. *The acquisition of syntax in children from 5 to 10*. Cambridge, Mass.: M.I.T. Press, 1969.

Chomsky, C. Reading, writing, and phonology. *Harvard Educational Review*, 1970, 40, 287-309.

Chomsky, C. Write first, read later. *Childhood Education*, 1971, 47, 296-299.

Chomsky, N., & Halle, M. *The sound pattern of English*. New York: Harper & Row, 1968.

Downing, J. *Evaluating the initial teaching alphabet*. London: Cassell & Co., Ltd., 1967.

Fodor, J., & Garrett, M. Some reflections on competence and performance. In J. Lyons & R. J. Wales (Eds.), *Psycholinguistics papers*. Edinburgh: Edinburgh University Press, 1966.

Fromkin, V. A. The non-anomalous nature of anomalous utterances. *Language*, 1971, 47, 27-52.

150

Gerritz, K. E. First graders' spelling of vowels: An exploratory study. Unpublished doctoral dissertation, Harvard University, 1974.

Graham, L. W., & House, A. S. Phonological oppositions in children: A perceptual study. *Journal of the Acoustical Society of America*, 1971, 49, 559-566.

House, A. S. On vowel duration in English. *Journal of the Acoustical Society of America*, 1961, 33, 1174-1178.

House, A. S., & Fairbanks, G. The influence of consonant environment upon the secondary acoustical characteristics of vowels. *Journal of the Acoustical Society of America*, 1953, 22, 105-113.

Jakobson, R. *Child language, aphasia and phonological universals.* A. P. Keiler (Trans.), The Hague: Mouton, 1968. (Originally published: *Kindersprache, Aphasie und allgemeine Lautgesetze.* Uppsala: Almqvist & Weksell, 1941.)

Jakobson, R., Fant, C. G. M., & Halle, M. *Preliminaries to speech analysis.* (2nd ed.) Cambridge, Mass.: M.I.T. Press, 1963.

Joos, M. (Ed.) *Readings in linguistics.* Washington, D.C.: ACLS, 1957.

Kamil, M. L., & Rudegeair, R. E. Methodological improvements in the assessment of phonological discrimination in children. *Child Development*, 1972, 43, 1087-1091.

Kenyon, J. S. *American pronunciation.* (10th ed.) Ann Arbor, Mich.: George Wahr Publishing Co., 1969.

Klima, E. S. How alphabets might reflect language. In J. F. Kavanagh & I. G. Mattingly (Eds.), *Language by ear and by eye: The relationships between speech and reading.* Cambridge, Mass.: M.I.T. Press, 1972.

Knafle, J. D. Auditory perception of rhyming in kindergarten children. *Journal of Speech and Hearing Research*, 1973, 16, 482-487.

Knafle, J. D. Children's discrimination of rhyme. *Journal of Speech and Hearing Research*, 1974, 17, 367-372.

Langacker, R. W. *Language and its structure: Some fundamental linguistic concepts.* (2nd ed.) New York: Harcourt Brace Jovanovich, 1973.

Liberman, A. M., Cooper, F. S., Shankweiler, D. P., & Studdert-Kennedy, M. Perception of the speech code. *Psychological Review*, 1967, 74, 431-461.

Malécot, A. Vowel nasality as a distinctive feature in American English. *Language*, 1960, 36, 222-229.

Massaro, D. W. Perceptual processes and forgetting in memory tasks. *Psychology Review*, 1970, 77, 555-567. (a)

Massaro, D. W. Preperceptual auditory images. *Journal of Experimental Psychology*, 1970, 85, 411-417. (b)

Massaro, D. W. Effect of masking tone duration on preperceptual auditory images. *Journal of Experimental Psychology*, 1971, 87, 146-148.

Massaro, D. W. Preperceptual images, processing time, and perceptual units in auditory perception. *Psychological Review*, 1972, 79, 124-145. (a)

Massaro, D. W. Stimulus information versus processing time in auditory pattern recognition. *Perception and Psychophysics*, 1972, 12, 50-56. (b)

Menyuk, P. Children's learning and reproduction of grammatical and nongrammatical phonological sequences. *Child Development*, 1968, 39, 849-859.

Messer, S. Implicit phonology in children. *Journal of Verbal Learning and Verbal Behavior*, 1967, 6, 609-613.

Miller, G. A., & Nicely, P. E. An analysis of perceptual confusions among some English consonants. *Journal of the Acoustical Society of America*, 1955, 27, 338-352.

Montessori, M. *The Montessori method*. New York: Schocken Books, 1964.

Morehead, D. Processing of phonological sequences by young children and adults. *Child Development*, 1971, 42, 279-289.

Moskowitz, B. A. On the status of vowel shift in English. In T. E. Moore (Ed.), *Cognitive development and the acquisition of language*. New York: Academic Press, 1973.

Olmsted, D. L. *Out of the mouth of babes: Earliest stages in language learning*. The Hague: Mouton, 1971.

O'Neil, W. A. The oral-formulaic structure of the Faroese Kvæði. *Fróðskaparrit*, 1970, **18**, 59-68.

Peterson, G. E., & Lehiste, I. Duration of syllable nuclei in English. *Journal of the Acoustical Society of America*, 1960, **32**, 693-703.

Pike, K. L. *Phonemics: A technique for reducing languages to writing.* Ann Arbor, Mich.: University of Michigan Press, 1947.

Pitman, J., & St. John, J. *Alphabets and reading: The initial teaching alphabet.* London: Sir Isaac Pitman & Sons, Ltd., 1969.

Read, C. Children's perceptions of the sounds of English: Phonology from three to six. Unpublished doctoral dissertation, Harvard University, 1970.

Read, C. Pre-school children's knowledge of English phonology. *Harvard Educational Review*, 1971, **41**, 1-34.

Read, C. Children's judgments of phonetic similarities in relation to English spelling. *Language Learning*, 1973, **23**, 17-38.

Read, C. Lessons to be learned from the pre-school orthographer. In E. H. & E. Lenneberg (Eds.), *Foundations of language development*, New York: Academic Press, 1975.

Rystrom, R. Perceptions of vowel letter-sound relationships by first-grade children. *Reading Research Quarterly*, 1973-1974, **9**(2), 170-184.

Sapir, E. Sound patterns in language. *Language*, 1925, **1**, 37-51.

Sapir, E. La réalité psychologique des phonèmes. *Journal de Psychologie Normale et Pathologique*, 1933, **30**, 247-265.

Savin, H. G., & Bever, T. G. The nonperceptual reality of the phoneme. *Journal of Verbal Learning and Verbal Behavior*, 1970, **9**, 295-302.

Shattuck, S. Speech errors and the sentence production process. Unpublished doctoral dissertation, Massachusetts Institute of Technology, 1974.

Singh, S. Perceptual similarities and minimal phonemic differences. *Journal of Speech and Hearing Research*, 1971, **14**, 106-112.

Singh, S., & Black, J. W. Study of twenty-six intervocalic consonants as spoken and recognized by four language groups. *Journal of the Acoustical Society of America*, 1966, **39**, 372-387.

Singh, S., & Woods, D. R. Perceptual structure of 12 American English vowels. *Journal of the Acoustical Society of America,* 1971, **49**, 1861-1866.

Steinberg, D. D., & Krohn, R. K. The psychological validity of Chomsky and Halle's vowel shift rule. Paper presented at the Annual Meeting of the Linguistic Society of America, San Diego, December 1973.

Templin, M. *Certain language skills in children: Their development and interrelationships.* Minneapolis: University of Minnesota Press, 1957.

Thorndike, E. L. *Thorndike Century Senior Dictionary.* New York: Scott, Foresman and Company, 1941.

Venezky, R. L. *The structure of English orthography.* The Hague: Mouton, 1970.

Venezky, R. L. The asymmetry of sound substitutions. *ASHA,* 1971, **13**, 538. (Abstract)

Weir, R. H., & Venezky, R. L. Spelling-to-sound patterns. In K. S. Goodman (Ed.), *The psycholinguistic nature of the reading process.* Detroit: Wayne State University Press, 1968.

Zhurova, L. Ye. The development of analysis of words into their sounds by preschool children. In C. A. Ferguson and Dan I. Slobin (Eds.), *Studies of child language development.* New York: Holt, Rinehart and Winston, 1973.

APPENDICES

APPENDIX A: SPELLINGS OF FORTY PHONE-TYPES

Table 1: Phoneme [a]

AGE:	UNDER 6		UNKNOWN		6 OR OVER		ALL	
SPELLING	FREQ	PCT	FREQ	PCT	FREQ	PCT	FREQ	PCT
O	74	59.2	18	46.2	58	63.0	150	58.6
(OMIT)	22	17.6	6	15.4	10	10.9	38	14.8
A	13	10.4	3	7.7	14	15.2	30	11.7
J	10	8.0	8	20.5	0	0.0	18	7.0
F	2	1.6	1	2.6	2	2.2	5	2.0
U	2	1.6	2	5.1	2	2.2	6	2.3
CO	1	0.8	0	0.0	4	4.3	5	2.0
OU	1	0.8	0	0.0	0	0.0	1	0.4
H	0	0.0	1	2.6	0	0.0	1	0.4
YO	0	0.0	0	0.0	1	1.1	1	0.4
AR	0	0.0	0	0.0	1	1.1	1	0.4
TOTALS	125	100.0	39	100.0	92	100.0	256	100.0

Table 2: Phoneme [b]

AGE:	UNDER 6		UNKNOWN		6 OR OVER		ALL	
SPELLING	FREQ	PCT	FREQ	PCT	FREQ	PCT	FREQ	PCT
B	126	96.2	68	100.0	82	88.2	276	94.5
MB	2	1.5	0	0.0	0	0.0	2	0.7
(OMIT)	1	0.8	0	0.0	1	1.1	2	0.7
P	1	0.8	0	0.0	0	0.0	1	0.3
BO	1	0.8	0	0.0	0	0.0	1	0.3
D	0	0.0	0	0.0	7	7.5	7	2.4
BR	0	0.0	0	0.0	1	1.1	1	0.3
BB	0	0.0	0	0.0	2	2.2	2	0.7
TOTALS	131	100.0	68	100.0	93	100.0	292	100.0

Table 3: Phoneme [č]

AGE:	UNDER 6		UNKNOWN		6 OR OVER		ALL	
SPELLING	FREQ	PCT	FREQ	PCT	FREQ	PCT	FREQ	PCT
CH	21	53.8	13	81.3	11	57.9	45	60.8
C	6	15.4	0	0.0	1	5.3	7	9.5
TCH	5	12.8	1	6.3	1	5.3	7	9.5
SH	2	5.1	1	6.3	2	10.5	5	6.8
(OMIT)	1	2.6	0	0.0	1	5.3	2	2.7
T	1	2.6	0	0.0	1	5.3	2	2.7
CHE	1	2.6	0	0.0	0	0.0	1	1.4
ES	1	2.6	0	0.0	0	0.0	1	1.4
THC	1	2.6	0	0.0	0	0.0	1	1.4
GE	0	0.0	0	0.0	1	5.3	1	1.4
CHA	0	0.0	1	6.3	0	0.0	1	1.4
TTG	0	0.0	0	0.0	1	5.3	1	1.4
TOTALS	39	100.0	16	100.0	19	100.0	74	100.0

Table 4: Phoneme [d]

AGE:	UNDER 6		UNKNOWN		6 OR OVER		ALL	
SPELLING	FREQ	PCT	FREQ	PCT	FREQ	PCT	FREQ	PCT
D	226	74.8	116	75.8	154	69.4	496	73.3
T	39	12.9	22	14.4	41	18.5	102	15.1
(OMIT)	10	3.3	4	2.6	5	2.3	19	2.8
TT	9	3.0	0	0.0	8	3.6	17	2.5
DE	7	2.3	3	2.0	9	4.1	19	2.8
DD	2	0.7	2	1.3	0	0.0	4	0.6
W	1	0.3	0	0.0	0	0.0	1	0.1
N	1	0.3	1	0.7	0	0.0	2	0.3
J	1	0.3	4	2.6	0	0.0	5	0.7
B	1	0.3	0	0.0	1	0.5	2	0.3
G	1	0.3	0	0.0	0	0.0	1	0.1
DA	1	0.3	0	0.0	0	0.0	1	0.1
ID	1	0.3	0	0.0	0	0.0	1	0.1
DT	1	0.3	0	0.0	0	0.0	1	0.1
LD	1	0.3	0	0.0	0	0.0	1	0.1
ED	0	0.0	1	0.7	4	1.8	5	0.7
TOTALS	302	100.0	153	100.0	222	100.0	677	100.0

Table 5: Phoneme [ɛ]

AGE:	UNDER 6		UNKNCWN		6 OR CVER		ALL	
SPELLING	FREQ	PCT	FREQ	PCT	FREQ	PCT	FREQ	PCT
A	96	49.7	32	34.0	63	38.7	191	42.4
E	72	37.3	40	42.6	80	49.1	192	42.7
I	11	5.7	6	6.4	8	4.9	25	5.6
(OMIT)	9	4.7	10	10.6	5	3.1	24	5.3
EE	2	1.C	2	2.1	1	C.6	5	1.1
AE	1	0.5	0	0.C	C	0.0	1	0.2
AI	1	C.5	0	0.0	0	0.0	1	0.2
EU	1	C.5	0	0.C	0	C.C	1	0.2
C	0	0.0	0	0.0	1	C.6	1	0.2
U	0	0.C	1	1.1	1	0.6	2	0.4
EI	0	0.0	1	1.1	C	0.C	1	0.2
EY	0	C.C	0	0.0	2	1.2	2	0.4
EA	0	C.C	1	1.1	2	1.2	3	0.7
EAR	0	C.0	1	1.1	0	C.C	1	0.2
TCTALS	193	1CC.C	94	100.0	163	100.0	450	100.0

Table 6: Phoneme [f]

AGE:	UNDER 6		UNKNCWN		6 OR OVER		ALL	
SPELLING	FREQ	PCT	FREQ	PCT	FREQ	PCT	FREQ	PCT
F	91	93.8	48	92.3	70	90.9	209	92.5
FF	5	5.2	2	3.8	2	2.6	9	4.0
TTH	1	1.C	0	0.C	0	C.0	1	0.4
(OMIT)	0	C.0	0	0.0	1	1.3	1	0.4
PH	0	0.C	1	1.9	3	3.9	4	1.8
FR	0	0.0	C	0.0	1	1.3	1	0.4
FA	0	C.0	1	1.9	0	0.C	1	0.4
TOTALS	97	1CC.C	52	1CC.0	77	1CO.C	226	100.0

Table 7: Phoneme [g]

AGE:	UNDER 6		UNKNCWN		6 OR CVER		ALL	
SPELLING	FREQ	PCT	FREQ	PCT	FREQ	PCT	FREQ	PCT
G	74	94.9	44	95.7	55	98.2	173	96.1
(OMIT)	2	2.6	1	2.2	C	C.0	3	1.7
W	1	1.3	0	0.0	0	C.C	1	0.6
X	1	1.3	0	0.0	0	0.0	1	0.6
GG	0	0.0	1	2.2	1	1.8	2	1.1
TCTALS	78	1CC.0	46	100.0	56	100.0	180	100.0

Table 8: Phoneme [h]

AGE:	UNDER 6		UNKNOWN		6 OR OVER		ALL	
SPELLING	FREQ	PCT	FREQ	PCT	FREQ	PCT	FREQ	PCT
H	85	94.4	47	100.0	57	98.3	189	96.9
(OMIT)	4	4.4	0	0.0	0	0.0	4	2.1
WH	1	1.1	0	0.0	1	1.7	2	1.0
TOTALS	90	100.0	47	100.0	58	100.0	195	100.0

Table 9: Phoneme [ɪ]

AGE:	UNDER 6		UNKNOWN		6 OR OVER		ALL	
SPELLING	FREQ	PCT	FREQ	PCT	FREQ	PCT	FREQ	PCT
I	157	64.9	82	69.5	110	73.8	349	68.6
E	55	22.7	18	15.3	20	13.4	93	18.3
(OMIT)	12	5.0	13	11.0	4	2.7	29	5.7
A	5	2.1	1	0.8	2	1.3	8	1.6
O	2	0.8	0	0.0	1	0.7	3	0.6
Y	2	0.8	0	0.0	1	0.7	3	0.6
EI	2	0.8	0	0.0	7	4.7	9	1.8
IE	2	0.8	0	0.0	0	0.0	2	0.4
EE	2	0.8	1	0.8	0	0.0	3	0.6
U	1	0.4	1	0.8	1	0.7	3	0.6
CH	1	0.4	0	0.0	0	0.0	1	0.2
OO	1	0.4	0	0.0	0	0.0	1	0.2
II	0	0.0	1	0.8	2	1.3	3	0.6
IA	0	0.0	0	0.0	1	0.7	1	0.2
LI	0	0.0	1	0.8	0	0.0	1	0.2
TOTALS	242	100.0	118	100.0	149	100.0	509	100.0

Table 10: Phoneme [ǰ]

AGE:	UNDER 6		UNKNOWN		6 OR OVER		ALL	
SPELLING	FREQ	PCT	FREQ	PCT	FREQ	PCT	FREQ	PCT
G	27	51.9	3	21.4	13	61.9	43	49.4
J	20	38.5	7	50.0	4	19.0	31	35.6
GE	2	3.8	0	0.0	3	14.3	5	5.7
D	1	1.9	0	0.0	0	0.0	1	1.1
CH	1	1.9	0	0.0	1	4.8	2	2.3
JJ	1	1.9	0	0.0	0	0.0	1	1.1
DG	0	0.0	2	14.3	0	0.0	2	2.3
JE	0	0.0	2	14.3	0	0.0	2	2.3
TOTALS	52	100.0	14	100.0	21	100.0	87	100.0

Table 11: Phoneme [k]

AGE:	UNDER 6		UNKNOWN		6 OR OVER		ALL	
SPELLING	FREQ	PCT	FREQ	PCT	FREQ	PCT	FREQ	PCT
C	131	45.6	77	55.8	78	35.5	286	44.3
K	112	39.0	41	29.7	107	48.6	260	40.3
(OMIT)	10	3.5	4	2.9	4	1.8	18	2.8
X	5	1.7	4	2.9	0	0.0	9	1.4
QH	5	1.7	0	0.0	0	0.0	5	0.8
CH	3	1.0	0	0.0	1	0.5	4	0.6
G	3	1.0	2	1.4	1	0.5	6	0.9
CG	3	1.0	0	0.0	0	0.0	3	0.5
CK	3	1.0	5	3.6	12	5.5	20	3.1
CE	2	0.7	1	0.7	9	4.1	12	1.9
KC	2	0.7	0	0.0	2	0.9	4	0.6
Q	2	0.7	0	0.0	4	1.8	6	0.9
KCE	1	0.3	0	0.0	0	0.0	1	0.2
KE	1	0.3	2	1.4	1	0.5	4	0.6
LK	1	0.3	0	0.0	0	0.0	1	0.2
CKE	1	0.3	0	0.0	1	0.5	2	0.3
CT	1	0.3	0	0.0	0	0.0	1	0.2
TC	1	0.3	0	0.0	0	0.0	1	0.2
L	0	0.0	2	1.4	0	0.0	2	0.3
TOTALS	287	100.0	138	100.0	220	100.0	645	100.0

Table 12: Phoneme [l]

AGE:	UNDER 6		UNKNOWN		6 OR OVER		ALL	
SPELLING	FREQ	PCT	FREQ	PCT	FREQ	PCT	FREQ	PCT
L	233	78.7	157	88.2	167	81.5	557	82.0
(OMIT)	28	9.5	4	2.2	2	1.0	34	5.0
LL	21	7.1	3	1.7	20	9.8	44	6.5
LE	4	1.4	2	1.1	6	2.9	12	1.8
E	3	1.0	6	3.4	2	1.0	11	1.6
LA	2	0.7	0	0.0	0	0.0	2	0.3
C	1	0.3	0	0.0	2	1.0	3	0.4
Y	1	0.3	0	0.0	0	0.0	1	0.1
H	1	0.3	0	0.0	0	0.0	1	0.1
AL	1	0.3	5	2.8	0	0.0	6	0.9
LLE	1	0.3	0	0.0	0	0.0	1	0.1
T	0	0.0	0	0.0	1	0.5	1	0.1
LER	0	0.0	1	0.6	0	0.0	1	0.1
OL	0	0.0	0	0.0	4	2.0	4	0.6
UL	0	0.0	0	0.0	1	0.5	1	0.1
TOTALS	296	100.0	178	100.0	205	100.0	679	100.0

APPENDIX A

Table 13: Phoneme [m]

AGE: SPELLING	UNDER 6 FREQ	PCT	UNKNOWN FREQ	PCT	6 OR OVER FREQ	PCT	ALL FREQ	PCT
M	179	90.9	63	82.9	118	88.1	360	88.5
(OMIT)	7	3.6	6	7.9	0	0.0	13	3.2
N	3	1.5	1	1.3	3	2.2	7	1.7
ME	2	1.0	4	5.3	3	2.2	9	2.2
MM	2	1.0	2	2.6	9	6.7	13	3.2
L	1	0.5	0	0.0	0	0.0	1	0.2
MB	1	0.5	0	0.0	0	0.0	1	0.2
MA	1	0.5	0	0.0	0	0.0	1	0.2
MN	1	0.5	0	0.0	0	0.0	1	0.2
MP	0	0.0	0	0.0	1	0.7	1	0.2
TOTALS	197	100.0	76	100.0	134	100.0	407	100.0

Table 14: Phoneme [n]

AGE: SPELLING	UNDER 6 FREQ	PCT	UNKNOWN FREQ	PCT	6 OR OVER FREQ	PCT	ALL FREQ	PCT
N	345	84.1	178	84.0	232	87.9	755	85.2
(OMIT)	50	12.2	16	7.5	16	6.1	82	9.3
NE	6	1.5	4	1.9	10	3.8	20	2.3
M	4	1.0	2	0.9	1	0.4	7	0.8
T	1	0.2	1	0.5	0	0.0	2	0.2
EN	1	0.2	0	0.0	0	0.0	1	0.1
NA	1	0.2	0	0.0	0	0.0	1	0.1
DN	1	0.2	1	0.5	0	0.0	2	0.2
GN	1	0.2	0	0.0	0	0.0	1	0.1
S	0	0.0	0	0.0	1	0.4	1	0.1
D	0	0.0	2	0.9	0	0.0	2	0.2
X	0	0.0	1	0.5	0	0.0	1	0.1
ND	0	0.0	3	1.4	0	0.0	3	0.3
NN	0	0.0	3	1.4	1	0.4	4	0.5
KN	0	0.0	0	0.0	1	0.4	1	0.1
NEAN	0	0.0	1	0.5	0	0.0	1	0.1
ENE	0	0.0	0	0.0	1	0.4	1	0.1
NY	0	0.0	0	0.0	1	0.4	1	0.1
TOTALS	410	100.0	212	100.0	264	100.0	886	100.0

162

APPENDIX A

Table 15: Phoneme [o]

AGE:	UNDER 6		UNKNCWN		6 OR OVER		ALL	
SPELLING	FREQ	PCT	FREQ	PCT	FREQ	PCT	FREQ	PCT
O	84	77.1	39	61.9	48	64.9	171	69.5
(OMIT)	5	4.6	1	1.6	3	4.1	9	3.7
OO	5	4.6	1	1.6	0	0.0	6	2.4
OW	4	3.7	18	28.6	7	9.5	29	11.8
OE	3	2.8	1	1.6	3	4.1	7	2.8
OU	2	1.8	0	0.0	2	2.7	4	1.6
A	1	0.9	1	1.6	1	1.4	3	1.2
U	1	0.9	0	0.0	3	4.1	4	1.6
L	1	0.9	0	0.0	0	0.0	1	0.4
IOW	1	0.9	0	0.0	0	0.0	1	0.4
OH	1	0.9	0	0.0	0	0.0	1	0.4
EW	1	0.9	0	0.0	0	0.0	1	0.4
E	0	0.0	0	0.0	2	2.7	2	0.8
OA	0	0.0	2	3.2	1	1.4	3	1.2
AC	0	0.0	0	0.0	1	1.4	1	0.4
OWE	0	0.0	0	0.0	2	2.7	2	0.8
EO	0	0.0	0	0.0	1	1.4	1	0.4
TCTALS	109	100.0	63	100.0	74	100.0	246	100.0

Table 16: Phoneme [p]

AGE:	UNDER 6		UNKNCWN		6 OR OVER		ALL	
SPELLING	FREQ	PCT	FREQ	PCT	FREQ	PCT	FREQ	PCT
P	132	93.0	109	96.5	99	90.0	340	93.2
(OMIT)	3	2.1	1	0.9	4	3.6	8	2.2
B	3	2.1	0	0.0	2	1.8	5	1.4
PP	3	2.1	0	0.0	1	0.9	4	1.1
PE	1	0.7	2	1.8	3	2.7	6	1.6
T	0	0.0	0	0.0	1	0.9	1	0.3
MP	0	0.0	1	0.9	0	0.0	1	0.3
TCTALS	142	100.0	113	100.0	110	100.0	365	100.0

Table 17: Phoneme [ʌ] not /_r

AGE:	UNDER 6		UNKNOWN		6 OR OVER		ALL	
SPELLING	FREQ	PCT	FREQ	PCT	FREQ	PCT	FREQ	PCT
U	65	45.8	32	44.4	40	33.6	137	41.1
O	43	30.3	26	36.1	45	37.8	114	34.2
A	12	8.5	2	2.8	19	16.0	33	9.9
I	9	6.3	5	6.9	1	0.8	15	4.5
(OMIT)	7	4.9	3	4.2	2	1.7	12	3.6
E	3	2.1	1	1.4	2	1.7	6	1.8
NI	1	0.7	0	0.0	0	0.0	1	0.3
W	1	0.7	3	4.2	1	0.8	5	1.5
Y	1	0.7	0	0.0	0	0.0	1	0.3
AA	0	0.0	0	0.0	1	0.8	1	0.3
N	0	0.0	0	0.0	1	0.8	1	0.3
AE	0	0.0	0	0.0	1	0.8	1	0.3
OUI	0	0.0	0	0.0	1	0.8	1	0.3
OU	0	0.0	0	0.0	2	1.7	2	0.6
UE	0	0.0	0	0.0	1	0.8	1	0.3
OO	0	0.0	0	0.0	1	0.8	1	0.3
M	0	0.0	0	0.0	1	0.8	1	0.3
TOTALS	142	100.0	72	100.0	119	100.0	333	100.0

Table 17a: Phoneme [ʌ]

AGE:	UNDER 6		UNKNOWN		6 OR OVER		ALL	
SPELLING	FREQ	PCT	FREQ	PCT	FREQ	PCT	FREQ	PCT
U	67	33.0	32	35.6	50	32.1	149	33.2
(OMIT)	53	26.1	9	10.0	11	7.1	73	16.3
O	46	22.7	26	28.9	49	31.4	121	26.9
I	15	7.4	11	12.2	4	2.6	30	6.7
A	12	5.9	4	4.4	20	12.8	36	8.0
E	6	3.0	4	4.4	12	7.7	22	4.9
W	1	0.5	3	3.3	1	0.6	5	1.1
R	1	0.5	0	0.0	0	0.0	1	0.2
Y	1	0.5	0	0.0	0	0.0	1	0.2
NI	1	0.5	0	0.0	0	0.0	1	0.2
N	0	0.0	0	0.0	1	0.6	1	0.2
M	0	0.0	0	0.0	1	0.6	1	0.2
AE	0	0.0	0	0.0	1	0.6	1	0.2
IE	0	0.0	1	1.1	0	0.0	1	0.2
OO	0	0.0	0	0.0	1	0.6	1	0.2
OU	0	0.0	0	0.0	2	1.3	2	0.4
AA	0	0.0	0	0.0	1	0.6	1	0.2
UE	0	0.0	0	0.0	1	0.6	1	0.2
OUI	0	0.0	0	0.0	1	0.6	1	0.2
TOTALS	203	100.0	90	100.0	156	100.0	449	100.0

Table 18: Phoneme [r]

AGE:	UNDER 6		UNKNCWN		6 OR OVER		ALL	
SPELLING	FREQ	PCT	FREQ	PCT	FREQ	PCT	FREQ	PCT
R	437	88.8	206	91.2	254	87.6	897	89.0
(OMIT)	42	8.5	12	5.3	10	3.4	64	6.3
L	2	C.4	C	0.0	0	C.0	2	0.2
RR	2	C.4	0	0.C	2	C.7	4	0.4
ER	2	C.4	0	0.0	1	0.3	3	0.3
T	1	0.2	0	0.C	1	C.3	2	0.2
B	1	C.2	0	0.0	0	C.0	1	0.1
RE	1	C.2	5	2.2	19	6.6	25	2.5
'	1	C.2	0	0.0	0	C.C	1	0.1
WR	1	C.2	0	0.0	0	0.0	1	0.1
RU	1	C.2	C	0.C	C	C.C	1	0.1
RER	1	0.2	0	0.0	0	C.C	1	C.1
I	0	0.C	0	0.0	1	0.3	1	0.1
W	0	C.C	0	0.0	2	C.7	2	0.2
N	0	0.0	3	1.3	0	0.0	3	0.3
TOTALS	492	10C.C	226	100.0	290	100.C	1008	100.0

Table 19: Phoneme [s]

AGE:	UNDER 6		UNKNCWN		6 OR CVER		ALL	
SPELLING	FREQ	PCT	FREQ	PCT	FREQ	PCT	FREQ	PCT
S	270	85.7	152	88.4	192	87.7	614	87.0
C	11	3.5	5	2.9	3	1.4	19	2.7
SE	11	3.5	6	3.5	10	4.6	27	3.8
(OMIT)	8	2.5	3	1.7	2	0.9	13	1.8
SS	7	2.2	1	0.6	5	2.3	13	1.8
ES	2	C.6	1	0.6	2	C.9	5	0.7
E	1	C.3	C	0.0	0	C.0	1	0.1
M	1	0.3	0	0.0	0	C.0	1	0.1
X	1	C.3	0	0.C	0	0.0	1	0.1
SH	1	C.3	0	0.0	0	0.0	1	0.1
SC	1	C.3	0	0.C	0	C.C	1	0.1
SU	1	0.3	0	0.0	0	0.0	1	0.1
O	0	C.C	0	0.0	1	C.5	1	0.1
CF	0	C.C	1	0.6	0	C.0	1	0.1
CC	0	C.C	3	1.7	0	0.0	3	0.4
SU	C	C.C	0	0.0	3	1.4	3	0.4
SSE	0	0.0	0	0.0	1	0.5	1	0.1
TOTALS	315	100.C	172	100.0	219	100.0	706	100.0

Table 20: Phoneme [t]

AGE:	UNDER 6		UNKNCWN		6 OR CVER		ALL	
SPELLING	FREQ	PCT	FREQ	PCT	FREQ	PCT	FREQ	PCT
T	292	83.4	119	80.4	210	84.7	621	83.2
(OMIT)	24	6.9	7	4.7	10	4.0	41	5.5
TE	11	3.1	9	6.1	13	5.2	33	4.4
D	8	2.3	7	4.7	4	1.6	19	2.5
TT	5	1.4	1	0.7	4	1.6	10	1.3
CH	4	1.1	2	1.4	1	0.4	7	0.9
N	1	0.3	0	0.0	0	0.0	1	0.1
R	1	0.3	0	0.0	0	0.0	1	0.1
H	1	0.3	0	0.0	0	0.0	1	0.1
ED	1	0.3	1	0.7	2	0.8	4	0.5
IT	1	0.3	0	0.0	0	0.0	1	0.1
TI	1	0.3	0	0.0	0	0.0	1	0.1
M	0	0.0	1	0.7	0	0.0	1	0.1
C	0	0.0	1	0.7	0	0.0	1	0.1
TU	0	0.0	0	0.0	1	0.4	1	0.1
ET	0	0.0	0	0.0	2	0.8	2	0.3
TED	0	0.0	0	0.0	1	0.4	1	0.1
TCTALS	350	100.0	148	100.0	248	100.0	746	100.0

Table 21: Phoneme [u]

AGE:	UNDER 6		UNKNCWN		6 OR CVER		ALL	
SPELLING	FREQ	PCT	FREQ	PCT	FREQ	PCT	FREQ	PCT
U	28	35.4	4	14.3	4	12.5	36	25.9
OC	20	25.3	8	28.6	14	43.8	42	30.2
O	10	12.7	7	25.0	6	18.8	23	16.5
(OMIT)	5	6.3	0	0.0	0	0.0	5	3.6
OW	5	6.3	2	7.1	3	9.4	10	7.2
W	2	2.5	0	0.0	0	0.0	2	1.4
CE	2	2.5	0	0.0	0	0.0	2	1.4
OU	2	2.5	0	0.0	1	3.1	3	2.2
E	1	1.3	0	0.0	0	0.0	1	0.7
EOW	1	1.3	1	3.6	0	0.0	2	1.4
UC	1	1.3	0	0.0	1	3.1	2	1.4
AW	1	1.3	0	0.0	0	0.0	1	0.7
LLW	1	1.3	0	0.0	0	0.0	1	0.7
D	0	0.0	0	0.0	1	3.1	1	0.7
ICW	0	0.0	3	10.7	0	0.0	3	2.2
AC	0	0.0	1	3.6	0	0.0	1	0.7
OCW	0	0.0	0	0.0	1	3.1	1	0.7
OCO	0	0.0	0	0.0	1	3.1	1	0.7
UCO	0	0.0	2	7.1	0	0.0	2	1.4
TCTALS	79	100.0	28	100.0	32	100.0	139	100.0

Table 22: Phoneme [v]

AGE:	UNDER 6		UNKNCWN		6 OR OVER		ALL	
SPELLING	FREQ	PCT	FREQ	PCT	FREQ	PCT	FREQ	PCT
V	71	95.9	28	77.8	48	94.1	147	91.3
(OMIT)	1	1.4	1	2.8	1	2.0	3	1.9
W	1	1.4	0	0.C	0	C.C	1	0.6
FC	1	1.4	0	0.C	0	.0.0	1	0.6
F	0	C.C	1	2.8	1	2.0	2	1.2
FF	0	C.C	1	2.8	0	0.C	1	0.6
VF	0	C.0	5	13.9	1	2.C	6	3.7
TCTALS	74	1CC.C	36	100.0	51	1CC.0	161	100.0

Table 23: Phoneme [w]

AGE:	UNDER 6		UNKNCWN		6 OR OVER		ALL	
SPELLING	FREQ	PCT	FREQ	PCT	FREQ	PCT	FREQ	PCT
W	142	94.C	48	90.6	117	91.4	307	92.5
WH	3	2.C	2	3.8	4	3.1	9	2.7
(OMIT)	2	1.3	2	3.8	6	4.7	10	3.0
Y	2	1.3	1	1.9	0	0.0	3	0.9
E	1	0.7	0	0.0	0	C.C	1	0.3
U	1	C.7	0	0.0	1	0.8	2	0.6
TOTALS	151	1CC.C	53	100.0	128	1C0.0	332	100.0

Table 24: Phoneme [y]

AGE:	UNDER 6		UNKNCWN		6 OR OVER		ALL	
SPELLING	FREQ	FCT	FREQ	PCT	FREQ	PCT	FREQ	PCT
(OMIT)	24	60.C	7	41.2	5	33.3	36	50.0
Y	14	35.0	8	47.1	8	53.3	30	41.7
E	1	2.5	0	0.0	0	0.0	1	1.4
U	1	2.5	2	11.8	0	0.0	3	4.2
C	0	C.0	0	0.0	2	13.3	2	2.8
TCTALS	40	1CC.C	17	100.0	15	100.0	72	100.0

Table 25: Phoneme [z]

AGE:	UNDER 6		UNKNOWN		6 OR OVER		ALL	
SPELLING	FREQ	PCT	FREQ	PCT	FREQ	PCT	FREQ	PCT
S	92	82.1	59	72.0	88	85.4	239	80.5
Z	5	4.5	6	7.3	0	0.0	11	3.7
(OMIT)	3	2.7	0	0.0	2	1.9	5	1.7
SE	3	2.7	10	12.2	8	7.8	21	7.1
ES	2	1.8	2	2.4	3	2.9	7	2.4
C	1	0.9	3	3.7	0	0.0	4	1.3
IS	1	0.9	0	0.0	0	0.0	1	0.3
X	1	0.9	0	0.0	0	0.0	1	0.3
ZS	1	0.9	0	0.0	0	0.0	1	0.3
SES	1	0.9	0	0.0	0	0.0	1	0.3
ZCS	1	0.9	0	0.0	0	0.0	1	0.3
SU	1	0.9	0	0.0	0	0.0	1	0.3
SS	0	0.0	2	2.4	1	1.0	3	1.0
ESE	0	0.0	0	0.0	1	1.0	1	0.3
TOTALS	112	100.0	82	100.0	103	100.0	297	100.0

Table 26: Phoneme [i]

AGE:	UNDER 6		UNKNOWN		6 OR OVER		ALL	
SPELLING	FREQ	PCT	FREQ	PCT	FREQ	PCT	FREQ	PCT
E	100	46.5	59	38.8	62	48.4	221	44.6
Y	36	16.7	43	28.3	34	26.6	113	22.8
(OMIT)	17	7.9	9	5.9	3	2.3	29	5.9
I	16	7.4	9	5.9	10	7.8	35	7.1
EY	14	6.5	2	1.3	1	0.8	17	3.4
AY	11	5.1	5	3.3	0	0.0	16	3.2
EE	10	4.7	11	7.2	5	3.9	26	5.3
A	5	2.3	0	0.0	1	0.8	6	1.2
EA	2	0.9	3	2.0	4	3.1	9	1.8
EI	1	0.5	0	0.0	0	0.0	1	0.2
IE	1	0.5	4	2.6	4	3.1	9	1.8
IEE	1	0.5	1	0.7	0	0.0	2	0.4
EYI	1	0.5	0	0.0	0	0.0	1	0.2
OY	0	0.0	4	2.6	0	0.0	4	0.8
IEY	0	0.0	1	0.7	0	0.0	1	0.2
AS	0	0.0	0	0.0	1	0.8	1	0.2
UE	0	0.0	0	0.0	1	0.8	1	0.2
YE	0	0.0	0	0.0	2	1.6	2	0.4
EAE	0	0.0	1	0.7	0	0.0	1	0.2
TOTALS	215	100.0	152	100.0	128	100.0	495	100.0

Table 27: Phoneme [e]

AGE:	UNDER 6		UNKNOWN		6 OR OVER		ALL	
SPELLING	FREQ	PCT	FREQ	PCT	FREQ	PCT	FREQ	PCT
A	87	73.7	48	57.1	56	71.8	191	68.2
AY	13	11.0	14	16.7	2	2.6	29	10.4
AE	4	3.4	2	2.4	6	7.7	12	4.3
E	3	2.5	6	7.1	2	2.6	11	3.9
AI	3	2.5	3	3.6	3	3.8	9	3.2
(OMIT)	2	1.7	4	4.8	1	1.3	7	2.5
EY	2	1.7	2	2.4	0	0.0	4	1.4
Y	1	0.8	2	2.4	4	5.1	7	2.5
AUY	1	0.8	0	0.0	0	0.0	1	0.4
OL	1	0.8	0	0.0	0	0.0	1	0.4
EEA	1	0.8	0	0.0	0	0.0	1	0.4
EE	0	0.0	1	1.2	1	1.3	2	0.7
EA	0	0.0	0	0.0	1	1.3	1	0.4
EAY	0	0.0	1	1.2	0	0.0	1	0.4
ALE	0	0.0	0	0.0	2	2.6	2	0.7
AL	0	0.0	1	1.2	0	0.0	1	0.4
TOTALS	118	100.0	84	100.0	78	100.0	280	100.0

Table 28: Phoneme [ə]

AGE:	UNDER 6		UNKNOWN		6 OR OVER		ALL	
SPELLING	FREQ	PCT	FREQ	PCT	FREQ	PCT	FREQ	PCT
(OMIT)	171	37.3	83	34.4	97	31.0	351	34.7
I	94	20.5	42	17.4	68	21.7	204	20.2
E	73	15.9	40	16.6	76	24.3	189	18.7
O	42	9.2	10	4.1	19	6.1	71	7.0
A	35	7.6	35	14.5	33	10.5	103	10.2
U	32	7.0	19	7.9	15	4.8	66	6.5
L	3	0.7	6	2.5	2	0.6	11	1.1
R	2	0.4	0	0.0	0	0.0	2	0.2
OE	2	0.4	0	0.0	0	0.0	2	0.2
N	1	0.2	1	0.4	0	0.0	2	0.2
EI	1	0.2	0	0.0	1	0.3	2	0.2
AI	1	0.2	0	0.0	0	0.0	1	0.1
RL	1	0.2	0	0.0	0	0.0	1	0.1
Y	0	0.0	1	0.4	0	0.0	1	0.1
DE	0	0.0	1	0.4	0	0.0	1	0.1
EE	0	0.0	2	0.8	0	0.0	2	0.2
OU	0	0.0	1	0.4	0	0.0	1	0.1
AP	0	0.0	0	0.0	1	0.3	1	0.1
EO	0	0.0	0	0.0	1	0.3	1	0.1
TOTALS	458	100.0	241	100.0	313	100.0	1012	100.0

Table 28a: Phoneme [ə] not /_r

AGE:	UNDER 6		UNKNOWN		6 OR OVER		ALL	
SPELLING	FREQ	PCT	FREQ	PCT	FREQ	PCT	FREQ	PCT
(OMIT)	86	28.6	37	24.0	45	19.7	168	24.6
I	83	27.6	32	20.8	67	29.4	182	26.6
E	39	13.0	29	18.8	58	25.4	126	18.4
O	34	11.3	7	4.5	17	7.5	58	8.5
A	26	8.6	22	14.3	27	11.8	75	11.0
U	25	8.3	16	10.4	9	3.9	50	7.3
L	3	1.0	6	3.9	2	0.9	11	1.6
EI	1	0.3	0	0.0	1	0.4	2	0.3
RL	1	0.3	0	0.0	C	0.0	1	0.1
AI	1	0.3	0	0.0	C	0.0	1	0.1
N	1	0.3	0	0.0	0	0.0	1	0.1
R	1	0.3	0	0.0	C	0.0	1	0.1
Y	0	0.0	1	0.6	0	0.0	1	0.1
AP	0	0.0	0	0.0	1	0.4	1	0.1
OU	0	0.0	1	0.6	C	0.0	1	0.1
EE	0	0.0	2	1.3	0	0.0	2	0.3
EO	C	0.0	0	0.0	1	0.4	1	0.1
DE	0	0.0	1	0.6	C	0.0	1	0.1
TOTALS	301	100.0	154	100.0	228	100.0	683	100.0

Table 29: Phoneme [ɔ]

AGE:	UNDER 6		UNKNCWN		6 OR CVER		ALL	
SPELLING	FREQ	PCT	FREQ	PCT	FREQ	PCT	FREQ	PCT
O	35	68.6	25	73.5	26	66.7	86	69.4
A	8	15.7	3	8.8	3	7.7	14	11.3
UO	2	3.9	4	11.8	0	0.0	6	4.8
E	1	2.C	0	0.C	0	C.0	1	0.8
U	1	2.0	1	2.9	0	0.0	2	1.6
(OMIT)	1	2.0	C	0.C	C	C.0	1	0.8
CW	1	2.C	0	0.0	C	0.0	1	0.8
OE	1	2.C	0	0.0	0	C.0	1	0.8
OO	1	2.C	C	0.0	0	C.0	1	0.8
AI	0	0.0	0	0.0	1	2.6	1	0.8
OU	0	C.C	0	0.0	2	5.1	2	1.6
AW	0	0.0	0	0.0	1	2.6	1	0.8
OA	0	0.0	0	0.0	1	2.6	1	0.8
AL	0	C.C	0	0.C	2	5.1	2	1.6
CL	0	0.0	0	0.C	1	2.6	1	0.8
ALE	0	C.C	0	0.0	1	2.6	1	0.8
AU	0	C.C	0	0.C	1	2.6	1	0.8
AR	0	0.C	1	2.9	0	0.0	1	0.8
TOTALS	51	1CC.C	34	1CO.0	39	100.0	124	100.0

Table 30: Phoneme [ʊ]

AGE:	UNDER 6		UNKNOWN		6 OR OVER		ALL	
SPELLING	FREQ	PCT	FREQ	PCT	FREQ	PCT	FREQ	PCT
U	9	39.1	3	23.1	9	22.5	21	27.6
O	4	17.4	3	23.1	12	30.0	19	25.0
(OMIT)	3	13.0	1	7.7	0	C.0	4	5.3
OC	3	13.0	3	23.1	15	37.5	21	27.6
E	1	4.3	0	0.0	0	C.0	1	1.3
K	1	4.3	0	0.0	0	0.0	1	1.3
OY	1	4.3	0	0.0	0	0.0	1	1.3
OOA	1	4.3	0	0.0	0	C.0	1	1.3
UO	0	C.0	0	0.0	1	2.5	1	1.3
OG	0	C.0	2	15.4	0	C.0	2	2.6
OU	0	C.0	1	7.7	1	2.5	2	2.6
AW	0	0.0	0	0.0	1	2.5	1	1.3
OUL	0	C.0	0	0.0	1	2.5	1	1.3
TOTALS	23	100.0	13	100.0	40	100.0	76	100.0

Table 31: Phoneme [aw]

AGE:	UNDER 6		UNKNOWN		6 OR OVER		ALL	
SPELLING	FREQ	PCT	FREQ	PCT	FREQ	PCT	FREQ	PCT
AOO	9	22.5	0	0.0	0	0.0	9	10.6
AW	8	20.0	0	0.0	1	4.2	9	10.6
O	7	17.5	9	42.9	2	8.3	18	21.2
OU	3	7.5	0	0.0	3	12.5	6	7.1
AO	3	7.5	0	0.0	0	C.0	3	3.5
U	1	2.5	0	0.0	1	4.2	2	2.4
OW	1	2.5	5	23.8	3	12.5	9	10.6
OE	1	2.5	0	0.0	1	4.2	2	2.4
AOW	1	2.5	3	14.3	1	4.2	5	5.9
OA	1	2.5	0	0.0	0	C.0	1	1.2
AWE	1	2.5	0	0.0	0	0.0	1	1.2
OOW	1	2.5	0	0.0	0	C.0	1	1.2
OUO	1	2.5	0	0.0	0	0.0	1	1.2
UCO	1	2.5	0	0.0	0	0.0	1	1.2
ECEY	1	2.5	0	0.0	0	C.0	1	1.2
A	0	0.0	3	14.3	4	16.7	7	8.2
E	0	C.0	1	4.8	0	C.0	1	1.2
OC	0	0.0	0	0.0	1	4.2	1	1.2
OLE	0	C.0	0	0.0	4	16.7	4	4.7
WW	0	C.0	0	0.0	1	4.2	1	1.2
OUW	0	C.0	0	0.0	1	4.2	1	1.2
HOWE	0	C.0	0	0.0	1	4.2	1	1.2
TOTALS	40	100.0	21	100.0	24	100.0	85	100.0

Table 32: Phoneme [θ]

AGE:	UNDER 6		UNKNOWN		6 OR OVER		ALL	
SPELLING	FREQ	PCT	FREQ	PCT	FREQ	PCT	FREQ	PCT
TH	26	68.4	8	80.0	23	100.0	57	80.3
T	9	23.7	1	10.0	0	0.0	10	14.1
F	2	5.3	0	0.0	0	0.0	2	2.8
(OMIT)	1	2.6	0	0.0	0	0.0	1	1.4
H	0	0.0	1	10.0	0	0.0	1	1.4
TOTALS	38	100.0	10	100.0	23	100.0	71	100.0

Table 33: Phoneme [ð]

AGE:	UNDER 6		UNKNOWN		6 OR OVER		ALL	
SPELLING	FREQ	PCT	FREQ	PCT	FREQ	PCT	FREQ	PCT
TH	67	82.7	40	87.0	55	90.2	162	86.2
T	12	14.8	4	8.7	5	8.2	21	11.2
(OMIT)	1	1.2	0	0.0	1	1.6	2	1.1
V	1	1.2	0	0.0	0	0.0	1	0.5
D	0	0.0	2	4.3	0	0.0	2	1.1
TOTALS	81	100.0	46	100.0	61	100.0	138	100.0

Table 34: Phoneme [ŋ]

AGE:	UNDER 6		UNKNOWN		6 OR OVER		ALL	
SPELLING	FREQ	PCT	FREQ	PCT	FREQ	PCT	FREQ	PCT
N	33	37.5	9	18.7	8	13.1	50	25.4
G	23	26.1	9	18.7	3	4.9	35	17.8
(OMIT)	19	21.6	6	12.5	10	16.4	35	17.8
NG	11	12.5	19	39.6	37	60.7	67	34.0
V	1	1.1	0	0.0	0	0.0	1	0.5
DE	1	1.1	1	2.1	0	0.0	2	1.0
NE	0	0.0	0	0.0	1	1.6	1	0.5
LIN	0	0.0	1	2.1	0	0.0	1	0.5
GN	0	0.0	2	4.2	1	1.6	3	1.5
NIN	0	0.0	0	0.0	1	1.6	1	0.5
NGE	0	0.0	1	2.1	0	0.0	1	0.5
TOTALS	88	100.0	48	100.0	61	100.0	197	100.0

Table 35: Phoneme [æ]

AGE:	UNDER 6		UNKNOWN		6 OR OVER		ALL	
SPELLING	FREQ	PCT	FREQ	PCT	FREQ	PCT	FREQ	PCT
A	139	89.7	67	77.9	78	94.0	284	87.7
(OMIT)	6	3.9	3	3.5	1	1.2	10	3.1
E	4	2.6	15	17.4	2	2.4	21	6.5
O	3	1.9	0	0.0	0	0.0	3	0.9
AE	1	0.6	0	0.0	0	0.0	1	0.3
AI	1	0.6	0	0.0	1	1.2	2	0.6
UA	1	0.6	0	0.0	0	0.0	1	0.3
I	0	0.0	1	1.2	0	0.0	1	0.3
AA	0	0.0	0	0.0	1	1.2	1	0.3
TOTALS	155	100.0	86	100.0	83	100.0	324	100.0

Table 36: Phoneme [ay]

AGE:	UNDER 6		UNKNOWN		6 OR OVER		ALL	
SPELLING	FREQ	PCT	FREQ	PCT	FREQ	PCT	FREQ	PCT
I	85	78.7	37	75.5	54	77.1	176	77.5
AY	7	6.5	0	0.0	0	0.0	7	3.1
Y	2	1.9	1	2.0	1	1.4	4	1.8
EI	2	1.9	0	0.0	0	0.0	2	0.9
IE	2	1.9	5	10.2	8	11.4	15	6.6
IY	2	1.9	1	2.0	1	1.4	4	1.8
UY	2	1.9	0	0.0	0	0.0	2	0.9
A	1	0.9	0	0.0	0	0.0	1	0.4
E	1	0.9	0	0.0	0	0.0	1	0.4
U	1	0.9	1	2.0	0	0.0	2	0.9
AIY	1	0.9	0	0.0	0	0.0	1	0.4
OY	1	0.9	0	0.0	0	0.0	1	0.4
UYE	1	0.9	0	0.0	0	0.0	1	0.4
(OMIT)	0	0.0	1	2.0	2	2.9	3	1.3
EY	0	0.0	0	0.0	1	1.4	1	0.4
IS	0	0.0	1	2.0	0	0.0	1	0.4
AI	0	0.0	0	0.0	2	2.9	2	0.9
IFY	0	0.0	1	2.0	0	0.0	1	0.4
IYE	0	0.0	0	0.0	1	1.4	1	0.4
EYF	0	0.0	1	2.0	0	0.0	1	0.4
TOTALS	108	100.0	49	100.0	70	100.0	227	100.0

Table 37: Phoneme [ɔy]

AGE:	UNDER 6		UNKNOWN		6 OR OVER		ALL	
SPELLING	FREQ	PCT	FREQ	PCT	FREQ	PCT	FREQ	PCT
O	1	50.0	0	0.0	0	0.0	1	33.3
OE	1	50.0	1	100.0	0	0.0	2	66.7
TOTALS	2	100.0	1	100.0	0	100.0	3	100.0

Table 38: Phoneme [š]

AGE:	UNDER 6		UNKNOWN		6 OR OVER		ALL	
SPELLING	FREQ	PCT	FREQ	PCT	FREQ	PCT	FREQ	PCT
SH	16	42.1	8	50.0	20	69.0	44	53.0
S	7	18.4	7	43.8	2	6.9	16	19.3
H	4	10.5	0	0.0	0	0.0	4	4.8
CH	2	5.3	0	0.0	2	6.9	4	4.8
HC	2	5.3	0	0.0	0	0.0	2	2.4
TI	2	5.3	0	0.0	1	3.4	3	3.6
(OMIT)	1	2.6	0	0.0	0	0.0	1	1.2
SC	1	2.6	0	0.0	0	0.0	1	1.2
ND	1	2.6	0	0.0	0	0.0	1	1.2
HS	1	2.6	0	0.0	0	0.0	1	1.2
SHT	1	2.6	0	0.0	0	0.0	1	1.2
TH	0	0.0	0	0.0	3	10.3	3	3.6
TT	0	0.0	0	0.0	1	3.4	1	1.2
SCH	0	0.0	1	6.3	0	0.0	1	1.2
TOTALS	38	100.0	16	100.0	29	100.0	83	100.0

Table 39: Phoneme [ž]

AGE:	UNDER 6		UNKNOWN		6 OR OVER		ALL	
SPELLING	FREQ	PCT	FREQ	PCT	FREQ	PCT	FREQ	PCT
SH	0	0.0	0	0.0	1	100.0	1	100.0
TOTALS	0	100.0	0	100.0	1	100.0	1	100.0

Table 40: Phoneme [yu]

AGE:	UNDER 6		UNKNOWN		6 OR OVER		ALL	
SPELLING	FREQ	PCT	FREQ	PCT	FREQ	PCT	FREQ	PCT
ə/U	20	71.4	3	42.9	2	33.3	25	61.0
Y/OO	4	14.3	0	0.0	0	0.0	4	9.8
Y/U	1	3.6	1	14.3	0	0.0	2	4.9
ə/ə	1	3.6	0	0.0	0	0.0	1	2.4
ə/E	1	3.6	0	0.0	0	0.0	1	2.4
ə/AW	1	3.6	0	0.0	0	0.0	1	2.4
O/U	0	0.0	0	0.0	1	16.7	1	2.4
ə/O	0	0.0	0	0.0	1	16.7	1	2.4
O/O	0	0.0	0	0.0	1	16.7	1	2.4
ə/UOO	0	0.0	2	28.6	0	0.0	2	4.9
Y/O	0	0.0	1	14.3	0	0.0	1	2.4
Y/OU	0	0.0	0	0.0	1	16.7	1	2.4
TOTALS	28	100.0	7	100.0	6	100.0	41	100.0

APPENDIX B: SCHWA [ə] BEFORE LIQUIDS AND NASALS

Table 1: Phonemes [ə]

AGE:	UNDER 6		UNKNOWN		6 OR OVER		ALL	
SPELLING	FREQ	PCT	FREQ	PCT	FREQ	PCT	FREQ	PCT
ə/R	75	59.1	37	56.1	49	63.6	161	59.6
E/R	31	24.4	11	16.7	15	19.5	57	21.1
O/R	6	4.7	3	4.5	2	2.6	11	4.1
ə/ə	4	3.1	1	1.5	1	1.3	6	2.2
I/R	4	3.1	10	15.2	1	1.3	15	5.6
A/R	2	1.6	2	3.0	0	0.0	4	1.5
A/ə	2	1.6	1	1.5	0	0.0	3	1.1
R/B	1	0.8	0	0.0	0	0.0	1	0.4
E/ə	1	0.8	0	0.0	2	2.6	3	1.1
U/R	1	0.8	1	1.5	3	3.9	5	1.9
ə/T	0	0.0	0	0.0	1	1.3	1	0.4
E/I	0	0.0	0	0.0	1	1.3	1	0.4
U/RE	0	0.0	0	0.0	2	2.6	2	0.7
TOTALS	127	100.0	66	100.0	77	100.0	270	100.0

Table 2: Phonemes [əl]

AGE:	UNDER 6		UNKNOWN		6 OR OVER		ALL	
SPELLING	FREQ	PCT	FREQ	PCT	FREQ	PCT	FREQ	PCT
ə/L	22	41.5	14	32.6	21	47.7	57	40.7
ə/ə	5	9.4	1	2.3	0	0.0	6	4.3
E/L	4	7.5	6	14.0	6	13.6	16	11.4
O/L	4	7.5	2	4.7	4	9.1	10	7.1
O/ə	4	7.5	0	0.0	0	0.0	4	2.9
L/E	3	5.7	6	14.0	2	4.5	11	7.9
A/L	3	5.7	5	11.6	1	2.3	9	6.4
I/L	2	3.8	1	2.3	2	4.5	5	3.6
ə/LL	1	1.9	0	0.0	1	2.3	2	1.4
U/L	1	1.9	5	11.6	3	6.8	9	6.4
U/LE	1	1.9	1	2.3	0	0.0	2	1.4
A/LL	1	1.9	0	0.0	1	2.3	2	1.4
A/LE	1	1.9	0	0.0	0	0.0	1	0.7
R/L	1	1.9	0	0.0	0	0.0	1	0.7
ə/LER	0	0.0	1	2.3	0	0.0	1	0.7
E/LL	0	0.0	0	0.0	1	2.3	1	0.7
I/LL	0	0.0	0	0.0	1	2.3	1	0.7
OU/L	0	0.0	1	2.3	0	0.0	1	0.7
EO/L	0	0.0	0	0.0	1	2.3	1	0.7
TOTALS	53	100.0	43	100.0	44	100.0	140	100.0

174

Table 3: Phonemes [əm]

AGE:	UNDER 6		UNKNOWN		6 OR OVER		ALL	
SPELLING	FREQ	PCT	FREQ	PCT	FREQ	PCT	FREQ	PCT
ə/M	3	33.3	0	0.0	1	14.3	4	23.5
E/M	2	22.2	C	0.0	C	0.0	2	11.8
A/M	2	22.2	0	0.0	0	0.0	2	11.8
U/MB	1	11.1	0	0.0	C	0.0	1	5.9
U/M	1	11.1	0	0.0	C	0.0	1	5.9
I/M	0	0.0	0	0.0	4	57.1	4	23.5
O/M	C	0.0	1	100.0	2	28.6	3	17.6
TOTALS	9	100.0	1	100.0	7	100.0	17	100.0

Table 4: Phonemes [ən]

AGE:	UNDER 6		UNKNOWN		6 OR OVER		ALL	
SPELLING	FREQ	PCT	FREQ	PCT	FREC	PCT	FREQ	PCT
I/N	40	40.4	16	29.6	24	40.7	80	37.7
ə/N	19	19.2	6	11.1	11	18.6	36	17.0
O/N	12	12.1	3	5.6	3	5.1	18	8.5
E/N	9	9.1	8	14.8	11	18.6	28	13.2
U/N	6	6.1	6	11.1	1	1.7	13	6.1
ə/ə	5	5.1	2	3.7	1	1.7	8	3.8
A/N	3	3.0	3	5.6	3	5.1	9	4.2
I/ə	2	2.0	1	1.9	C	0.0	3	1.4
E/ə	1	1.0	1	1.9	C	0.0	2	0.9
I/T	1	1.0	0	0.0	C	0.0	1	0.5
N	1	1.0	0	0.0	C	0.0	1	0.5
Y/X	0	0.0	1	1.9	C	0.0	1	0.5
I/M	0	0.0	1	1.9	C	0.0	1	0.5
I/NE	0	0.0	0	0.0	1	1.7	1	0.5
A/NN	C	0.0	0	0.0	1	1.7	1	0.5
O/NE	0	0.0	0	0.0	2	3.4	2	0.9
ə/NE	0	0.0	1	1.9	C	0.0	1	0.5
A/ə	0	0.0	2	3.7	C	0.0	2	0.9
EI/N	0	0.0	C	0.0	1	1.7	1	0.5
N/T	0	0.0	1	1.9	C	0.0	1	0.5
DE/N	0	0.0	1	1.9	C	0.0	1	0.5
I/D	0	0.0	1	1.9	C	0.0	1	0.5
TOTALS	99	100.0	54	100.0	59	100.0	212	100.0

Table 5: Phonemes [əŋ]

AGE:	UNDER 6		UNKNOWN		6 OR OVER		ALL	
SPELLING	FREQ	PCT	FREQ	PCT	FREC	PCT	FREQ	PCT
TOTALS	0	100.0	0	100.0	C	100.0	0	100.0

APPENDIX C: [n] BEFORE OBSTRUENTS

Table 1: Phonemes [nt]

AGE:	UNDER 6		UNKNOWN		6 OR OVER		ALL	
SPELLING	FREQ	PCT	FREQ	PCT	FREQ	PCT	FREQ	PCT
N/T	30	44.8	19	54.3	39	75.0	88	57.1
ə/T	19	28.4	8	22.9	7	13.5	34	22.1
N/ə	9	13.4	0	0.0	2	3.8	11	7.1
ə/ə	4	6.0	2	5.7	1	1.9	7	4.5
N/TE	2	3.0	0	0.0	1	1.9	3	1.9
N/D	1	1.5	1	2.9	1	1.9	3	1.9
T/IT	1	1.5	0	0.0	0	0.0	1	0.6
N/CH	1	1.5	0	0.0	0	0.0	1	0.6
X/T	0	0.0	1	2.9	0	0.0	1	0.6
N/C	0	0.0	1	2.9	0	0.0	1	0.6
N/TU	0	0.0	0	0.0	1	1.9	1	0.6
M/ə	0	0.0	1	2.9	0	0.0	1	0.6
ə/TE	0	0.0	1	2.9	0	0.0	1	0.6
T	0	0.0	1	2.9	0	0.0	1	0.6
TOTALS	67	100.0	35	100.0	52	100.0	154	100.0

Table 2: Phonemes [nd]

AGE:	UNDER 6		UNKNOWN		6 OR OVER		ALL	
SPELLING	FREQ	PCT	FREQ	PCT	FREQ	PCT	FREQ	PCT
N/D	24	60.0	18	78.3	19	76.0	61	69.3
ə/D	9	22.5	3	13.0	1	4.0	13	14.8
N/ə	2	5.0	1	4.3	1	4.0	4	4.5
ə/ə	1	2.5	0	0.0	1	4.0	2	2.3
NE/ə	1	2.5	0	0.0	0	0.0	1	1.1
M/ə	1	2.5	0	0.0	0	0.0	1	1.1
ə/DD	1	2.5	0	0.0	0	0.0	1	1.1
M/W	1	2.5	0	0.0	0	0.0	1	1.1
N/T	0	0.0	0	0.0	1	4.0	1	1.1
N/DE	0	0.0	0	0.0	2	8.0	2	2.3
NN/ə	0	0.0	1	4.3	0	0.0	1	1.1
TOTALS	40	100.0	23	100.0	25	100.0	88	100.0

Table 3: Phonemes [n s]

AGE:	UNDER 6		UNKNOWN		6 OR OVER		ALL	
SPELLING	FREQ	PCT	FREQ	PCT	FREQ	PCT	FREQ	PCT
N/S	11	52.4	22	88.0	12	80.0	45	73.8
ə/S	6	28.6	1	4.0	1	6.7	8	13.1
N/C	4	19.0	1	4.0	0	0.0	5	8.2
N/CE	0	0.0	1	4.0	0	0.0	1	1.6
N/SS	0	0.0	0	0.0	2	13.3	2	3.3
TOTALS	21	100.0	25	100.0	15	100.0	61	100.0

Table 4: Phonemes [nz]

AGE:	UNDER 6		UNKNOWN		6 OR OVER		ALL	
SPELLING	FREQ	PCT	FREQ	PCT	FREQ	PCT	FREQ	PCT
N/S	18	81.8	4	36.4	8	80.0	30	69.8
ə/ə	1	4.5	0	0.0	0	0.0	1	2.3
DN/S	1	4.5	1	9.1	0	0.0	2	4.7
N/ES	1	4.5	0	0.0	2	20.0	3	7.0
ə/S	1	4.5	0	0.0	0	0.0	1	2.3
N/Z	0	0.0	1	9.1	0	0.0	1	2.3
ND/S	0	0.0	2	18.2	0	0.0	2	4.7
N/SE	0	0.0	2	18.2	0	0.0	2	4.7
D/SE	0	0.0	1	9.1	0	0.0	1	2.3
TOTALS	22	100.0	11	100.0	10	100.0	43	100.0

Table 5: Phonemes [nš]

AGE:	UNDER 6		UNKNOWN		6 OR OVER		ALL	
SPELLING	FREQ	PCT	FREQ	PCT	FREQ	PCT	FREQ	PCT
TOTALS	0	100.0	0	100.0	0	100.0	0	100.0

Table 6: Phonemes [nč]

AGE:	UNDER 6		UNKNOWN		6 OR OVER		ALL	
SPELLING	FREQ	PCT	FREQ	PCT	FREQ	PCT	FREQ	PCT
N/TCH	2	40.0	0	0.0	0	0.0	2	40.0
N/SH	1	20.0	0	0.0	0	0.0	1	20.0
ə/CH	1	20.0	0	0.0	0	0.0	1	20.0
N/CH	1	20.0	0	0.0	0	0.0	1	20.0
TOTALS	5	100.0	0	100.0	0	100.0	5	100.0

Table 7: Phonemes [nǰ]

AGE:	UNDER 6		UNKNOWN		6 OR OVER		ALL	
SPELLING	FREQ	PCT	FREQ	PCT	FREQ	PCT	FREQ	PCT
N/G	4	50.0	0	0.0	2	100.0	6	60.0
N/J	2	25.0	0	0.0	0	0.0	2	20.0
N/JJ	1	12.5	0	0.0	0	0.0	1	10.0
ə/G	1	12.5	0	0.0	0	0.0	1	10.0
TOTALS	8	100.0	0	100.0	2	100.0	10	100.0

APPENDIX D: [m] BEFORE STOPS

Table 1: Phonemes [mp]

AGE:	UNDER 6		UNKNOWN		6 OR OVER		ALL	
SPELLING	FREQ	PCT	FREQ	PCT	FREQ	PCT	FREQ	PCT
M/P	4	44.4	0	0.0	1	25.0	5	31.3
a/P	3	33.3	3	100.0	0	0.0	6	37.5
M/a	2	22.2	0	0.0	2	50.0	4	25.0
MP/T	0	0.0	0	0.0	1	25.0	1	6.3
TOTALS	9	100.0	3	100.0	4	100.0	16	100.0

Table 2: Phonemes [mb]

AGE:	UNDER 6		UNKNOWN		6 OR OVER		ALL	
SPELLING	FREQ	PCT	FREQ	PCT	FREQ	PCT	FREQ	PCT
M/B	6	75.0	2	66.7	4	36.4	12	54.5
a/B	2	25.0	1	33.3	0	0.0	3	13.6
M/D	0	0.0	0	0.0	6	54.5	6	27.3
N/D	0	0.0	0	0.0	1	9.1	1	4.5
TOTALS	8	100.0	3	100.0	11	100.0	22	100.0

APPENDIX E: [ŋ] BEFORE STOPS

Table 1: Phonemes [ŋk]

AGE:	UNDER 6		UNKNOWN		6 OR OVER		ALL	
SPELLING	FREQ	PCT	FREQ	PCT	FREQ	PCT	FREQ	PCT
ə/K	4	26.7	4	44.4	4	36.4	12	34.3
ə/C	4	26.7	1	11.1	4	36.4	9	25.7
N/C	3	20.0	0	0.0	0	0.0	3	8.6
N/K	2	13.3	2	22.2	0	0.0	4	11.4
ə/KCE	1	6.7	0	0.0	0	0.0	1	2.9
ə/Q	1	6.7	0	0.0	0	0.0	1	2.9
N/G	0	0.0	0	0.0	1	9.1	1	2.9
N/ə	0	0.0	1	11.1	0	0.0	1	2.9
NG/K	0	0.0	0	0.0	1	9.1	1	2.9
N/L	0	0.0	1	11.1	0	0.0	1	2.9
ə/ə	0	0.0	0	0.0	1	9.1	1	2.9
TOTALS	15	100.0	9	100.0	11	100.0	35	100.0

Table 2: Phonemes [ŋg]

AGE:	UNDER 6		UNKNOWN		6 OR OVER		ALL	
SPELLING	FREQ	PCT	FREQ	PCT	FREQ	PCT	FREQ	PCT
ə/G	8	66.7	1	20.0	0	0.0	9	47.4
N/G	2	16.7	2	40.0	2	100.0	6	31.6
ə/ə	1	8.3	0	0.0	0	0.0	1	5.3
NG/W	1	8.3	0	0.0	0	0.0	1	5.3
LIN/G	0	0.0	1	20.0	0	0.0	1	5.3
N/GG	0	0.0	1	20.0	0	0.0	1	5.3
TOTALS	12	100.0	5	100.0	2	100.0	19	100.0

APPENDIX F: VOWELS BEFORE [r]

Table 1: Phonemes [ɚ]

AGE:	UNDER 6		UNKNOWN		6 OR OVER		ALL	
SPELLING	FREQ	PCT	FREQ	PCT	FREQ	PCT	FREQ	PCT
ə/R	75	59.1	37	56.1	49	63.6	161	59.6
E/R	31	24.4	11	16.7	15	19.5	57	21.1
Ɔ/R	6	4.7	3	4.5	2	2.6	11	4.1
I/R	4	3.1	10	15.2	1	1.3	15	5.6
ə/ə	4	3.1	1	1.5	1	1.3	6	2.2
A/R	2	1.6	2	3.0	0	0.0	4	1.5
A/ə	2	1.6	1	1.5	0	0.0	3	1.1
R/B	1	0.8	0	0.0	0	0.0	1	0.4
U/R	1	0.8	1	1.5	3	3.9	5	1.9
E/ə	1	0.8	0	0.0	2	2.6	3	1.1
ə/T	0	0.0	0	0.0	1	1.3	1	0.4
E/I	0	0.0	0	0.0	1	1.3	1	0.4
U/RE	0	0.0	0	0.0	2	2.6	2	0.7
TOTALS	127	100.0	66	100.0	77	100.0	270	100.0

Table 2: Phonemes [ɝ]

AGE:	UNDER 6		UNKNOWN		6 OR OVER		ALL	
SPELLING	FREQ	PCT	FREQ	PCT	FREQ	PCT	FREQ	PCT
ə/R	46	75.4	6	33.3	9	24.3	61	52.6
I/R	6	9.8	5	27.8	3	8.1	14	12.1
E/R	3	4.9	3	16.7	8	21.6	14	12.1
Ɔ/R	3	4.9	0	0.0	4	10.8	7	6.0
U/R	1	1.6	0	0.0	9	24.3	10	8.6
R/L	1	1.6	0	0.0	0	0.0	1	0.9
U/ə	1	1.6	0	0.0	0	0.0	1	0.9
A/R	0	0.0	2	11.1	0	0.0	2	1.7
A/ə	0	0.0	0	0.0	1	2.7	1	0.9
I/RE	0	0.0	1	5.6	0	0.0	1	0.9
IE/R	0	0.0	1	5.6	0	0.0	1	0.9
E/ə	0	0.0	0	0.0	1	2.7	1	0.9
E/RE	0	0.0	0	0.0	1	2.7	1	0.9
U/RR	0	0.0	0	0.0	1	2.7	1	0.9
TOTALS	61	100.0	18	100.0	37	100.0	116	100.0

Table 3: Phonemes [ɪr]

AGE:	UNDER 6		UNKNOWN		6 CR OVER		ALL	
SPELLING	FREQ	PCT	FREQ	PCT	FREQ	PCT	FREQ	PCT
E/R	3	37.5	2	22.2	7	70.0	12	44.4
I/R	3	37.5	4	44.4	C	0.0	7	25.9
A/R	1	12.5	0	0.0	C	0.0	1	3.7
EE/R	1	12.5	2	22.2	C	0.0	3	11.1
ə/R	0	0.0	0	0.0	1	10.0	1	3.7
UE/RE	0	0.0	0	0.0	1	10.0	1	3.7
Y/R	0	0.0	1	11.1	C	0.0	1	3.7
E/RE	0	0.0	0	0.0	1	10.0	1	3.7
TOTALS	8	100.0	9	100.0	1C	100.0	27	100.0

Table 4: Phonemes [ɛr]

AGE:	UNDER 6		UNKNOWN		6 OR OVER		ALL	
SPELLING	FREQ	PCT	FREQ	PCT	FREQ	PCT	FREQ	PCT
A/R	26	48.1	6	27.3	11	35.5	43	40.2
E/R	15	27.8	8	36.4	10	32.3	33	30.8
ə/R	6	11.1	0	0.0	C	0.0	6	5.6
EE/R	1	1.9	1	4.5	C	0.0	2	1.9
AI/R	1	1.9	0	0.0	0	0.0	1	0.9
A/RR	1	1.9	0	0.0	1	3.2	2	1.9
E/ə	1	1.9	0	0.0	C	0.0	1	0.9
E/RR	1	1.9	0	0.0	0	0.0	1	0.9
A/RER	1	1.9	0	0.0	C	0.0	1	0.9
EU/T	1	1.9	0	0.0	C	0.0	1	0.9
A/RE	0	0.0	1	4.5	4	12.9	5	4.7
I/RE	0	0.0	0	0.0	1	3.2	1	0.9
ə/ə	0	0.0	1	4.5	0	0.0	1	0.9
U/R	0	0.0	1	4.5	1	3.2	2	1.9
I/N	0	0.0	3	13.6	C	0.0	3	2.8
EAR	0	0.0	1	4.5	C	0.0	1	0.9
EA/R	0	0.0	0	0.0	2	6.5	2	1.9
E/RE	0	0.0	0	0.0	1	3.2	1	0.9
TOTALS	54	100.0	22	100.0	31	100.0	107	100.0

Table 5: Phonemes [ar]

AGE:	UNDER 6		UNKNOWN		6 OR OVER		ALL	
SPELLING	FREQ	PCT	FREQ	PCT	FREQ	PCT	FREQ	PCT
ə/R	20	58.8	6	31.6	8	28.6	34	42.0
A/ə	5	14.7	0	0.0	0	0.0	5	6.2
O/R	4	11.8	8	42.1	10	35.7	22	27.2
A/R	1	2.9	2	10.5	8	28.6	11	13.6
I/R	1	2.9	2	10.5	0	0.0	3	3.7
O/ə	1	2.9	1	5.3	0	0.0	2	2.5
A/'	1	2.9	0	0.0	0	0.0	1	1.2
U/ə	1	2.9	0	0.0	0	0.0	1	1.2
E/R	0	0.0	0	0.0	2	7.1	2	2.5
TOTALS	34	100.0	19	100.0	28	100.0	81	100.0

Table 6: Phonemes [ɔr]

AGE:	UNDER 6		UNKNOWN		6 OR OVER		ALL	
SPELLING	FREQ	PCT	FREQ	PCT	FREQ	PCT	FREQ	PCT
O/R	26	60.5	12	66.7	11	44.0	49	57.0
ə/R	3	7.0	0	0.0	2	8.0	5	5.8
OE/R	3	7.0	0	0.0	0	0.0	3	3.5
OO/R	3	7.0	1	5.6	0	0.0	4	4.7
OU/R	2	4.7	0	0.0	0	0.0	2	2.3
O/ə	1	2.3	3	16.7	1	4.0	5	5.8
A/RE	1	2.3	1	5.6	0	0.0	2	2.3
OO/ə	1	2.3	0	0.0	0	0.0	1	1.2
U/R	1	2.3	0	0.0	2	8.0	3	3.5
EW/R	1	2.3	0	0.0	0	0.0	1	1.2
O/RU	1	2.3	0	0.0	0	0.0	1	1.2
E/R	0	0.0	0	0.0	1	4.0	1	1.2
A/R	0	0.0	0	0.0	1	4.0	1	1.2
ə/ə	0	0.0	1	5.6	0	0.0	1	1.2
O/RE	0	0.0	0	0.0	4	16.0	4	4.7
ə/RE	0	0.0	0	0.0	1	4.0	1	1.2
OW/R	0	0.0	0	0.0	1	4.0	1	1.2
E/ə	0	0.0	0	0.0	1	4.0	1	1.2
TOTALS	43	100.0	18	100.0	25	100.0	86	100.0

Table 7: Phonemes [awr]

AGE:	UNDER 6		UNKNOWN		6 OR OVER		ALL	
SPELLING	FREQ	PCT	FREQ	PCT	FREQ	PCT	FREQ	PCT
AWE/R	1	100.0	0	0.0	0	0.0	1	12.5
O/R	0	0.0	1	33.3	0	0.0	1	12.5
A/RE	0	0.0	2	66.7	3	75.0	5	62.5
HOWE/R	0	0.0	0	0.0	1	25.0	1	12.5
TOTALS	1	100.0	3	100.0	4	100.0	8	100.0

APPENDIX G: [ʌ] BEFORE LIQUIDS AND NASALS

Table 1: Phonemes [ɝ]

AGE:	UNDER 6		UNKNOWN		6 OR OVER		ALL	
SPELLING	FREQ	PCT	FREQ	PCT	FREQ	PCT	FREQ	PCT
ə/R	46	75.4	6	33.3	9	24.3	61	52.6
I/R	6	9.8	5	27.8	3	8.1	14	12.1
O/R	3	4.9	0	0.0	4	10.8	7	6.0
E/R	3	4.9	3	16.7	8	21.6	14	12.1
U/R	1	1.6	0	0.0	9	24.3	10	8.6
U/ə	1	1.6	0	0.0	0	0.0	1	0.9
R/L	1	1.6	0	0.0	0	0.0	1	0.9
I/RE	0	0.0	1	5.6	0	0.0	1	0.9
A/R	0	0.0	2	11.1	0	0.0	2	1.7
IE/R	0	0.0	1	5.6	0	0.0	1	0.9
ʌ/â	0	0.0	0	0.0	1	2.7	1	0.9
U/RR	0	0.0	0	0.0	1	2.7	1	0.9
E/RE	0	0.0	0	0.0	1	2.7	1	0.9
E/ə	0	0.0	0	0.0	1	2.7	1	0.9
TOTALS	61	100.0	18	100.0	37	100.0	116	100.0

Table 2: Phonemes [ʌl]

AGE:	UNDER 6		UNKNOWN		6 OR OVER		ALL	
SPELLING	FREQ	PCT	FREQ	PCT	FREQ	PCT	FREQ	PCT
A/L	1	50.0	0	0.0	0	0.0	1	33.3
ə/L	1	50.0	0	0.0	0	0.0	1	33.3
O/L	0	0.0	1	100.0	0	0.0	1	33.3
TOTALS	2	100.0	1	100.0	0	100.0	3	100.0

Table 3: Phonemes [ʌm]

SPELLING	UNDER 6 FREQ	PCT	UNKNOWN FREQ	PCT	6 OR OVER FREQ	PCT	ALL FREQ	PCT
O/M	11	37.9	1	5.6	11	31.4	23	28.0
U/M	10	34.5	9	50.0	7	20.0	26	31.7
ə/M	3	10.3	1	5.6	2	5.7	6	7.3
U/ə	2	6.9	0	0.0	0	0.0	2	2.4
A/ME	1	3.4	0	0.0	0	0.0	1	1.2
O/MM	1	3.4	0	0.0	0	0.0	1	1.2
A/M	1	3.4	0	0.0	8	22.9	9	11.0
A/N	0	0.0	0	0.0	1	2.9	1	1.2
O/ME	0	0.0	2	11.1	2	5.7	4	4.9
O/ə	0	0.0	4	22.2	0	0.0	4	4.9
W/M	0	0.0	0	0.0	1	2.9	1	1.2
U/ME	0	0.0	0	0.0	1	2.9	1	1.2
U/MP	0	0.0	0	0.0	1	2.9	1	1.2
E/ME	0	0.0	1	5.6	0	0.0	1	1.2
M	0	0.0	0	0.0	1	2.9	1	1.2
TOTALS	29	100.0	18	100.0	35	100.0	82	100.0

Table 4: Phonemes [ʌn]

SPELLING	UNDER 6 FREQ	PCT	UNKNOWN FREQ	PCT	6 OR OVER FREQ	PCT	ALL FREQ	PCT
U/N	12	36.4	1	16.7	5	31.3	18	32.7
O/N	6	18.2	1	16.7	3	18.8	10	18.2
U/ə	4	12.1	0	0.0	1	6.3	5	9.1
A/N	3	9.1	0	0.0	4	25.0	7	12.7
I/N	3	9.1	0	0.0	0	0.0	3	5.5
O/ə	2	6.1	0	0.0	1	6.3	3	5.5
W/N	1	3.0	3	50.0	0	0.0	4	7.3
Y/N	1	3.0	0	0.0	0	0.0	1	1.8
E/ə	1	3.0	0	0.0	0	0.0	1	1.8
UE/ə	0	0.0	0	0.0	1	6.3	1	1.8
E/N	0	0.0	0	0.0	1	6.3	1	1.8
O/NE	0	0.0	1	16.7	0	0.0	1	1.8
TOTALS	33	100.0	6	100.0	16	100.0	55	100.0

Table 5: Phonemes [ʌŋ]

SPELLING	UNDER 6 FREQ	PCT	UNKNOWN FREQ	PCT	6 OR OVER FREQ	PCT	ALL FREQ	PCT
U/N	1	50.0	1	25.0	0	0.0	2	28.6
U/ə	1	50.0	0	0.0	0	0.0	1	14.3
O/N	0	0.0	2	50.0	0	0.0	2	28.6
O/ə	0	0.0	1	25.0	0	0.0	1	14.3
OUI/NG	0	0.0	0	0.0	1	100.0	1	14.3
TOTALS	2	100.0	4	100.0	1	100.0	7	100.0

APPENDIX H: VOWELS BEFORE [nt]

Table 1: Phonemes [ænt]

AGE:	UNDER 6		UNKNOWN		6 OR OVER		ALL	
SPELLING	FREQ	PCT	FREQ	PCT	FREQ	PCT	FREQ	PCT
A/ə/T	6	85.7	2	100.0	0	0.0	8	72.7
A/N/ə	1	14.3	0	0.0	0	0.0	1	9.1
A/N/T	0	0.0	0	0.0	2	100.0	2	18.2
TOTALS	7	100.0	2	100.0	2	100.0	11	100.0

Table 2: Phonemes [ʌnt]

AGE:	UNDER 6		UNKNOWN		6 OR OVER		ALL	
SPELLING	FREQ	PCT	FREQ	PCT	FREQ	PCT	FREQ	PCT
U/N/ə	3	16.7	0	0.0	0	0.0	3	12.0
O/N/T	2	11.1	0	0.0	0	0.0	2	8.0
A/N/ə	2	11.1	0	0.0	1	33.3	3	12.0
U/N/T	2	11.1	0	0.0	1	33.3	3	12.0
U/ə/ə	2	11.1	0	0.0	0	0.0	2	8.0
O/N/ə	1	5.6	0	0.0	0	0.0	1	4.0
A/N/T	1	5.6	0	0.0	0	0.0	1	4.0
I/N/T	1	5.6	0	0.0	0	0.0	1	4.0
E/ə/ə	1	5.6	0	0.0	0	0.0	1	4.0
O/ə/T	1	5.6	0	0.0	0	0.0	1	4.0
W/N/CH	1	5.6	0	0.0	0	0.0	1	4.0
U/ə/T	1	5.6	0	0.0	0	0.0	1	4.0
W/N/T	0	0.0	3	75.0	0	0.0	3	12.0
O/N/C	0	0.0	1	25.0	0	0.0	1	4.0
O/ə/ə	0	0.0	0	0.0	1	33.3	1	4.0
TOTALS	18	100.0	4	100.0	3	100.0	25	100.0

Table 3: Phonemes [Int]

AGE:	UNDER 6		UNKNOWN		6 OR OVER		ALL	
SPELLING	FREQ	PCT	FREQ	PCT	FREQ	PCT	FREQ	PCT
I/N/T	1	100.0	0	0.0	0	0.0	1	50.0
I/ə/T	0	0.0	1	100.0	0	0.0	1	50.0
TOTALS	1	100.0	1	100.0	0	100.0	2	100.0

Table 4: Phonemes [ɛ nt]

AGE:	UNDER 6		UNKNOWN		6 OR OVER		ALL	
SPELLING	FREQ	PCT	FREQ	PCT	FREQ	PCT	FREQ	PCT
E/N/T	3	30.0	0	0.0	1	5.6	4	14.3
A/N/T	2	20.0	0	0.0	13	72.2	15	53.6
ə/N/T	1	10.0	0	0.0	0	0.0	1	3.6
A/ə/T	1	10.0	0	0.0	1	5.6	2	7.1
I/N/T	1	10.0	0	0.0	1	5.6	2	7.1
I/ə/T	1	10.0	0	0.0	0	0.0	1	3.6
E/ə/T	1	10.0	0	0.0	1	5.6	2	7.1
A/N/D	0	0.0	0	0.0	1	5.6	1	3.6
TOTALS	10	100.0	0	100.0	18	100.0	28	100.0

Table 5: Phonemes [ənt]

AGE:	UNDER 6		UNKNOWN		6 OR OVER		ALL	
SPELLING	FREQ	PCT	FREQ	PCT	FREQ	PCT	FREQ	PCT
ə/N/T	3	21.4	3	15.0	1	8.3	7	15.2
I/N/T	3	21.4	7	35.0	2	16.7	12	26.1
A/N/T	1	7.1	0	0.0	0	0.0	1	2.2
O/N/T	1	7.1	1	5.0	1	8.3	3	6.5
I/N/ə	1	7.1	0	0.0	0	0.0	1	2.2
E/ə/ə	1	7.1	0	0.0	0	0.0	1	2.2
I/T/IT	1	7.1	0	0.0	0	0.0	1	2.2
U/N/T	1	7.1	1	5.0	0	0.0	2	4.3
ə/ə/T	1	7.1	1	5.0	0	0.0	2	4.3
E/N/ə	1	7.1	0	0.0	0	0.0	1	2.2
A/ə/T	0	0.0	1	5.0	0	0.0	1	2.2
I/ə/T	0	0.0	1	5.0	0	0.0	1	2.2
Y/X/T	0	0.0	1	5.0	0	0.0	1	2.2
E/N/T	0	0.0	1	5.0	6	50.0	7	15.2
ə/N/TE	0	0.0	0	0.0	1	8.3	1	2.2
ə/N/ə	0	0.0	0	0.0	1	8.3	1	2.2
E/ə/T	0	0.0	1	5.0	0	0.0	1	2.2
I/M/ə	0	0.0	1	5.0	0	0.0	1	2.2
ə/N/D	0	0.0	1	5.0	0	0.0	1	2.2
TOTALS	14	100.0	20	100.0	12	100.0	46	100.0

Table 6: Phonemes [a nt]

AGE:	UNDER 6		UNKNOWN		6 OR OVER		ALL	
SPELLING	FREQ	PCT	FREQ	PCT	FREQ	PCT	FREQ	PCT
O/N/T	5	71.4	1	33.3	9	56.3	15	57.7
O/ə/T	2	28.6	1	33.3	5	31.3	8	30.8
ə/N/T	0	0.0	0	0.0	1	6.3	1	3.8
U/N/T	0	0.0	1	33.3	0	0.0	1	3.8
O/N/TU	0	0.0	0	0.0	1	6.3	1	3.8
TOTALS	7	100.0	3	100.0	16	100.0	26	100.0

APPENDIX I: VOWELS BEFORE [nd]

Table 1: Phonemes [ænd]

AGE:	UNDER 6		UNKNOWN		6 CR CVER		ALL	
SPELLING	FREQ	PCT	FREQ	PCT	FREQ	PCT	FREQ	PCT
A/N/D	12	57.1	2	66.7	1	50.C	15	57.7
A/ə/D	6	28.6	C	0.0	C	C.C	6	23.1
A/N/ə	1	4.8	0	0.C	C	C.C	1	3.8
A/M/ə	1	4.8	C	0.C	C	C.C	1	3.8
A/M/W	1	4.8	0	0.C	0	C.C	1	3.8
A/ə/ə	C	C.0	0	C.C	1	5C.C	1	3.8
I/N/ə	0	0.0	1	33.3	C	C.C	1	3.8
TOTALS	21	100.0	3	1C0.C	2	1C0.C	26	1CC.C

Table 2: Phonemes [ʌnd]

AGE:	UNDER 6		UNKNCWN		6 CR CVER		ALL	
SPELLING	FREQ	PCT	FREQ	PCT	FREQ	PCT	FREQ	PCT
I/N/D	2	50.0	C	0.0	0	0.C	2	2C.C
U/N/D	1	25.0	0	0.0	2	33.3	3	30.0
U/ə/DD	1	25.0	0	0.0	0	C.C	1	10.C
A/N/D	0	C.0	0	C.0	2	33.3	2	2C.C
O/N/D	0	0.0	C	0.C	1	16.7	1	1C.C
U/ə/D	0	0.0	0	0.0	1	16.7	1	1C.C
TOTALS	4	1CC.0	C	100.0	6	100.C	1C	1C0.C

Table 3: Phonemes [Ind]

AGE:	UNDER 6		UNKNCWN		6 CR CVER		ALL	
SPELLING	FREQ	PCT	FREQ	PCT	FREQ	PCT	FREQ	PCT
I/ə/D	1	50.0	2	18.2	0	0.C	3	20.0
E/ə/ə	1	50.0	C	C.C	C	0.C	1	6.7
ə/N/D	0	0.0	1	9.1	0	C.C	1	6.7
E/N/D	0	0.0	1	9.1	C	C.C	1	6.7
I/N/D	0	0.0	6	54.5	2	1C0.C	8	53.3
I/NN/ə	0	C.0	1	9.1	C	C.C	1	6.7
TOTALS	2	100.0	11	1C0.C	2	100.C	15	1C0.0

Table 4: Phonemes [ɛnd]

AGE:	UNDER 6		UNKNCWN		6 CR CVER		ALL	
SPELLING	FREQ	PCT	FREQ	PCT	FREQ	PCT	FREQ	PCT
A/N/D	4	66.7	0	0.0	4	66.7	8	53.3
E/N/D	1	16.7	2	66.7	0	0.0	3	20.0
E/ə/D	1	16.7	0	0.0	0	0.0	1	6.7
I/N/D	0	0.0	1	33.3	0	0.0	1	6.7
I/N/DE	0	0.0	0	0.0	1	16.7	1	6.7
E/N/ə	0	0.0	0	0.0	1	16.7	1	6.7
TOTALS	6	100.0	3	100.0	6	100.0	15	100.0

Table 5: Phonemes [ərd]

AGE:	UNDER 6		UNKNCWN		6 OR CVER		ALL	
SPELLING	FREQ	PCT	FREQ	PCT	FREC	PCT	FREQ	PCT
I/N/D	1	33.3	1	25.0	0	0.0	2	22.2
E/N/ə	1	33.3	0	0.0	0	0.0	1	11.1
I/ə/D	1	33.3	0	0.0	0	0.0	1	11.1
A/N/D	0	0.0	2	50.0	0	0.0	2	22.2
E/N/D	0	0.0	0	0.0	1	50.0	1	11.1
I/N/T	0	0.0	0	0.0	1	50.0	1	11.1
A/ə/D	0	0.0	1	25.0	0	0.0	1	11.1
TOTALS	3	100.0	4	100.0	2	100.0	9	100.0

Table 6: Phonemes [and]

AGE:	UNDER 6		UNKNCWN		6 CR CVER		ALL	
SPELLING	FREQ	PCT	FREQ	PCT	FREQ	PCT	FREQ	PCT
O/N/D	1	100.0	0	0.0	0	0.0	1	100.0
TOTALS	1	100.0	0	100.0	0	100.0	1	100.0